Janette Benaddi is a 52-year-old businesswoman from Leeds. She is married with two children.

Helen Butters is an NHS communications expert from North Yorkshire. She is 46 years old, married and has two children.

Frances Davies is a solicitor running her own law firm in Leeds. She is 48 years old, married with two sons and lives in York.

Niki Doeg runs her own business and is a qualified rugby coach. She is 46 years old and lives in York with her husband and their two sons.

Four Mums in a Boat

Janette Benaddi, Helen Butters, Niki Doeg and Frances Davies

ONE PLACE. MANY STORIES

HQ
An imprint of HarperCollinsPublishers Ltd
1 London Bridge Street
London SE1 9GF

This paperback edition 2018

1

First published in Great Britain by HQ, an imprint of HarperCollinsPublishers Ltd 2017

A catalogue record for this book is available from the British Library.

ISBN: 978-0-00-821484-5

Printed and bound in Great Britain by
CPI Group (UK) Ltd, Croydon, CR0 4YY

This book is dedicated to you. We hope it will inspire you to conquer your own 'ocean', whatever it may be.

JANETTE, HELEN, FRANCES AND NIKI

'You can never cross the ocean unless you have the courage to lose sight of the shore.'

CHRISTOPHER COLUMBUS

Contents

CHAPTER I

La Gomera

'To be is to do.'
SOCRATES

30 November 2015, San Sebastián Marina, La Gomera

'This', said Frances, shaking her head slowly as she stared at the waves smashing into the harbour wall below us, 'is not an entry-level ocean.'

Standing next to her, looking at the violent swell just outside San Sebastián Marina in La Gomera, the rest of us – Janette, Helen and Niki – were inclined to agree. The waves were enormous and the distance we were about to row was substantial. Who on earth could have possibly thought this was a good idea? Collectively, we were about to leave four husbands, eight children, five dogs, two cats, two snakes and a gerbil and row 3,000 miles across one of the most dangerous oceans in the world. It is said that more people have travelled into space or climbed Mount Everest than have crossed the Atlantic in a rowing boat.

And not one of them, to be frank, was a middle-aged working mother from Yorkshire, firmly the wrong side of 40 (or 50), with little or (more accurately) no sporting prowess.

In fact, there was not a single Olympic athlete, extreme sportsman or endurance nut among the four of us. None of us had marched to a Pole or bivouacked on the side of a mountain or lived in a cave drinking nothing but rainwater with only a small rodent for company. That said, we weren't totally unfit, sofa-bound sloths; Frances had done the Coast to Coast race from Nairn to Glen Coe, and Janette once did a 5-kilometre 'fun run' where she got covered in pink paint as she jogged around the grounds of Castle Howard. But essentially we were four mums who had met on the school run and decided to row an ocean.

And now, standing here, that decision to enter the Talisker Whisky Atlantic Challenge – one of the toughest races on earth – made after a few too many glasses of Pinot on a cold winter's night in York back in January 2013, looked like a moment of total madness. It had taken us nearly three long, hard years to get to this day. We had always said to each other that the hardest part of the race, the toughest challenge, would be getting to the start line in the Canary Islands in the first place. And we'd managed that. We'd done the difficult bit. We'd raised the money, won over enough sponsors and managed to convince enough people that we were serious and worth backing. But now, here we were, staring into a cauldron of currents and tides, with hurricane-force winds and waves up to 60 feet high, not to mention the giant shipping tankers who could take out our little rowing boat at a moment's notice. We were also trying hard not to think of the sharks, the whales and the marlins, which had been known to skewer through the hulls of boats in the middle of the night, plus the scorching hot sun, the driving rain, the injuries, the sores, the exhaustion and the endless, endless rowing. It would be two hours on, two hours off – eat, sleep, row, repeat – which we estimated we would need to keep doing for at least 50 days, or possibly a touch longer. We'd certainly need the emergency bottle of mango gin we were planning to squirrel into the hold.

'It'll be fine,' said Helen with a rictus grin and an exaggerated shrug, just as another huge wave hit the rocks below. 'We know we'll make it to Antigua.' She nodded.

'We just all have to think positive,' said Niki.

'The strength of our team is each individual member. The strength of each member is our team.' Janette was quoting from our 'On-board Values' sheet that she'd presented for our perusal and approval 3,000 miles away in Yorkshire.

Standing there, staring at those powerful waves, we were all desperately trying to be positive, think positive and breathe positive, whereas deep down we were all wondering: why the bloody hell have we decided to row across an ocean in the first place? We all knew there was a chance we wouldn't make it across. But now was not the time to dwell on the negative. This was going to be life-changing. But we knew that. We were all in this adventure not to escape life, but for life not to escape us. And this was it. The sun was beating down, the salt air filled our nostrils; it was Helen who eventually broke the silence.

'And', she added firmly, 'no one is allowed to cry.'

We arrived in La Gomera on the last day of November 2015, two weeks before the start of the Talisker Whisky Atlantic Challenge. The four of us were about to row 3,000 miles from our base in the Canary Islands over to Antigua in the West Indies. We'd been told that preparation was one of the most important parts of the race and we had been determined to get to the Canaries in good time to sort out and organise our stuff, and also to make sure that there would still be the necessary essential supplies left in the few shops on the tiny volcanic island.

BBC Breakfast had decided to film us leaving the UK, saying goodbye to our back-up team, friends (lots of friends), family (lots of family) and supporters at Manchester Airport. Out of the 26 teams making the Atlantic crossing this year they had chosen us – Yorkshire Rows – as the team to follow. We were naturally thrilled as we were desperate to make as much money as possible for our chosen charities: Maggie's Cancer Care and Yorkshire Air Ambulance.

The TV cameras were rolling as we stood at the Thompson check-in to Tenerife, surrounded by friends, relatives and our piles of suitcases, packed with a water pump, bags of brazil nuts, wet-weather gear and chafe-free pants, hoping they wouldn't make us pay for excess luggage, when we were approached by the strappingly good-looking former Olympic champion James Cracknell, who had famously rowed the same race with Ben Fogle, off the telly, some years before.

Exuding ebullient charm, he had been sent by the BBC as our surprise guest to see us off and deliver some last-minute pearls of wisdom. Unfortunately, no one had told Janette, and in the confusion of suitcases, faces and bright lights, she waved at him to move away.

'Shhh,' she warned, index finger in the air. 'The BBC are filming over there.'

'But –' began James, looking a little confused.

'Can't you see the camera?'

Not recognising the handsome rower, Janette was convinced he was another competitor in the race.

'They are trying to get their shots.' She was squinting a little into the light. 'Could you just keep quiet until they are finished.'

'I was just –' the handsome Cracknell ventured again.

'Shhh,' she replied.

Eventually, finally, Janette was introduced to her dashing interlocutor, and after red-faced, profuse apologies, James was allowed to deliver his final words to camera, which were that we would all hate each other one day and love each other the next, and that this would be a recurring pattern until we finished crossing the ocean. He warned us we'd have blisters where we never thought we could have blisters, and he added that he thought we'd make it, as we had all been through a far worse experience: childbirth.

With his encouragement ringing in our ears, we set off for the Canaries – our chafe-free pants securely in the hold and at no extra cost!

On our journey to get to the Canaries we had been helped, not only very significantly by our families, but also by so many extraordinarily generous people along the way. One of these was 88-year-old Ron from Halifax, who owned a haulage company in Yorkshire and an apartment in Tenerife. He'd read about us in the *Yorkshire Post* and had contacted us via our fundraising website offering his services as our official meet-and-greeter in Tenerife. Having never met him before, we, of course, had no idea what to expect as this charming, diminutive elderly chap met us at the airport. Not only did he manage to pack all our hugely heavy suitcases into his car, but he also then proceeded to take us all out to lunch in Santa Cruz before depositing us at the ferry to catch the boat over to La Gomera island itself.

Less than an hour later and the marina at San Sebastián was buzzing with energy as we arrived. We checked in at the headquarters for the race and were handed our access passes to the harbour. As we made our way through the giant security gates at the harbour entrance, the first thing that hit us was the noise: shouting, chattering, laughter, the sound of sawing, blowtorches, hammers. There was so much work going on.

'Is anyone else feeling nervous and excited?' asked Niki.

'I can't believe we're here,' said Helen.

'I can't believe we've got this far,' added Janette.

'At last,' smiled Frances.

There were crews of rowers for the race everywhere, boats lined up alongside each other. The teams were from all over the world: pairs, solo rowers and, like us, other teams of four. There were 26 teams in total, all preparing for the race and wandering up and down the jetties. Their huge piles of kit, ropes, buckets, grab bags, water pumps, drogues, sea anchors, radios, flares and first-aid kits were strewn about the wooden planks in a form of very ordered chaos, ready to be scrutinised by the race organisers – a painstakingly precise process in which each and every piece of equipment is checked, along with the competitor's ability to use them. It is not only an inventory of the boat; it also tests her and the team's seaworthiness. Anyone failing this process is not allowed to race.

Bang in the middle of it all was *Rose* – our beautiful Rannoch ocean-going racing boat and very much the fifth member of the team – 8 metres long and 1.5 metres wide, and glowing white in the sunshine. We were so eager to see her we picked our way through the teams to find her. We had missed her since she'd been packed onto a cargo ship and sent south two months earlier. Finally we spotted her, sleek and shiny with new Glide Coat paint to help her speed through the Atlantic. She was moored up next to a bold green boat powered by the only other all-female crew in the race – Row Like a Girl. We immediately climbed aboard and, like concerned parents, began to check her over just in case she had been knocked or bashed about on her journey. Fortunately she was perfect. In fact, compared to a lot of the boats in the marina she looked fabulous.

'Not to be rude,' whispered Helen, looking up and down the line of boats, 'but none of these other boats are a patch on *Rose*!'

'You're right,' confirmed Niki, also up on deck. '*Rose* is one of the more modern boats here.'

But it wasn't just the age and size of the boats that differed; it was what the other crews had done to them. As we wandered up and down the jetties, chatting to the other crews and introducing ourselves, it became apparent that quite a lot of the other teams had effectively 'pimped their rides'.

'The Antiguans have got a little cooker,' said Janette. 'They've taken out one of their rowing seats and put it in the middle.'

'They've got rods as well,' added Niki. 'Apparently they're planning to fish their way across.'

'Fish?' asked Helen.

'They'll get there when they get there, or that's what they're saying,' continued Niki, looking extremely perplexed.

'Team Beyond are taking gallons of olive oil to drink,' shared Frances.

'Doesn't that give you diarrhoea?' asked Helen.

'Ocean Reunion have packed masses of peanut butter in a bag!'

As we went up and down the boats, checking everyone out, we began to seriously doubt our preparation. Did we need a little cooker? Should we be fishing? Eating peanut butter, while glugging back the olive oil? What were we doing? What were we thinking? We didn't belong here, among this group of extreme athletes. We were four mums from Yorkshire who really didn't have any idea.

'Enough is enough,' declared Frances firmly. 'We've done what we've done and we're here now. Let's get on with it.'

With so many rowers, support crews and race organisers crammed onto such a small island, accommodation was at a premium. Fortunately, Janette had been to La Gomera the year before with her husband, Ben, on a recce for the team. So she'd tested out some of the restaurants and truffled out a couple of bars. She'd even spotted a glamorous five-star hotel high on the hill that she'd fancied for the trip, but Frances had other ideas and found a distinctly less salubrious but certainly more practical apartment for the four of us to hole up in until the rest of our families arrived to wish us well before the start of the race.

An estate agent might have generously described the first-floor apartment as 'characterful'. Helen optimistically described it as having 'Spanish charm', but then she had managed to secure the best bedroom – or perhaps that should be the *only* bedroom – with a double bed and a large wardrobe, right next to the bathroom. Janette ended up on the sofa bed in the lounge, while Frances and Niki slept in the 'attic' – a mezzanine open to the elements. They were forced to pee in buckets (much to the amusement of the neighbours), as climbing down the rickety ladder in the middle of the night was not an ideal way to avoid injury. And we could not afford injuries. Not now. Not after all our hard work, when we were so close to the race itself.

On our first night, we had a meeting about how much kit we should take onto the boat. Obviously, the more kit we had, the heavier the boat and the more slowly we would be able to row. It was in our interest to keep everything to a minimum. There were essentials like the spare rudder and the hand-operated watermaker that simply could not be left behind, but Helen's hair straighteners and family-sized glitter shower gel were certainly being sent back home before the race with her husband, Richard, as they were strictly a La Gomera 'essential' only. As indeed, it appeared, were our pants.

'We only really need two pairs,' announced Janette.

'Two?' asked Niki.

Janette nodded. 'We have to start somewhere, so it may as well be the knickers. We won't be wearing them anyway.'

'Why only two?' asked Helen.

'The weight.'

'Knickers don't weigh very much,' continued Helen.

'I know, but added to everything else you want, you'll end up with a boat so heavy we can't row.'

'There are probably bigger and heavier items we should be arguing about. Like snack packs.'

Niki flinched. During the long build-up to the race we had each, at various different times and stages, been assigned roles or duties. And Niki had been placed in charge of snack packs. It was one of the many jobs she is well suited to. For, despite the fact that she is slim and as svelte as you like, she likes her food. She has an extremely fast metabolism and when she is not eating, she is quite often thinking about what she might want to be eating next. So she was the logical person to put in charge of food, particularly snacks.

Sufficient calorie intake on such a strenuous and mammoth journey is, needless to say, essential, and Niki researched her task impeccably with the razor-sharp precision that she brings to everything. Rules of the challenge stipulate that each boat must carry 60 days' worth of rations per person, and with us burning anything between 6,000 and 10,000 calories a day, we obviously needed a lot of meals and plenty of snacks in between them. In fact, we'd been told that as the high-calorie ration packs themselves would soon bore us into not bothering or wanting to eat anything, the snacks were more than a treat; they could end up keeping us going through an especially long night out at sea or a miserable moment of depression, and could therefore end up saving our lives. And Niki had definitely investigated all avenues and scenarios. She had gone through what we should bring, and what could survive the sweaty, salty, damp journey. She had asked us what we liked, and what we might want to eat in the middle of a force-eight gale. Unfortunately, when Niki had emailed us all, none of us had really focused on her question.

'We don't mind,' we all said politely. 'It's up to you.' Turns out that was a decision we would certainly live to regret.

Janette's kit cull was ruthless, and knickergate rumbled on with talk of a mutiny and a plan to stash a secret bag of pants on the boat. But our overriding memory of those first few days as we tinkered with our boat, stuck the names of our sponsors on *Rose*'s hull and ran through the list of essentials we needed to find space for on-board was the incredible 'can-do' attitude of the other competitors. It was truly a different world.

We were moored up next to Row Like a Girl – a fantastic group of stunningly attractive women who were, frankly, young enough to be our daughters. They were bright and capable and had bags of adventurous sporting experience behind them.

'Even if I lost two stone I'd never look like that,' said Janette, watching the girls slap on some suntan lotion. Further down the jetty, a couple of the other crews started wolf whistling at the girls. 'I'm not sure we'd get the same reaction,' she mused.

'No,' agreed Frances. 'In fact, I'd say quite the opposite!'

We spent those early days racing around town, trying to find a chandlery to buy ropes and pads for seat covers, while chatting to the girls next door – Olivia, Gee, Bella and Lauren.

'Yoga mats make the best seat padding,' suggested Lauren helpfully, from the deck of her boat.

'Really?' said Helen.

'They're nice and soft – good for the bottom,' she added.

It transpired, as we readied our boats and covered our hull in the sponsorship stickers, that Lauren had already tried and failed to cross the Atlantic two years previously as part of a double, with her teammate Hannah Lawton. Having suffered some of the worst conditions ever experienced in the race's history, she'd ended up capsizing, losing all power to her boat and drifting for 40 days in the ocean. She spent a total of 96 days at sea before returning to the UK some 111 days after she started, having been rescued by a cargo ship en route from Canada. The fact that she was back here again, to exorcise her demons, was extraordinary. And her story was a salutary one. Enough to cut through the bravado as we coiled ropes on deck. And enough to make us all think quietly about exactly what we were letting ourselves in for. What were we doing, leaving eight children, with ages ranging from 8 to 18 years old, behind in Yorkshire? Were we being selfish? Insane? Can women of a certain age with jobs and responsibilities really go off and have an adventure? Are they allowed? Who on earth did we think we were?

Amazingly, no one here asked us those questions. No one ever asked what we were doing. Or who the hell we thought we were. Or questioned our motives. They merely accepted that we were. We could not help thinking as we moved among these extraordinary can-do people who encouraged us, rather than discouraged us, that there really should be more of them in this world. It is a rare feeling of empowerment for a woman, not to be judged.

Having said that, the inspirational crew Row2Recovery – a four made up of single- and double-amputee soldiers: Cayle, Lee, Paddy and Nigel – did once give us 'the look', like we had no idea what we were doing. In their defence, we were playing the uplifting anthem 'Let It Go' from the kids' movie *Frozen* at full volume at the time as we cleaned the boat. They moaned, groaned, covered their ears and begged us to turn it off – just as Greg Maud, a solo rower who's climbed Everest and Kilimanjaro and completed the Marathon des Sables, loudly joined in on the chorus as he walked past, his arms outstretched as he sang.

'LET IT GO-O-O! LET IT GO-O-O!' He paused. 'What can I say?' He shrugged at the appalled faces of the Row2Recovery team. 'I have a daughter.'

As race day edged a little closer, so the atmosphere in the town got a little headier; the tension increased, as did the amount of gins consumed in The Blue Marlin.

The unofficial race bar, The Blue Marlin – a tiny watering hole in a side street of La Gomera whose walls are graffitied with the last words of adventurers past – was where all the rowers and their support teams would gather after a long, hard day of packing and repacking their boats. A veritable hub of all things transatlantic and rowing, it smelt of salt and spilt beer and was the place where friendships were formed and hangovers were made. As the days ticked by, the talk turned from past adventures, tall waves and tall stories to the present. We'd talk in intense detail about how to distribute the weight properly around the boat, how to deploy a para-anchor (a giant parachute of an anchor used in storms to stop the boat being blown around in the sea) and when exactly you should launch a drogue (in very rough seas and currents, apparently). Later in the evening, as a few more rums slipped down, the singing and the guitar playing became a little louder and would sometimes carry on until two or three in the morning.

Frances was in her element. Having been at university in Southampton, she was right back there, loving every minute, reliving her student days. Normally quite reserved, she was now talking to all the competitors, thriving on everyone's positive attitude. Of course we were all going to make it across! Of course it was possible! Of course! Of course!

There was the small matter of passing our scrutineering test first. We knew the race organisers would not allow a boat into the water until it had passed this very intensive check. Every tiny piece of kit, from survival suits to safety lines right the way down to the number of plasters in the medical kit, had to be laid out in a particular format next to the boat and checked off the 11-page list of mandatory kit. The day of our final scrutineering was nerve-racking. It took us nearly the whole day to lay everything out by *Rose*. Would we have all the kit? Were the ropes the right diameter? Did we have the right splint in our medical kit? Will our daily food packages have enough calories in them? All the other crews were obviously in the same boat, so when someone was missing something or needed something there was a lot of sharing – things were flying from one boat to the next and the sense of community spirit was fantastic. Everyone was willing to help out others. It was inspiring.

However, keeping occupied while Lee from Atlantic Campaigns slowly and methodically went through the kit was a nightmare.

'Shall we just pace up and down on the quayside?' suggested Helen.

'Go for a cup of coffee?' asked Frances.

'I'm too nervous,' said Niki. 'What if we're missing something?'

Eventually we took it in turns to answer Lee's questions, otherwise the two or so hours he spent going through each tiny item of kit would have been excruciating. Our hearts were pounding. Our mouths were dry. Eventually. Finally. At last. We passed! Never before has a group of four working mothers been so thrilled to have sourced 35 sticky plasters in their lives! We were race-ready and could launch *Rose*. We booked a slot the next morning to get her into the water.

We were on a high. Nothing could hold us back now.

However, our first practice run out with *Rose* was a different story. The rules of the challenge stipulate that you must have at least 24 hours of sea experience in the boat before heading off, and even though we had already ticked that box, we were keen to know what she felt like in the Atlantic. How would she handle? How would she feel? It was also a good idea to run through a few manoeuvres – like getting the watermaker going – while we still had time to make any adjustments on the luxury of dry land. Anything that went wrong once we'd started the race would have to be fixed at sea. And we all knew how difficult that would be. So any problem we identified now would, in theory, be a bit of a bonus.

Less than an hour outside the harbour wall the first fly in our ointment became apparent: Helen. The seas were big, the waves were choppy and coming at us from all angles, and the boat was bouncing around like a ping-pong ball in a Jacuzzi. We'd been warned that for the first few weeks out of La Gomera the sea would be fast, furious and terrifying, but we had only just left the harbour and already the ocean was throwing us around like a toy.

'I'm going to be sick,' announced Helen as she deposited her breakfast down the side of the boat.

'And again.' She hurled.

Poor Helen suffers from chronic seasickness, which is not an ideal affliction in an ocean rower. We all knew she suffered from it and we had discussed it many times before. She wasn't the only one. Frances was not immune to the odd vomit either, but the difference between the two of them was that when Frances was sick, she felt better and was able to continue rowing. She would simply pause mid-stroke in order to throw up over the side of the boat and then carry on. Whereas Helen was out cold. Helen could not move, she could not row, she could not get out of the cabin. All she could do was lie there, making strange lowing noises like a cow about to give birth, unable to sit up, speak or swallow.

And she tried everything: pills, potions, ginger pegs… She'd even been given, in case of great emergency, a seriously strong anti-emetic, that a doctor friend of ours, Caroline Lennox, had suggested we pack should we desperately need it. Helen had shown it to the handsome, God-like race doctor, Thor Munsch, who advised against taking it. His counsel was simple. She was going to be sick; she should go with it until it was out of her system, and then she would be fine. But Helen was desperate to find a remedy. Today she was trying out a special pair of 'travel shades' that blocked vision in one eye, which the company who had provided them said might do the trick.

'They are not working,' she said, declaring the obvious as she held onto the side, retching. 'All that is happening is that I'm being sick while looking out of one eye!'

She turned to look at Janette, who was steering the boat as Frances and Niki rowed. It was tempting to laugh. She was clinging onto the side of the boat, her long brown hair all over the place, wearing a pair of glasses with a patch over one eye. The effect was faintly ridiculous.

'I'm going back to the Stugeron travel sickness tablets,' she announced as she vomited again and disappeared back down into the tiny cabin below.

The problem with having a member of the crew completely incapacitated with seasickness is twofold. Not only do the rest of the crew have to pick up the slack, which is impossible when there is simply no room for passengers on a small boat in the middle of a race to cross the Atlantic, but also if the boat is in danger and all hands are needed on deck then our power to deal with a difficult situation and our capacity to row ourselves out of trouble are severely diminished.

And it wasn't long before that happened. About an hour and a half into our practice the winds, the waves and the currents suddenly turned against us and we were heading towards the rocks just outside the harbour.

'One! Two!' Janette was urging Niki and Frances to dig their oars in deep to help turn the boat away from the rocks. The waves were slapping at the boat from all angles, drenching us. 'Pull!' she yelled, tugging on the rudder, trying to keep the boat from careering towards the collection of sharp black rocks just visible above the foam.

'Helen!' yelled Janette. 'Helen! We need you! We're heading for the rocks!'

Then, 'Helen, will you get on those oars, or we are going to crash into those rocks!'

And, 'Helen, if you don't come out now and help us, we'll all die. Row or die!'

There was a seriousness in her voice. The idea that we could have come all this way only to smash the boat to pieces, or at the very least severely damage the hull, before the race had even started would be such a waste.

'Helen!'

Helen hauled herself out of the cabin, looked up from the back of the boat, glancing over the waves towards the black rocks beyond. She swallowed, still wearing her patched glasses; she could barely speak.

'We're fine!' she managed to mumble over the sound of the surf. 'Suicide Steve is over there and he's much closer than we are. We are nowhere near them!'

'He's much closer to the harbour wall, where there's much less wind. If you took that damned patch off your eye you might be able to see!'

As we made our way back to port with Helen still lying prone on deck, she and Janette looked at each other. Helen had always insisted, despite her chronic seasickness, that she could do it. She would not let anyone down. She would be the trooper who'd carry on rowing no matter what. But in that moment, there was a look of doubt in her eye. Fear, even. Could she really do this? There were plenty of stories of strapping rowers who'd had to be rescued off their boats due to extreme dehydration. All it took was a few days of copious vomiting to reduce a powerful 17-stone professional rower to a useless, quivering, weeping wreck. Could Helen – all 9 stone 3 of her – really make it across? And how on earth was she going to do it if she couldn't last an afternoon in the Atlantic? There were 3,000 miles to go.

'I'll take the Stugeron tablets,' she reassured the rest of us as we moored up next to Row2Recovery. 'I'll eat the Queezibics. I'll get through it.' As we all watched her slowly move her still-shaking body off the boat, we prayed she was right.

A few days later our families arrived, along with our eight children. Met by the lovely Ron from Halifax, they arrived in La Gomera on a wave of unconditional support and excitement. It was fantastic to have them there; they were a welcome distraction from the growing nerves and anxiety surrounding the race. And to show them around the place was a moment we had all been waiting for.

We were hoping that our idea to row the Atlantic would rub off on them. In a world that is full of Instagram negativity and cynical Snapchat, we really wanted to show our children the power of positivity. That if you wanted something enough and you worked hard enough, anything is possible. And there's nothing more positive than hanging out with a group of rowers, all about to cross the Atlantic. With all sorts of creeds, colours and different backgrounds among them, each having been dealt a myriad of different hands in life, they were all here for the same purpose. There's a saying that we'd heard a few times on our journey to the Canaries: 'If you ask the question, "Why cross the Atlantic?" then you won't understand the answer.' The answer, of course, is, 'Because it is there.' And everyone sipping beers at night in The Blue Marlin understood that. As did all the crews packing their ready-meals, fiddling with their equipment and making anxious jobs for themselves as we all waited around for the start of the race.

Our families also made themselves useful. Ben, and Niki's dad, Pete, were fantastic at doing the heavy lifting, lugging around the rudder and packing the giant para-anchor and endlessly giving us instructions on how to use a power tool or fix the watermaker. Memorably one evening, Ben very kindly went through the logistics and intricacies of the watermaker as we sat down in The Blue Marlin nursing our gin and tonics. He was very specific about how many times we should change the filter and how exactly we should do it. (Check it once a week and change it if it turns yellow, apparently.)

'Yes, absolutely,' declared Janette, taking a sip from her glass.

'Great,' nodded Helen.

'Of course,' said both Frances and Niki.

Later we were to realise that it would have perhaps been helpful if at least one of us had listened.

Our other husbands, Richard, Gareth and Mark, had a lot of corralling to do, keeping their eye on our gang – Helen's two kids, Henry (13) and Lucy (16); Niki's Aiden (9) and Corby (12); Janette's Safiya (14) and James (18); and Frances's Jack (13) and Jay (14). Although some of the children, due to their ages, were more useful than others, going backwards and forwards to the supply shops to pick up last-minute scissors or coils of rope, the others did what we'd always hoped they would – they mixed with the crews, heard their stories and came back all shiny-eyed and inspired. They were, of course, most fascinated by the collection of spare limbs left on the dock by the boys from Row2Recovery. They found it extraordinary that a group of men could overcome so many obstacles to row an ocean. They were the embodiment of the power of positive thinking.

However, much as we loved having our families with us, there were also a great many moments when we felt torn. The plan had been to fly them out on the Wednesday and Thursday before the race and for them to leave on the Sunday, with the race itself starting on Tuesday. With so much to check and go through, most of the days were spent with *Rose*, and it was only in the evenings that we really got to see our children.

We'd discussed many times how we wanted to leave the harbour on the day of the race, what our exit strategy would be, and we had all agreed, except Janette, that we would rather be rowing towards our children in Antigua, rather than away from them in La Gomera. So we didn't want a send-off. We didn't want to watch weeping nine-year-olds on the quay, frantically calling out their mothers' names as they disappeared off into the distance. Equally, we also didn't want to be waving and crying and shouting 'I love you!' right back across the waves as our families became small dots on the horizon. And, as Niki pointed out, none of us wanted to say the wrong thing. It would be difficult enough to say goodbye without saying something we would regret over the next three months, stuck on the ocean, with plenty of time to ruminate, churn and analyse from every angle what was said or not said. It was also psychologically smarter that every stroke we took would be one step closer towards them, rather than one step further away.

So it was decided that the majority would leave on the Sunday, taking all our luggage with them. (Janette's family, being a little older and more used to her travelling abroad and being away for long periods of time, were staying until 1 p.m. on the Tuesday to wave us all off for the start of the race. They were keen to give us a send-off and Janette was keen to have them around.) We would only have a small plastic bag of toothbrushes, toothpaste and two pairs of chafe-free pants (Janette won the argument!), which would see us through the next three months until we got to Antigua.

The Saturday before everyone left, there was a party in a cave behind the harbour with some dubious-tasting crabsticks and a seafood-flavoured Swiss roll and quite a lot of beer. We all talked about how we were feeling about the row, what we wanted to get out of it and how we thought it might change us.

'I don't want to worry as much,' said Niki. 'I want to be less organised – enough of the OCD.'

'I want to be much MORE organised,' said Helen. 'I also want to prove that being a working mother doesn't stop you from living your dreams.'

'I don't think I'll change at all,' declared Frances, taking a sip of her beer. 'I shall probably come back exactly the same. The journey to get here has changed me already.'

'I want to live in the moment,' said Janette. 'And', she added, presenting a very small pair of turquoise shorts with green fluoro piping around the legs, 'I am determined to fit into these!'

'What size are they?' shrieked Helen as we all laughed.

'Medium,' Janette replied solemnly. 'They are a little tight.'

We all watched, laughing, as Janette wriggled and struggled, snaking her hips from side to side, as she tried to edge the teeny tiny shorts over her knees. But they refused to budge and stood firm.

'Mmm,' said Frances, looking her slowly up and down. 'This is going to be quite a long trip.'

The next day we said farewell to our families. The tears flowed, the hugs were tight and the goodbyes were painful.

Niki, whose children are the youngest, was perhaps the most upset. It was obvious by her abject silence and the firm grip she had on Gareth's hand that she was trying extremely hard to keep it together. Her teeth were gritted and the smile on her face was tight to the point of rictus.

'If I speak, I will cry,' she said very quietly to her husband as they slowly walked towards the ferry.

Aiden and Corby were also none too keen to leave. They'd loved the boats and the sunshine, and spending Christmas without their mum was going to be hard. Christmas really was their thing. Their magic time of year. Niki was queen of Christmas and now she wasn't going to be there.

'Bye, Mum. See you after Christmas. Good luck,' they said, hugging Niki as tightly as they could. Having kept it together over breakfast and smiling as brightly as she could all the way to the ferry, this proved too much for Niki. The tears started to roll. Try as she might, she could not stop them.

'It won't be long,' Gareth whispered in her ear. 'We'll be thinking of you all the time. And just think of how it will feel in Antigua. We'll be waiting for you.'

They hugged one last time before they boarded the ferry. Niki waved cheerfully as the tears poured down her cheeks.

Meanwhile, Helen was desperately trying to be bright and jolly, endlessly talking extremely quickly about anything at all other than the row, and trying to say positive things to Henry and Lucy.

'Don't forget your GCSEs,' she said to Lucy. 'Keep working hard. It's only seven months to go. They'll fly by. You can do it. You can nail them, smash them... And you –' She turned to Henry. 'You can enjoy school and make me proud. I am already proud... even more proud... if it's possible to be prouder...'

And with one final kiss to Richard and the children, Helen wished them all a Happy Christmas as she waved them onto the boat.

Frances's boys were much less keen on making a fuss. After some strong, brave hugging, she simply kissed Jay, Jack and Mark and waved them goodbye as everyone boarded the ferry back to Tenerife.

It was an odd feeling as our families left. The sadness was balanced by fear and the excitement of what was about to happen. All the waiting, the focus and the hard work was about to come to fruition and we were ready to go. We wanted to get out there and get on with it. It was then, when we got back to the marina, that we discovered the race had been cancelled. Not cancelled as such, but delayed, and delayed by a whole five days. It was a huge shock, but there was nothing to be done. The southerly winds were too strong – they'd blow us all back into the Canaries, or worse, and we wouldn't stand a chance of getting to Antigua no matter how hard we rowed. The harbour master and the race officials were adamant we would have to wait for a better weather window before they would allow us to leave. We might have been desperate to get going, but the ocean clearly had other plans.

Most of the crews took it quite well – nearly every other race before us had suffered some sort of delay, so it was not unexpected. Except we, of course, had not quite thought that possibility through and found ourselves turfed out of our 'deluxe' Spanish apartment with only a plastic bag of toothpaste and pants to our name. Fortunately, Janette had a plan. As her family was staying on a little longer, she'd managed to find a hotel up the hill. The Parador – a five-star, no less – where they viewed us with deep suspicion as we shuffled into their smart reception area, wearing nothing but our rowing vests and black Lycra shorts, swinging our carrier bags.

The delay sadly meant that Janette had to say goodbye to her family too before the start of the race. They had their flights booked to leave on Tuesday after we were supposed to have set off. There was talk of Ben, Safiya and James staying on, but in the end it was decided that they, too, should leave. The start was currently five days delayed, but it could change. There was no point in them waiting in limbo, especially this close to Christmas. So they said their goodbyes, with Janette keeping it as light as possible.

'Good luck, Mum,' said Safiya, with a wave.

'Watch out for the sharks!' joked James. Janette hates sharks, so much so that she almost never swims on holiday.

'No! I'm not setting foot in that ocean!'

'Don't take too long,' smiled Ben.

'I won't!' laughed Janette.

'Row hard and you'll get there sooner!' he suggested.

'Never thought of that!' quipped Janette.

'Bye!' they waved.

'Bye!' she waved.

Janette carried on smiling and waving as they boarded the ferry, before walking around the corner and collapsing against the wall of the ticket office, where she promptly burst into tears.

So now we were alone. Just us and *Rose*. Occasionally a giant cruise ship would dock in the harbour and we'd hear people shouting.

'Look, that's them! The Yorkshire Rows. There they are. With their tiny little boat.'

It seems our little stint on the telly with James Cracknell had been a bit of a hit back home.

'Good luck!' they'd yell, waving at us. 'We're thinking of you!'

It was wonderful to think that we had some support out there. We were, after all, trying to raise money for charity, so any interest we gained along the way was incredibly helpful. But it was an odd time, sitting around and making jobs for ourselves, waiting to hear when we were going to set off.

So the arrival of Wayne and Tracy was a welcome relief. Close friends of Janette's, they had been on a trip of a lifetime to go and see the

Northern Lights in Iceland for the past 10 days. They had never flown before and were first-time owners of a passport. They had been gutted not to be able to see Janette off in the first place, as they were away. However, having read about the delayed start to the race, they decided to change planes in London (they were clearly 'liking the flying thing') and come to La Gomera. None of us believed they would make it until we saw Tracy tottering down the pontoon towards us, waving frantically, still wearing her Northern Lights outfit.

'Yoo-hoo!' she yelled, picking her way past the boats in her fur boots and heavy jacket, with lots of blonde hair. 'Here we are!' She was followed by Wayne, who, a few years younger than Tracy, was also dressed for the frozen wastes of Iceland. 'We're here!' he grinned. 'We had to come and see you off!'

And they did. Come race day they were the ones waving and shouting goodbye as we slowly edged our way out of the port.

SHIP'S LOG:

'Prepare and prepare again. Whatever you do in life, throw yourself into it, learn everything you can and be ready for the ride of your life. Believe in yourself and believe in the special people around you, because they believe in you.'

(JANETTE/SKIPPER)

CHAPTER 2

Holding On

'The sky is not my limit … I am.'
T. F. HODGE

20 December 2015, San Sebastián Marina, La Gomera

The day itself started early: there was a briefing at 7 a.m. Not that the early start mattered that much, as none of us had really slept the night before. It was more than nerves. It was a terrifying feeling, not being able to stop something we had put in motion all that time ago. We had been waiting for this day for so long and now it was here. Very early, we enjoyed a 'last breakfast' at a café on the seafront, quietly savouring the last proper meal we would eat for possibly the next three months and deep in our own thoughts. We were lingering – it was as if no one quite wanted to leave.

Janette piped up into the silence.

'I feel so nervous, as if I'm about to get married again!'

'What the *hell* are we doing?' asked Helen.

'Who knows?' replied Niki. And we all looked at one another.

'Well, come on then!' said Frances, standing up. As the one who'd got us into all of this, she wasn't going to allow us to sit around as if there was nowhere else we should be. 'Let's do this!' And with that, she led us out, leaving the table and, indeed, her sunglasses behind.

The briefing room was silent, but we were worried and disconcerted to see that Lauren from Row Like a Girl was visibly upset as we listened to Carsten Heron Olsen, CEO and race director, run through his last-minute safety list. Quite apart from how sorry we felt for her, she was one of the few who knew what it was really like out there. And the gift given to each of the boats in the race from the people of La Gomera did not help much either. It was a gladdening picture of the Holy Mary to stick on the wall of the cabin, which (we noticed) no one refused. It was like we were being read our last rites. What the hell had we let ourselves in for?

The silent, tense atmosphere of the briefing was in massive contrast to the noise outside. We walked, blinking, into the sunlight to be faced with cheering, waving crowds and a loud local band. The sound was overwhelming and as the deafening drums beat out some unrecognisable tune, we all processed in silence behind.

Yorkshire Rows had been given the honour of going first out of the harbour. The fours were leading out and we'd been chosen to head the race out of San Sebastián into the Atlantic. It would probably be the only time we would be leading the race itself and we felt extremely proud and sick with nerves as we walked towards *Rose*, moored up on the pontoon. Our hearts were pounding. Our hands were sweating. This was it. There was no turning back. Helen, who is normally one of the most garrulous of us all, was completely silent. We were trying to focus. Then, what had begun in apparent slow motion began to frantically speed up. Suddenly it felt like a panic, as we all started asking if we had everything. Where was this? That? Frances had lost her sunglasses. Where the hell were they? Janette was fumbling with the tiller, making those last-minute skipper checks – battery levels, harnesses and comms. Niki's feet wouldn't fit in her shoes and Helen was looking for some sort of sign that everything was going to be fine.

Looking for signs is Helen's thing. She has a very close friend, Dawn, who reads angel cards and tarot.

'It was through her that I learnt about looking for signs,' she once explained to the rest of us. 'You just have to open your eyes to see them, whereas before I would have my head down and didn't look at what was around me and didn't see the opportunities or the potential in any situation. But she taught me that actually you've got to look, and there's always someone ready to help you, supporting you. But you have to look and listen.'

In the run-up to the race Helen was seeing signs all the time. She'd go into restaurants and there would be oars on the wall. She went on holiday to a cottage in Robin Hood's Bay only to find a great big blade in the kitchen. But feathers are really her thing. She sees them everywhere. They are small indications of affirmation and support.

'Helen!' shouted Sarah, one of the PR girls working for Talisker, as we were poised at the oars, about to set off. 'Look! Look in the water beside you!' We all turned and there, sure enough, floating in the water right next to Helen, was a large white feather.

'There you go!' she smiled as she nodded down at the sea. 'It will all be fine. We will make it across! Just you wait and see…

And so we set off towards the start line. With Janette at the helm, we rowed with all three of us up on the oars, with as much style and panache as we could manage. We were very conscious that our families would be watching the start on *BBC Breakfast*, curled up on the sofa at home, five days before Christmas and without their mums. We wanted to give them a bit of a show.

'Okay, ladies,' grinned Janette as we lined up at the start, surrounded by small boats, larger vessels, TV crews, a circling helicopter, shouting, waving crowds and Wayne and Tracy. 'Let's show them how it's done!'

We were poised to go. Janette held onto the mooring line with Carsten gripping the other end. This was the only thing that was stopping us from leaving. Carsten kissed Janette on the cheek.

'Good luck,' he said. 'I'll see you in Antigua.' He let go of the rope. Our last contact with land.

Janette pulled it on board. It felt strange. This was it. We were leaving. Our hearts were pounding. It was nerve-racking. It was our last touch. Our last bit of contact with land, with anyone else.

From now on it would be just us four. It was going to be tough, but we were going to make damn sure we managed it.

Janette stood tall. She was ready to steer the way. She knew we'd give it everything we could to show to the world we were ready, we were strong and we were women.

'Come on, girls,' she urged, her blonde hair whipping around her face. 'Let's do this!'

Carsten sounded the klaxon and the loud, shrieking blast echoed around the harbour. The crowds roared and we were off, rowing in unison, giving it our best in our black Lycra rowing shorts and our Talisker vests, pulling our oars through the water powerfully and in time, together.

'One! Two!' shouted Janette from the helm. 'Smile!' she urged. 'I feel like Queen Boadicea in the middle of her slaves!' She laughed. 'We're Amazons!'

'Quite elderly Amazons,' said Frances, as she slid back and forth on her seat.

'Middle-aged,' corrected Niki.

'Middle-aged Amazons!' agreed Helen. 'Who ARE going to cross an ocean!'

The boats left La Gomera at 15-minute intervals, and it wasn't long before we watched Row Like a Girl power past us. We had held the lead in the race for precisely half an hour! Possibly less. Not that we minded; we were more interested in hitting the first waypoint (a marker), which we had dutifully programmed into our GPS system and were trying to head towards, despite the ever-increasing swell. The problem, we soon realised, with being first out of the harbour is that you have no one to follow! And it didn't take long before all the other rowers had also left La Gomera and disappeared.

One moment we could see an ocean littered with boats – friends that we had made over the three weeks that we had spent on the island. And then, all of a sudden, we were alone. It was like an oceanic game of hide and seek. We were on our own.

There was no time to worry about this, for even with land still firmly in sight, the ocean had plans. The waves were growing and the current grew stronger, and *Rose* was being pulled along in it. Time and again we tried to row, and time and again the oars were being wrenched out of our hands. It was painful. The sea was so strong that we could not get any purchase in the waves, and when we did the oars would shoot out of the water, sending us and them flying backwards, hitting us in the legs and the thighs, garrotting us or, even worse, whacking us extremely hard in the pubic bone. It was agony, and not what we had trained for at all. It was also cold, freezing cold, as wave after 40-foot wave broke over us, dousing us in icy salt water. We were being lashed from left and right, the oars flying everywhere. It was truly a baptism of fire; we were taking our wet-weather gear on and off constantly, and clinging onto the boat for dear life. And we had only just gone out to sea.

'Call this a rowing race?' shouted Frances as she held onto the side of the boat, as we rode yet another wall of 40-foot waves. 'This is just holding on!'

'I hate these waves,' said Helen. 'I can't believe they are SO big.'

'These aren't big!' shouted Janette. 'This is nothing – 40 foot is noth-ing – 40 foot is easy.' She smiled. 'We're perfectly safe.'

'It's like the best rollercoaster ride!' grinned Niki, who, out of all four of us, was the one loving it the most. We were hitting 3.5 knots without even putting an oar in the water. Who knew she was such a speed freak?

Meanwhile, everything was an effort. Moving around on the boat was so difficult. Constrained by our bulky wet-weather gear and the extreme rocking with the waves, even the smallest thing seemed impossible. Cooking was actually dangerous. The simple task of boiling some water and then trying to rehydrate a bag of chicken curry or beef stew could take up to 45 minutes at a time, as splashes of scalding hot water sloshed all over the place.

But going to the toilet was the worst. We had two buckets – one for washing in and the other for doing our business. Being resourceful ladies we had naturally customised our toilet bucket with a grey plastic lav seat for a more comfortable experience. However, it is difficult to do one's business with your weatherproof salopettes around your ankles while riding a rollercoaster wave, with a biodegradable wet wipe in your hand. Not forgetting the audience. In the front row.

Not that any of us really cared about that. We'd seen each other in all forms of undress in the build-up to the race. We had shared more dodgy hotel rooms with badly plumbed bathrooms than we cared to remember. So performing on a bucket in front of the group was not the problem; staying on the bucket was. And keeping the contents of the bucket from flying back into the boat after you hurled it overboard or avoiding spilling it all over your fellow rower was something of a challenge. Also, remembering to fill it with a little water before sitting on it was clearly trickier for some members of the crew than for others. Helen was always the one having to scrub out her bucket after being surprised by her sudden need to go to the loo.

Despite the huge waves and the strong current, we were sticking to our plan of rowing two hours on, two hours off. We were on the oars in our pairings of Frances and Niki, and Janette and Helen, keeping to our schedule and pointing the bow towards Antigua, 3,000 miles away.

Even Helen. Every two hours she would come out of the diminutive cabin she was sharing with Niki and she would throw up, get on the oars, throw up, either row or not row, throw up. And she would remain there for the next two hours, being battered by the waves and throwing up, before it was her turn to go back into the cabin. Then she would get off her seat, throw up, knock on the cabin door to get Niki out of bed, throw up again, before dragging herself into the cabin, where she would lie, without moving, until she was called back up on deck again two hours later.

The only two things that kept Helen going during those first few days were mugs of Ultra Fuel (an all-singing, all-dancing liquid meal-replacement drink, developed from extreme sports) and Niki. Every time Helen came off shift, Niki made her a mixture of Ultra Fuel and water, which Helen would sip in tiny mouthfuls, while lying motionless, for the next two hours. Oddly, Helen was not sick when she was lying down, and those precious minutes allowed her to metabolise the nutrients in the drink and prevent total dehydration. And dehydration on the ocean can be fatal, or at least fatal to your ambitions of finishing the race, as once it kicks in it is extremely difficult to combat. Which is exactly what happened to poor Nick Khan in the Latitude 35 team – after 10 days of chronic seasickness, he had to be medivacked off the boat when he was found deliriously shouting at the sea and saying he wanted to die. He had no choice but to leave the boat (along with another crew member who'd decided it was no longer safe for him to continue), leaving the remaining pair to row the four-man boat without them.

So we all kept an eye on Helen. Well, Niki did. Sympathy, or indeed empathy, is not something that courses freely through the veins of either Janette or Frances. They are more Yorkshire than pudding, and their suffering of fools and vomitus is limited to say the least. But what neither of them could fault Helen on was her absolute determination to keep on going during those first 72 hours. She was not so much 'eat, sleep, row, repeat'; more 'puke, sleep, puke, row, puke, repeat'. It was impressive. Her eyes were glazed, her conversation was non-existent, but still she managed to row. The waves crashed against the side of the boat and Helen stood firm. 'Just a few more days,' we all kept on thinking; just a few more days and we hoped Helen would be able to crack a smile and keep down the all-in-one breakfast-in-a-bag.

But it was about 2 a.m. in the morning on the third day when disaster struck. The boat was lurching from side to side in the huge waves, the few lights we had on board were flickering and it was Helen's turn up on the oars.

'Five minutes!' yelled Niki, knocking on the door to the sealed cabin.

'What do you think?' asked Janette through the darkness, sliding back and forth on her seat. 'Do you think Helen is any better?'

'A bit,' said Niki, holding onto the boat while trying to slip out of her wet-weather gear. 'She is being very brave. Stick to the Ultra Fuel and I'm sure she'll pull through, eventually.'

Just then a huge wave hit the side of the boat, sending Niki flying. With one leg still in her trousers, she didn't stand a chance as she was hurled against a metal peg that sank hard into the base of her spine.

'Oh my GOD!' she screamed in the darkness. 'Oh my GO-O-OD!'

'Are you okay?' Janette leapt off the oars.

Niki was writhing around in the water at the bottom of the boat, screaming and clutching the base of her spine. Both Frances and Helen appeared, from either end of the boat.

'No! NO! I am not!'

'Are you hurt?'

'Yes! My bum, my bum –'

Niki was shaking and stammering with cold and pain.

'Have you broken anything? Cut anything? Is there blood?' asked Janette, scrabbling about in the darkness.

'No. I don't know… my back, my coccyx, my pelvis. It's agony… Aaaah – this is worse than childbirth! Worse… than… bloody… childbirth!'

'Here,' shouted Frances, staggering towards her. 'Here's the medical bag.'

'Okay, okay,' said Janette, leaning over and grabbing the bag. 'On a scale of one to ten. One to ten, remember. What is your pain?'

'Oh, Jesus Christ!' spat Niki. 'Once a nurse, always a bloody nurse.' Janette was indeed once a nurse.

'It's a ten! Of course it's a ten!'

'Okay, okay,' said Janette, fumbling through the bag in the darkness. 'How about… paracetamol? No. Tramadol? Or…' She strained to read the label in the dark. 'Diclofenac?'

'What's that?'

'It's a painkiller and an anti-inflammatory.'

'What will it do?' gasped Niki.

'Make you go… um, diclofuckit?' suggested Janette.

'I'll have two diclofuckits,' said Niki desperately.

'Two,' nodded Janette in agreement.

'And I don't know what you're looking at,' said Niki, lying flat at the bottom of the boat, staring up at Frances as yet another wave crashed overhead. 'It's all your fault we're here!'

'Yeah!' agreed Helen, speaking for the first time in 24 hours. 'This is the last time I listen to any of your bright ideas.'

SHIP'S LOG:

'We were holding on, yet at the same time we were letting go. The first 24 hours of our row were about letting go – letting go of life enough so that we could venture into the unknown. Each of us had to eventually stop looking at the outline of the land and turn instead towards the vast open ocean. That first stroke of the oars away from the shore was our first step into an unknown world. It takes courage to let go of what you are familiar with. Once the step has been taken, there is no knowing how the ride will go – and that's the fun part.'

(JANETTE/SKIPPER)

CHAPTER 3

The Beginning

'A dream you dream alone is only a dream. A dream you dream together is reality.'

YOKO ONO

3 May 2013, Leeds

It was just past seven in the morning as Frances Davies, a 45-year-old lawyer from York, was driving down Whitehall Road, Leeds, listening to Stan Graham, a favourite folk singer of hers.

She'd been up since 5.30 a.m., as she had been every working day for the past 20 years. As a busy mother of two, it was the only time when she could have a moment to herself. The house was quiet and her husband, Mark, and their two children, Jay and Jack, would be asleep, so she would potter around their Victorian terraced house in the centre of York, listening to motivational TED talks on her computer, soaking up the words and ideas of Diana Nyad, who, at 60, was the only person to swim from Cuba to Florida without a shark cage. Either that, or Frances would sneak in an extra chapter of a book, with her yoghurt and fruit, reading about ex-headmistress Anne Mustoe's account of cycling around the world at the age of 50. And then she'd kiss everyone goodbye while they were still asleep in their beds, get into the car and drive the 25-mile journey to the office and the job she'd had for the past 13 years.

Sitting at the traffic lights that morning, dressed in her grey suit and white shirt, with her chin on the steering wheel, she watched the same old man walk the same elderly dog across the same road at the same time as he did every day. She looked up the road towards her looming office building and across at all the other commuters sitting in their cars. She thought of Patrick Swayze from one of her favourite films – *Point Break* – and those 'dead souls inching along the freeways in their metal coffins'.

There were only a few lights on in the office – she'd be one of the first in, again, and one of the last to leave. She'd miss school drop-off and pick-up as usual. She'd probably have to stop for a drink with a client at the end of the day and wouldn't be home until well past nine that evening.

'*Who knows what's around the bend? A brand-new start or the bitter end?*' sang Stan Graham in *Easy Street*.

Frances glanced at the radio, her palms feeling clammy, her heart beating harder in her chest. A brand-new start? Or the bitter end? The bitter end. 'Will this be my entire adult working life?' she thought to herself. Wearing the same old groove? Going on the same journey 25 miles in and 25 miles out of Leeds? Every. Single. Day?

'That's it,' she said to herself, pushing herself back in her seat. 'I am asking them again. They can only say no.' She put the car into gear. Her mother had died at the age of 58 from breast cancer. Frances was 28 years old at the time and her mother's passing left a huge hole in her life. Her mother had lost her battle with cancer when she was little older than Frances is now. She had not lived long enough to meet Mark or her grandchildren – a loss that Frances had always felt very keenly.

'We are only here once,' she reasoned. 'We should make the most of our short time here. I'm fed up with going to things and hearing how "busy" everyone is. I don't care who is "busy" or who is not "busy". What is admirable about being busy? I don't care about any of that. I want to get out and do something else.'

One of the things about the death of her mother that had always inspired Frances was how she never gave up – she always carried on fighting. For years she battled cancer with a serenity that was humbling. Her courage against all the odds was overwhelming.

So, after refuelling with a weak, tepid coffee from the office kitchen, she sat down at her desk and wrote this email:

From: Frances Davies
Sent: 03 May 2013 08:19
To: Janette Benaddi; Niki Doeg; Helen Butters; Caroline Lennox
Subject: Atlantic Campaigns | Atlantic Rowing | TALISKER Whisky Atlantic Challenge | Atlantic Rowing Race – Helen – don't delete!

http://www.atlanticcampaigns.com/

Morning,
Do you remember my suggestion at the boat club dinner? I thought I would forward this to all of you. I do see that it sounds very silly, but I think we could do this race. Other people have done it and we must be just as good as they are.

I think it's possible to enter as 1, 2, 4, 5 or 6, so any combination of us could enter. It's quite pricey and, of course, would mean taking a couple of months out of our regular lives! We would need sponsorship. Mark obviously thinks I'm ridiculous, but I have sold it to the boys on the basis that they get to go to Antigua to meet us at the finish!

It would be amazing and probably life-changing, and we definitely won't want to go back to work afterwards – we could maybe sign up for it if we get very drunk in France in September.

Anyway, have a think about it.

For those racing this weekend – good luck.

Have a great weekend

F xx

She pressed send, sighed and waited. Shuffling through the papers she needed for her first meeting that morning, she kept her eye on the screen.

It took Janette precisely 13 minutes to reply:

From: Janette Benaddi

Sent: 03 May 2013 08:32

To: Frances Davies; Niki Doeg; Helen Butters; Caroline Lennox

Subject: RE: Atlantic Campaigns | Atlantic Rowing | TALISKER Whisky Atlantic Challenge | Atlantic Rowing Race – Helen – don't delete!

Life's for living, so let's really live. I am definitely up for it.

J

Janette Benaddi

That was so very typical of Janette. An impetuous force of nature, she is a self-made businesswoman who has been running her own clinical trials company for the past 20 years. Married to Ben, a French-Moroccan, whom she met dancing in her sister's sitting room, she has never knowingly taken a duvet day in her life. Even after the birth of her first child, James, she didn't take any time off. Not even a day! It wasn't meant to happen that way, but she'd been booked to give a talk in London. She had originally thought she'd be fine. She'd have her baby; he would be two weeks old and she'd leave him with Ben for the day while she popped down to London to talk at the conference and popped back up to York again. But James was a first baby and first babies are often late. He was two weeks late. Janette had no choice, not unless she didn't want to be paid, and anyway, she didn't want to let them down. So she gave birth at 8 a.m. on the Tuesday after a long 36-hour labour with gas, air and ventouse. Come 8 a.m. on the Wednesday, she was on the train to London, leaving Ben in charge of their newborn son. During a break at the conference, there were a few doctors milling around, drinking tea and eating biscuits, and one of them approached Janette.

'Do you have any children?' she asked, smiling politely and nibbling the corner of a custard cream.

'Oh yes!' replied Janette, beaming with new-mother pride. 'A son.'

'How lovely,' replied the doctor. 'How old is he?'

'Oh,' replied Janette, her brain whirring, not wanting to lie that much. 'Um… two weeks?' she ventured.

'Two weeks!' The doctor was horrified; the crumbs went flying. 'What are you doing here? Are you mad! You should be at home!'

Little did she know that, back in Selby, Ben was busy explaining Janette's absence to an equally appalled midwife, who turned up to weigh the baby and was completely astonished to find no sign of the mother.

But Janette has never been one to conform. She left school at 16 with two O levels and eventually became a trained nurse, after putting herself through night school while working in a doctor's surgery. As a nurse she became frustrated, as there was never enough time to do the job properly, never enough time to speak to the patients or give them the care they needed. Gradually, she found herself moving into the world of medical technology, travelling the length and breadth of the country, selling dressings and syringes to doctors, hospitals and surgeries.

The second of four girls, her childhood was peripatetic, and financially it was either feast or famine. Her father was also no stranger to graft, and had at any one time an HGV business, a bingo hall, a coach business and a tyre business. 'Some Christmases there were loads of presents and sometimes there was very little.' So when Janette got the chance she worked, and she worked hard. She took the plunge and set up a clinical trial business, although it wasn't exactly good timing as her husband Ben had just started university. 'We were really strapped for cash. Every month was absolutely tight – we'd go to the wire, scrabbling around for change, because neither of us was really making anything. It was very hard for us for the first couple of years until the business got going. We didn't have any holidays – a lot of people don't, I know, but we didn't for years. We had an old blue Nissan car and Ben used to make a lot of meals that were full of potatoes so we wouldn't feel hungry.'

But Janette was very focused. 'I was once one of those kids who had free school meals. It was so obvious, the kids who were on free meals. We had different-coloured tickets from the rest of them and it was like a taboo was attached to you. It was like being put into a box, and I was desperate to break out of that box. Why should I be put into a box in the first place?'

So then, together, she and Ben bought some old offices in Selby, which they stripped of paint every night until two in the morning, with one heater on and James asleep in a carry-cot. They mortgaged themselves to the hilt and worked all hours while Ben also put himself through university. The idea was to do up the building, rent out parts of it and start a business.

'I always thought, "What's the worst that can happen? We lose our house? So what – we have lots of family and friends who would take us in."'

One night the stripping and the painting got a little boring, and nine months later Safiya was born. More mouths to feed, more work to be done. Fortunately, the business was beginning to grow, Ben graduated from university with a first-class honours degree and they took on their first employee: Janette's mum! Eventually Janette's clinical trial business broke through and then her life changed and became a lot more comfortable; she and Ben were able to send their children to private school.

Haunted by the memory of having to conceal a romance for two years – even having to hide in the back of a car – because her boyfriend's posh parents didn't want him consorting with the likes of her, Janette wanted something different for her own children.

'Obviously his mother didn't want a Catholic girl like me to be involved with her son,' she remembers. 'Little things that happen in your life like that can either go one way or the other. They either knock you down so low that you never get up again, or they make you more determined.'

And it was at the children's school, St Peter's in York, established in AD 627, that we all met. Not in the car park, as you might expect, as half of us aren't around to do the school run, but at the Guy Fawkes' Boat Club (so named because one of St Peter's illustrious alumni was Mr Fawkes himself) one drizzly Saturday in September 2012.

Our children were all attending school on Saturdays, so we each had the mornings free. We could either lie in bed with a cup of tea and a newspaper, sit googling nice things to wear or put on a pair of wellies, a woolly hat and some Lycra shorts and learn to row. All four of us chose the latter.

Quite why we each of us decided to spend those spare mornings freezing on a muddy riverbank instead of eating a muffin in a coffee shop in town is a question in itself.

For Janette the answer was simple. Baby James was now grown up and had descended into his non-communicative teenage years. He was in a rowing team at school, so Janette concluded that if she also learnt to row, they'd have something to talk about, and she might lose some weight in the process.

For Frances it was a question of a sudden gap opening up in her schedule (her youngest, Jack, had just started going to school on Saturdays), which urgently needed to be filled. She is not someone who can sit still. Even during the ad breaks while watching television she has a burning desire to do something. So the idea that she would have nothing to do on a Saturday morning, nothing at all, while both of her sons were now at school was enough motivation in itself. She'd done the 10-kilometre runs, the Coast to Coast races and already joined the BSAC (British Sub Aqua Club), diving Stoney Cove in Leicestershire and over the harbour wall at St Abbs on the east coast of Scotland, so signing up to the Guy Fawkes' Boat Club would be no giant leap at all.

And she and Niki Doeg knew each other from book club. Their sons, Corby and Jack, have been friends since they were in nursery together – so why wouldn't Niki also want to fill a small window on a Saturday morning? In between running her finance business with her husband, Gareth. And training to be a rugby coach. While looking after two small boys. Her plate was simply not full enough already! So leaving Aiden (her youngest) behind with Gareth, Niki turned up at the boathouse at 8.20 a.m. (just after drop-off) on that first Saturday morning at the start of a new school year.

Helen Butters bumped into Niki and Frances dressed in their tracksuits after their first session as she was picking up her son, Henry (who was also in the same class as Corby and Jack). She insists that she'd been thinking about learning a new skill when she saw them, that she'd been wanting something to do on a Saturday morning as she was only currently working three days a week for the NHS in Wakefield. Not that rowing or getting wet was particularly Helen's thing, but she does not like to be bored. She'd been a stay-at-home mother once before, for four years, and it had driven her ever so slightly to distraction. She maintains that there is only so much sitting around in 'cream kitchens, in pretty houses with very thick carpets, in a bubble of niceness' that she can cope with. The 'Cashmere Mafia' with their champagne breakfasts, their Pilates classes and their meeting for afternoon coffee drove her to set up a small business with a friend, Rebecca. It was a loyalty-based card scheme, 'My High Street Card', and they went from shop to shop like contestants in *The Apprentice*, getting local retailers to join up. The scheme was successful for a while, before Helen gave it up to re-join the NHS. 'I was a much better mother when I worked than when I was at home full-time, because then I would get frustrated and extremely grumpy.'

So it was effectively the second week of rowing club when we all finally met. Well, actually, when we all finally met Janette. It was a dank autumn morning. The air was cold enough to leave a conversation hanging, long after the sound had disappeared. The pretty wooden-slatted school boat house was bustling with women, sorting out their bags, stamping in their boots, keen to get out onto the nearby River Ouse. When, through the early-morning mist, a plump vision in blue and pink rubber sailing boots with a hat as tight as a diaphragm over her blonde head came tramping down the towpath towards us, with a nervous grin on her face. It was Helen who noticed her first.

'Who's that weird woman in the boots and hat?' she asked, zipping up her fleece.

'I'm not sure,' frowned Frances. 'Have you ever seen her before?'

And to her credit, despite not knowing anyone, Janette came over and introduced herself, and within a few minutes she had squeezed her ample derrière into the back of a very thin, very unstable, very wobbly boat, her hat pulled down over her ears. Her reasoning being that if she sat at the back then no one would notice her. It was obvious that all the other women knew each other, except her. She was more than a little worried that she wouldn't fit in. Fortunately, there was no time to ponder the social niceties and her insecurities before the no-nonsense, bellowing tones of the coach took over.

We limped into the middle of the river, splashing and thrashing our oars as we went, and for the next two hours the coach whipped our behinds, shouting commands and bemoaning our lack of talent, technique and knowledge of anything whatsoever to do with rowing.

'Feather!'

'Square!'

'Feather!'

'Square!'

'More on stroke!'

'More on bow!'

'Half!'

'Quarter!'

'What the hell's a square?' whispered Janette as she wobbled about in the back.

'No idea!' hissed Helen as she wobbled about in the seat in front. 'What's a sodding feather?'

'Christ!' shrieked Janette as she splashed herself in the face with what felt like a bucket of freezing, fetid river water. 'What are we doing?'

None of the coach's words meant anything to us. Clearly his favourite method of teaching was total immersion, or indeed a baptism. He bawled and begged us, telling us we were letting the whole boat down by our awful ineptitude. We should whip back and forth on our seat using our strong legs, our blades should glide through water. We should have strength and style. And all the while, all we wanted to focus on was trying to remain out of the water as the boat listed precariously from side to side in the freezing River Ouse.

At the end of the lesson, we crawled – exhausted and decidedly damp – up the muddy riverbank. We all had pink cheeks, runny noses, painful hands and wet backsides, but it was immediately obvious who was going to be coming back the following week. Half the women looked miserable, like it had been the worst two hours of their lives, and there were a few, like us, who were clearly invigorated and excited, adrenalised and very much alive.

'Who fancies a cup of coffee at The Grange?' suggested Niki, looking across the expansive playing fields towards the small Georgian hotel next door to the school.

'Great,' said Frances.

'Absolutely,' agreed Helen.

'Janette?' asked Niki, looking over at her.

'Me?'

And that was it. We would meet every Saturday after that, come rain or shine (mainly rain), and we'd row up and down the Ouse, falling in, getting back into the boat, only to be shouted at by the coach over and over. And then we would retire to The Grange and drink coffee and eat as many biscuits as was politely possible in a smart four-star hotel, while we talked about our husbands, our children and our lives.

People mostly thought we were mad. Our husbands thought we were a little eccentric. Why would four middle-aged women want to spend their Saturday mornings freezing their breasts off rowing, rather poorly, up and down a river? There was the exercise element. And, of course, we were all learning a new skill, but truthfully, after a while it became about the friendship.

We are four completely different characters. Janette is the go-getter with a very dry sense of humour. Helen is always the cheerful one – gossipy, full of stories and tall tales of angels, feathers and the universe. Frances is very laid-back, sanguine and calm; it takes a lot to rile her. And then there's Niki, the serious, dependable one, who is never knowingly out of wet wipes, with a handbag to rival Mary Poppins, right down to the hat stand.

Our backgrounds could also not be more diverse. Niki was born in Nassau in the Bahamas. Her parents were schoolteachers who travelled all over the world, and Niki lived in Mexico, Dubai, Sri Lanka and Saudi Arabia before she was sent to boarding school near York at the age of 10. Rebellious at school, with dyed hair and an attitude to match, she managed to pass her A levels before getting a job at the nascent First Direct bank during her gap year. Having toyed with the idea of joining the Army, she never took up her place at university, preferring to work her way up through the bank and meeting her future husband, Gareth, at the Mansion Pub in Roundhay Park, Leeds, on New Year's Eve when she was 20. 'He was quite drunk, I was quite drunk, and he was asking girls for New Year's Eve kisses. I refused, saying I would only kiss him at midnight.' And they have been together ever since. Literally. They bought a house together quite soon afterwards and have barely – almost never – spent a day apart. They finally got married in 1999. The theme was fancy dress: Cavaliers Only! Gareth was dressed in high boots and a tabard and Niki came down the aisle in a fabulous corseted gold frock with a feathered mask.

Helen is married to Richard, a former barrister who is currently the Director of Public Prosecutions on the Isle of Man. A Catholic grammar school girl, she attended Notre Dame School in Leeds before turning down a place at the London School of Fashion to work at LTHT (Leeds Teaching Hospital Trust). She worked her way up to management level, only to give up her job to get married and have children.

'I met Richard in an All Bar One and it was time,' she said. 'I had got to a point when all I was doing was finishing work on a Friday and going out for a few glasses of wine. I remember I was waiting for the bus and this man selling *The Big Issue* was standing next to me. He asked me to look after his dog and we ended up chatting. He was selling the magazine, while I was holding the dog, and I just thought, "Maybe, Helen, the universe is trying to tell you something." This was not the best use of my Friday night, after all. So subconsciously, I believe, I must have put it out there that I really wanted to find someone. I wanted to settle down. It was only a few weeks later when Richard walked into All Bar One and started to talk to me. He was very funny and bright and clearly one of those people who knows what he wants and gets it and, *boof*, that was it. Before I knew it, we were married. It was all a bit of whirlwind.'

Frances, on the other hand, grew up in Denby Dale, a quiet village in West Yorkshire in the rolling hills outside Huddersfield. Her mother (a school teacher) and her father (a chemical engineer) got together in their twenties and settled down to family life in Yorkshire, raising Frances and her older brother, Robert. Her parents were not ones to stray too far from the county borders: her father made a single cross-Channel trip for business and her mother visited France once on a school trip. Family holidays were spent in the Lake District and Wales. Exotic travel was not high on the family's agenda, nor adrenaline-fuelled experiences...

Running was Frances's escape as a teenager. She ran for Longwood Harriers on the track and in cross-country events, and loved nothing better in the evenings and at weekends than a run across the local hills and along the back lanes around neighbouring villages. Running gave Frances a sense of freedom and independence, and the space to let her mind wander. 'I just love that feeling of almost leaving the real world when a racing gun has started. You are in this no man's land. Such a feeling of flow. Then there's the finish line and the elation when you cross it.'

Perhaps her parents shouldn't have been so shocked, then, when Frances chose to go away from Yorkshire, all the way to Southampton University, for her degree course. After completing her chemistry degree, Frances studied law in Manchester and qualified as a solicitor, moving to Leeds to join a commercial law firm. Here she met and married her husband Mark, a lawyer at the same firm. 'Mark has always said that I have a restless soul. One of our first dates was abseiling (my idea), and shortly after that I persuaded him to join me in having a go at paragliding. I think I took him out of his comfort zone, but he must have liked it given that we were married within 18 months of getting together!'

They managed to fit in a trek in Nepal and a London Marathon, and then plans for more ambitious adventures had to be put on hold in 2001 with the birth of their son, Jay, who was closely followed by his brother, Jack, the following year.

'When the boys were little we used to go to libraries a lot and one day at Acomb Library in the York suburbs, while they took out picture books, I borrowed Debra Veal's *Rowing it Alone*, the story of a woman who rowed the Atlantic solo after setting off with her husband. He had to abandon the trip when he couldn't cope with being out at sea. I also read books by Anne Mustoe and Dervla Murphy – they were my armchair adventures. I would read all these books and dream and think, "I'd love to do that one day."'

Instead, she channelled her energies into her legal career and raising her family. With the routines of daily life eating away at any spare time, Frances's thirst for adventure had to be satisfied by taking part in occasional running, cycling or open-water swimming races. But while she was taking part in these races she still dreamed of bigger adventures.

And Janette? Well, her husband Ben's father was in the French Foreign Legion. Moroccan by birth, Ben was brought up in Paris by his young mother and older father. He was only 15 years old when his father decided to move the family back to Morocco. Ben refused to come, electing instead to stay with his elder brother in Paris, only for him to be turfed out onto the streets when his brother's girlfriend moved in. He found himself living in a monastery and training to be a Catholic priest – a vocation he thankfully passed up for what was supposed to be a brief sojourn in Yorkshire. Janette always says he came into her life at completely the right time. A vision in white jeans and cowboy boots, he danced into her life in her sister's sitting room – an inauspicious entrance for a guardian angel who rescued her from a life of impecunious partying. Janette's sister, Maria, ran what turned out to be a rather posh squat in the middle of Selby, which was responsible for many parties and many international relationships and indeed marriages. Janette's other sister, Jane, had met her Spanish husband while Samba-ing around the sofa, and as soon as Ben opened his mouth to speak in his thick French-Yorkshire accent, Janette knew he was the man for her! He was invited to her father's fiftieth birthday party (by Janette's sister); they moved in together soon after and were married two years later.

So here we were: four completely different women, brought together through our mutual love of biscuits and adventure by a school rowing club in the middle of York.

To start off with we didn't venture far. We'd go north to Poppleton and back, which was a mere six miles – of blood, sweat and swearing. Or we'd pootle up the Ouse simply admiring the pretty bridges and stunning architecture of York. Sometimes we'd row south to Bishopthorpe and back, another five or so miles of grunting and groaning, and that would be sufficient to exhaust us and send us on our hands and knees to The Grange for a large latte and a plate of shortbread.

We did manage one trip to Newton-on-Ouse, which involved a 10-mile row there and a 10-mile row back, but it was fortunately broken up by a lengthy pub lunch in between. Apart from us four, there was a small group of hardcore Fawkes regulars, including Joan, Sally, Liz and a close friend of ours, Dr Caroline Lennox, and it wasn't too long before we all thought we might branch out, move it up a gear and enter a few races.

Not that we fancied our chances. Truth be told, we knew we were appalling, though perhaps not quite as appalling as our first outing proved to be.

Obviously it was not our fault and, frankly, it would have been better had we not invited most of our families to line the riverbank to bear witness to our fabulous rowing prowess. But we were keen to prove that we had not been wasting our Saturday mornings, and anyway it was quite a nice day and the race was in York, at the rowing club, so it wasn't far for anyone to go.

We arrived, dressed in our regulation rowing-club blue-and-white skin-tight Lycra onesies, very much looking and feeling the part. Janette and Helen, who were in the first boat of eight to race, were exuding a little bit of confidence until they saw their cox. He was rather a large chap, with a fuller chest than any of us – not the usual light, pint-sized peanut you hope to have steering the boat.

'Why have we got the big cox?' whispered Janette.

'I suppose we're beginners and no one really wants to steer us,' ventured Helen.

'Well, I hope he knows what he's doing,' said Janette.

Sadly, the cox appeared to know even less about rowing than we did, and no sooner had we all parked our behinds on the seats and laced our feet into our shoes than we ploughed straight into the riverbank. The Ouse was obviously quite busy with crews of fours and eights all heading up the river to the start of the race, so the going was tricky. It required skill and forethought to negotiate the traffic, neither of which our increasingly sweaty cox appeared to have.

'Number 48!' an umpire, marching along the bank, shouted through a megaphone. 'Number 48! Watch yourselves!'

'Is that us?' asked Janette as we careered into another boat.

'Yup!' replied Helen right behind her.

'Number 48!' the woman shouted again as we ricocheted off the boat and into the bank. 'I really think you need to come off the river.'

'I think we need to come off the river,' repeated the cox, his round face pale with sweat as he frantically looked around him.

'This', declared Janette, as she whipped back and forth on her seat, pulling at her oar, 'is our first ever race and we are not, I repeat not, coming off the river for anyone. We have family watching.' She glanced over her shoulder at the crowd. 'We are not coming off!'

On seeing the determined look on Janette's face, the cox panicked. We hit the side of another boat and zigzagged straight into the bank.

'Number 48!' wailed the megaphone. 'You are a danger to yourselves and a danger to everyone else on the river! We're launching the safety boat!'

And that was that. We were towed off the river in front of all the spectators; we limped back to the boathouse in full view of our home crowd, and all the while the safety officer kept asking us what was wrong. Janette kept blaming it on a fault with the steering system, while avoiding the chubby cox's eye.

'Well,' she explained as we shoved our wellington boots back on again, 'there's no point in blaming him, the poor sod. He knows as much about rowing as we do!'

SHIP'S LOG:

'Four very different women brought together through a love of rowing and none of us would ever have imagined we would join a rowing club. Trying something new or choosing a different path to the one you normally take can definitely lead to amazing and wonderful adventures, including new friendships to be treasured.'

(JANETTE/SKIPPER)

CHAPTER 4

The Team

'That's a little further than Poppleton.'
DR CAROLINE LENNOX

Over the next few months we entered a few more races and actually made it to the starting line. Turns out we were the first 'senior women' to enter any races at all in the history of the club. Not that there hadn't been any mum rowers before, but they had all mostly been recreational rowers, joining the club for social reasons – for the chat, the barbecues and the club ball. It had been the fathers who had raced before, and now we were joining them, and quite often racing with them in the same boat.

Frances and Niki were, to be honest, rather better than Helen and Janette. Helen had a tendency to talk a lot while rowing and Janette was a little too unconcerned with technique and could often disappear into her own world or, to put it less politely, lose interest while on the river. 'I liked the idea of being part of a team, while still being with my thoughts.' Frances and Niki were a little less slapdash – Niki liked the 'precision' of the strokes and the technique, whereas Frances just loved being out on the water, away from the office, the telephone and the meetings.

There was one race at Shipley Glen in Bradford where Niki and Frances were put together as a pair, and another where they raced as a four with two other members of the Guy Fawkes' Boat Club, Charles and Nigel. The second race was in York – the Head Race – and there were hundreds at the staggered start. The weather was kind when the four set off up to the head of the river, waiting for their allotted slot, but during the 45 minutes they had to wait, hanging onto a tree by the riverbank, the heavens opened. 'Rain, hail, high winds, the lot, and we were sat there getting soaked in nothing but our Guy Fawkes onesies.'

And it wasn't just the rowing that kept pulling us together. Helen and Frances had spent the whole of that summer jogging every Monday evening. They each had a child in the York Athletics squad and they would have to drive to an athletics track over the other side of York at 7 p.m., for an hour.

'All the other mothers would sit and gossip with their flasks of coffee, but Helen used to bring the dog and we'd run around the trading estate. We'd do two circuits while the children were doing their athletics and then come home,' explained Frances. 'There's an hour right there. We're not going to sit about and watch our children when we could be doing something else. Not that there is anything wrong with watching your children; it's a good thing. But we saw an hour that we could usefully use, and so we usefully used it. I like to be busy.'

Come January 2013, we were fast becoming extremely close friends. Our husbands, on the other hand, had barely met each other. And if we are a diverse band, then our husbands are even more so.

Back then Richard, Helen's husband, was still a barrister, whereas Mark, Frances's other half, had given up his career as a solicitor to become a stay-at-home father instead.

The truth of the matter was that Mark worked all hours of the day and Frances, who officially finished work at 2p.m., usually left work just in time to be about 15 minutes late to collect her children from school.

'They would be swept into prep club because I was too late to pick them up and they would not be allowed out until five,' said Frances. 'I was always in trouble. Something had to give, and as I was earning more money than Mark, and Mark was seriously disillusioned with his job, it was decided that I would continue to work and he would stay at home. The results are a very well-walked Jackadoodle called Daisy, a much happier family and some well-seasoned pasta carbonara on the stove,' she laughed.

'Actually, Mark cooks everything from scratch every day. Even when it is my turn to host book club, he is the one who does the cooking. I don't even pretend that it's me any more. I used to be the one who did everything. I used to finish work at two, then I'd come home, get the children, do tea for them, do dinner for us separately and then I'd start work again. In the evenings I was either working or I had gone to bed. We weren't seeing each other and it was a bit joyless. Often I would cook dinner and he wouldn't be back to eat it. He'd still be out. He was a banking lawyer and the transactions happen late and the hours are ridiculous; he often wasn't home until 11 p.m. We just weren't seeing each other at all. And then he'd come home on Fridays after a few drinks and then be hungover on Saturday and then you'd think, "Well, that's Saturday." It just wasn't working, so we did something about it. We changed it. I am a great believer in changing things that aren't working.'

Janette's husband, Ben, has a degree in IT and does consultancy work and property development, and has also taken on most of the childcare. 'He cooks, he cleans, he irons, he does the whole bloody lot. He's much better at it than I am.'

Gareth, on the other hand, runs a wealth management company with Niki. He was already a financial advisor, running his own business, when Niki took voluntary redundancy from her job at Orange, where she had been their UK and Indian broadband account manager, and put all her eggs into Gareth's company. 'We are 50-50 partners.'

So the St Peter's Boat Club dinner in the Merchant Taylor's Hall in January 2013 was something of a leap of faith. Would the husbands get on? Would they manage to be polite to each other? Would we even like each other's husbands? Or would it be one of those buttock-clenching nights when no one says anything, we all drink too much cheap red wine for want of something better to do and the conversation hics and trips, stilted to the point of rigor mortis?

The first problem was that Niki was ill. She'd had pleurisy and, as an asthma sufferer, had been in and out of hospital all that week, and couldn't make it.

So in the end our table of ten became an eight, with Caroline and her husband Mike, as well as Janette and Ben, Frances and Mark, and Richard and Helen all sitting down at the back of the oak-panelled room. With its high-beamed ceilings and glittering chandeliers, the Merchant Taylor's Hall was a glamorous venue for a black-tie dinner in aid of a school boat club. Somewhat confusingly, we'd presumed the dinner was in aid of the Guy Fawkes' club, which was for past pupils as well as parents and friends of the school, when in fact it was in aid of the rowing achievements by the pupils of St Peter's School, so we were rather surprised when we were put at the back of the hall, away from a gang of well-scrubbed-up school students in their party frocks. Of the hundred or so people at the dinner, our rowing club only had about three tables, very much placed towards the back.

Before dinner, the captain of the school boat club stood up and gave a speech, giving an annual review of races won and lost, and of various sporting achievements accrued by members of the school rowing squad.

'I can't believe how confident they all are,' said Frances. 'It's a delight to watch.' The dinner continued, the champagne flowed and weirdly everyone seemed to get on.

'I normally hate all of Helen's friends,' announced Richard, as he poured out some more champagne. 'But I like you lot.'

'It's true,' confirmed Helen. 'He does hate MOST of my friends.'

Frances was equally honest. 'I don't think we'd have naturally been friends when we were children,' she said to Janette. 'We were so very different. At school we'd have been in different sets. I was a swot – I worked really hard at school.'

'And I didn't,' replied Janette.

'My mother used to have to lock me out of the house to stop me from revising for my exams.'

'And my mother could never get me to come home!'

'But as adults we've really hit it off,' laughed Frances. 'As you get older, I think, who cares about where you've been, what your background is, what job you've got, any of that? I don't. It's all about your sense of humour and… you make me laugh.'

We drank a few more glasses of wine and the evening became even more convivial. Eventually, by the time they started calling the raffle numbers it was a little difficult to focus. Fortunately, Ben was more on the ball than the rest of us and every time the winning tickets were announced he was the one who could tell us.

'Frances, I think that's your ticket.'

'Janette, that's yours.'

In the end, we rather embarrassingly seemed to win everything, right down to the case of wine that Janette had brought along herself as a prize. It was just one of those nights where the stars seemed to align in our favour and the tickets to *The Great Gatsby* ballet kept wending their way to our table. We were all getting on, we were drinking lots of wine and our barriers were down. We were all having a very nice time. So perhaps it was no surprise that Frances suddenly made a suggestion.

'I've got an idea,' she began. 'Why don't we do something together, a challenge? Why don't we row the Atlantic?'

'That's a little further than Poppleton,' replied Caroline.

'No, I'm serious!' continued Frances. 'I've been reading about this race, it goes from the Canary Islands to Antigua.'

'I like Antigua,' said Helen.

'Rowing?' asked Janette.

'Yes,' nodded Frances.

'Let's do it,' said Janette. 'Even though we can barely get to the pub and back.'

'I don't see why we *can't* do it,' said Frances. 'I've read about the race. It's called the Talisker Atlantic Challenge. It doesn't look that hard, honestly. It's only rowing. Why don't we? Why don't we just do it and change things a bit? I'm up for the challenge!'

'You know me, I'm always up for a challenge,' said Janette.

'So am I,' added Helen.

'Me too,' said Caroline.

'It's been a dream of mine to do this since I read Debra Veal's book,' said Frances with glee, raising her glass.

'A dream?' chipped in Richard. 'Honestly, if we all followed our dreams where would we be?'

But no one was listening to Richard, or Ben, or Mark, or Mike. We were carried away with the excitement of the idea. Why couldn't we? Why couldn't some amateur rowers, who had only ever pootled up and down the River Ouse, make it across the Atlantic? Stranger things have happened, surely? We clinked glasses and toasted our ambition and Frances's idea. What a ride! What a journey! What a trip that would be!

That night, rather the worse for wine, Helen posted excitedly on her Facebook page. 'I can't believe I have just agreed to row the Atlantic!' And Frances spoke animatedly to Mark as they walked home.

'I can't believe I asked them to row the Atlantic with me and they said yes! Isn't that great?'

'No,' he replied. 'It is not great. It's not great at all.' But then he paused and looked over at her. 'But if you really want to go and you really want to do it, then it's okay by me. However, I want you to know that the idea does not make me jump for joy. Not one little bit.'

Perhaps our partners were all hoping we'd forget about it, that the plan would simply disappear, like most plans discussed after a few bottles of wine. They expected it would evaporate along with the hangover.

And for a long time, they were right. We did vaguely discuss the possibility of rowing across an ocean the following Saturday over cups of coffee at The Grange. Helen told Niki the story and we had a laugh on the sofa at the foolishness of it all.

'Rowing the Atlantic?' she asked. 'That's a long way.'

'I know!' agreed Helen. 'That's what Richard said!'

'We'd drunk quite a lot of wine by then,' added Caroline.

'Ben is positively encouraging me to go, the sod!' said Janette.

Only Frances stayed silent, thinking. The problem with saying something like 'I want to row an ocean' and declaring your dream, revealing your innermost desires, is that it can't be unsaid. And once the genie was out of the bottle, it was all Frances could think about. She was determined to do it.

It was fairly obvious what Mark thought about the idea, and indeed all the other husbands. Their surprised, incredulous faces that night around the dinner table said it all. Not one of them believed we could pull it off. Four mums rowing an ocean? It was clearly a ridiculous idea and, anyway, who was going to do the washing if we went?

But Frances mulled, she daydreamed, she googled the hell out of the event and she quietly would not give up. She kept mentioning it to Mark, as a way of getting him used to the idea.

'I thought if I kept talking about it, slipping it into conversation, he'd believe that I was serious. That I really *could* do it. The seed that had been sown by reading all those books from the library years before was finally germinating. Why couldn't I have an adventure? Does being a mother of two mean you can no longer dream? No longer do anything for yourself?'

So that Friday morning in May, she could not control it any more and she emailed them all. 'It was the grey suits, the grey road, the grey everything, and I wanted a bit of sunshine and a bit of memory-making. I was feeling increasingly frustrated and underappreciated at work. I just kept thinking, "Am I going to do this for another 10 years and then retire? Is this it? My life?"'

Janette, of course, replied almost immediately. But the others did not. There was nothing but radio silence, so much so that Frances began to think that perhaps she'd misjudged the mood. It was, after all, her idea, her mid-life crisis! Maybe the others wanted nothing to do with it…

At least Janette was up for it. In fact, Janette was so up for it that she was ready to row that Christmas. She was a little disappointed to learn that the two of them weren't taking off in six months' time but in two years.

'We've got to plan, we've got to train, we've got to get a boat – we can't possibly be ready this year!' explained Frances as the two of them trawled the Talisker website, working out how to register. And register they did. Just the two of them. It was 500 euros each. They were the first to register for the 2015 race. In fact, they were the only team to register for quite a long time. Whatever was going to happen, Frances and Janette were going to row an ocean. There was a small matter of some training and a boat, but they were on their way.

Janette immediately signed herself up to a five-day practical RYA (Royal Yachting Association) Day Skipper at Sea programme in Spain. Of course she did. 'Well, I was definitely going to row the Atlantic, so I thought I should get started. Also we did have a yacht already, so we thought it was a good idea to do some sort of professional training!

She and Ben flew to Girona, Spain, where they were joined by an elderly chap from Australia who wanted to work on cruise ships in his retirement and a young girl who was keen to work on yachts, and that was it. For five days they learnt how to reverse, turn, hoist sails and get them down again.

'To be frank, I wasn't very good. I was rubbish. Ben was trying to help me so that I could pass the test. He was whispering things in my ear, telling me which way to go. At one point we were in a man-overboard situation where they'd thrown a fender into the sea to simulate a body, which I then proceeded to mow down. The skipper wasn't pleased.'

'Now, Janette,' she said, 'if that was a person, they would be dead by now.'

'I also launched the 40-foot yacht headlong into the pontoon. I have never seen anyone move so fast in their life when she realised I was about to plough the whole boat into the dock. She grabbed the joystick out of my hand and plunged it into reverse.'

Both Janette and Ben got their International Certificate of Competence and another one in marine VHF (very high frequency) radio.

'It was a bit of a joke, really, as I was completely incompetent, but the one thing I really did learn that week was the incredible power of the sea. It really opened my eyes. It gave me a flavour of what the ocean could do. We left port one day for a practice and we had to turn back because the weather was so bad and the seas were so big. I had no idea it could get that rough out there. I had no idea how strong and powerful the ocean could be.'

If Frances and Janette were fully signed up to the idea of crossing the Atlantic, the rest of us were most certainly not.

'Have you heard that this lot are still going on about this ridiculous idea?' asked Richard as we all sat down to dinner at Helen's house one evening towards the end of June. We thought the rowing dinner had gone so well, we'd decided to get everyone together again for a plate of lasagne and some wine. Although this was not quite the feedback Frances and Janette were after! 'It's madness. You can't row the Atlantic! I don't know who you lot think you are. You're a bunch of nutters!'

'We are,' agreed Janette, sitting down next to Richard and taking a mouthful of lasagne. 'Total nutters!'

'But we are going to do it,' insisted Frances.

'And you're letting her go?' Richard asked Mark, pointing at Frances with his fork. 'Are you?'

'It's not for me to say yes or no,' said Mark. 'It's always been her dream to go, to row across the Atlantic.'

'Yes, but like I said,' replied Richard, 'if we all followed our dreams, where would we be?'

'I think we'd all be happy, Richard,' said Mark.

'It's utter fantasy,' said Richard, shaking his head.

'We all agree it is lunacy,' added Ben, pouring the wine. 'Total lunacy. But who am I to stand between my wife and her dreams?' And the conversation moved on.

But then something very odd happened. Helen is always looking for signs in life, little indicators that the path you want to choose or the idea that you had is the correct one. And then, just at the right time, a sign appeared. It was the first week in July, 10 days after the dinner, and St Olave's, the junior school to St Peter's senior school, were having their prize-giving. Usually they would book some sort of dignitary, an after-prize speaker to talk to the parents for a bit and pad out the hour or so between the most improved and the best in show. But this year it was different. This year, unbeknown to us, they had invited along Alastair Humphreys.

An adventurer, blogger and motivational speaker, Humphreys, as well as completing a four-year cycle trip around the world, walking across India, competing in the Marathon des Sables and being National Geographic Adventurer of the Year, had also rowed across the Atlantic.

We weren't sitting together in the hall that day as he started his talk. Actually, not all of us were even there. But those who were sat dotted around the room. Frances was near the back, Janette was to the side and Helen was closer to the front. Humphreys started to explain his new project – microadventures. A pioneering scheme that tries to encourage people to get outside, get out of their comfort zone and go somewhere they've never been before. He was an exciting speaker who exuded the sort of positivity that Frances was always talking about. He regaled the room with stories about his cycling trip around the world and about how he broke his foot in the Marathon des Sables. And then, in among his stories of his trips and his experiences, he said something that made our hearts skip a beat.

'If anyone ever asks you to row an ocean,' he said, 'don't hesitate. Don't even think about it. Just do it. It is a chance in a lifetime. It's a moment. And it is something that you will never, ever forget.'

Janette turned around to look at Frances and smiled. And Frances smiled back. And then, through the sea of neatly combed hair and smart jackets, Frances saw Helen turn around. She was beaming – she slowly nodded, a large grin all over her face. She then turned to look at Janette and did the same. Helen was in. She was going to be on that boat. No matter what.

SHIP'S LOG

'Just say yes. If someone presents you with an opportunity in life, always say yes. You can figure out afterwards how you will manage it. If you say no straight away, the opportunity passes you by and you might not be asked again.'

(JANETTE/SKIPPER)

CHAPTER 5

Making It Happen

'If you don't ask, the answer is always no. If you don't
step forward, you're always in the same place.'
NORA ROBERTS, TEARS OF THE MOON

If Helen was on board, Richard was still most adamantly not. Not unreasonably, he was worried. Worried that Helen might have to give up her job (the NHS would surely never give her four months off), worried about money and worried about what would happen to the children if Helen upped-sticks and launched herself on the ocean. While Frances's and Janette's husbands were being super-supportive, Helen found herself faced with a wall of silence. 'He just would not talk about it. He would just say no. No, you can't possibly leave your job. No, you can't leave the children. No, you can't do it. Just no. He was concerned about the money we would lose. About how we were going to manage to pay the bills and the mortgage. All very natural for him to be so worried. I'm glad now that one of us was!'

But Helen was convinced she was doing the right thing, and of course saw signs and inspiration everywhere. 'Even on TV. I remember watching *I'm a Celebrity… Get Me Out of Here*! with Melanie Sykes and watching her beating all the contestants who were younger than her. She is my age and I remember thinking, "Look at her, being all feisty and fabulous. I would love to do something that would test my limits. I would love to do something like that." Then I realised that this challenge – to row the Atlantic – had come to me. I'd asked for it, and now it had come, so I just had to do it. Even if Richard was not happy about it.'

So Helen used the gentle art of 'familiarity breeds acceptance'. Instead of giving up, she printed off the Atlantic Campaigns material and left it on the kitchen table. And there it sat for days, weeks, months, like a giant unanswered question or a very tacit challenge. Periodically, it would be opened and closed, but it never left the table. 'Every time I went near it, Richard would walk out of the room, but he never actually threw it in the bin.'

Although Niki and Gareth had started discussing the challenge, the idea itself was a little problematic. 'We're very close; we have the sort of relationship where we talk about anything and everything. I don't think he wanted me to be gone for so long.'

Emotional attachment aside, they also had a business together. 'He has a very strong work ethic, so he also could not understand why I would want to take time away from our business or how it could work without me.'

Also, Niki's children were younger than the rest of ours. Unlike Janette's, who were fairly self-sufficient, Corby was 11 and Aiden was 7 at the time, and despite the fact that Niki's parents – Bunny and Peter – lived right next door to them, there was still the question of childcare, the school run, homework and tea. But once the idea had been suggested, Niki found it difficult to let it go.

'I just really wanted the challenge. I think when you go through life you are lots of different people, depending on what you're doing and where you are going,' said Niki. 'I'd been the child, then I'd been the wife, and I'd been the career woman and I'd been the mum. And they are all different people. You behave and act differently in each of those roles. The professional role is very different to the mum role, and the married role is different to how I was as a child. I think, for me, it was about really trying to understand who the real Niki was underneath all of that, because you have all of these different layers and these different roles, and I was just trying to understand who I was again. So I was not going to give up that easily.'

Towards the end of that summer, after many conversations, some sort of compromise was reached. They decided that there was too much for Niki to do at home in York – she had too many responsibilities and too many people depending on her – so she would be involved, but she would be ground crew. She would help with setting up the trip, organising the sponsorship, helping the others get to La Gomera, but come the actual challenge, she would not get on the boat. She would not be there. She would stay behind with Gareth and the children, running the business, doing the drop-off and packing the rugby kit.

In the last week of September 2013, Janette invited the team and the support crew, which at that time consisted of Niki and Dr Caroline Lennox, to come and stay in her house near Perpignan in France. It had been booked as a girls' trip, as it was around the time of Helen's and Frances's birthdays. For fun, she'd planned a week of rowing tuition on a nearby lake, at a rather swish boat club, Perpignan Aviron 66, which had reportedly even trained some Olympic rowers.

'Some Olympic rowers, and now us,' declared Janette as we turned up at a beautiful stretch of water, about an hour's drive from the seaside house that Janette and Ben had bought as a wreck and spent every family summer slowly doing up.

'My poor children smelt paint stripper more than they inhaled the salt of the sea, and spent more time in Leroy Merlin, the builders' merchants, than they did on the beach!'

We were standing around at the boathouse, wearing various scruffy, unsporty outfits and waiting for our coach to arrive, when a team of what looked like female gazelles turned up. The French four sauntered straight past us with barely a backward glance. They were long-limbed, stunning and dressed in fabulously flattering team colours. We were transfixed and a little slack-jawed as they walked up to their moored boat, pushed off gently from the jetty and then, in a synchronised move that could only be performed better by the Bolshoi Ballet, leapt into the boat and with a swish of their oars and a flick of their shiny long hair rowed off in sequence.

'Holy shit,' said Janette. 'I've never seen anything like it.'

Ten minutes later and it was our turn to leave the boathouse. The huffing, puffing, splashing and shouting were mortifying. We were like a group of OAPs struggling to get off a tour bus.

'Hang on! Wait there!'

'Hold on!'

'Hold it!'

'Move the blade.'

'The *blade*!'

'It's going to get stuck!'

'We're stuck.'

'Jesus!'

'Ouch!'

'Was that really necessary?'

It took us a full 15 minutes to leave the jetty. No wonder, then, that our coach, François, thought we were a bunch of lunatics who had no idea what we were doing. But then, out of the blue, Helen really caught his eye. Or Hélène, as he insisted on calling her. She was rowing along with Caroline in a double scull (although judging by the amount of attention she was getting from the frankly rather ridiculously handsome coach, she could quite well have been rowing alone).

'Oh, Hélène,' he said. 'Come see, it is like zis.'

'Oh, Hélène,' he would say again. 'You stroke soft like zat.'

'Oh Hélène, zat is good!'

'Oh Hélène, don't you worry!'

'Oh Hélène, let me 'elp you.'

And all the while Hélène was making cooing incompetent noises, giggling, flicking her hair and generally batting her eyelashes. François helped Hélène into the boat. He helped Hélène out of the boat. He showed Hélène how to turn, what to do, where to go. He was *très* attentive.

'What am I?' demanded Caroline at one point, just as he sorted another one of Hélène's 'little problems'. 'Bloody invisible?'

The following morning, Janette came down to breakfast in a cloud of Chanel perfume, armed with a low plunge-necked vest and a very sturdy, barely hidden push-up bra.

'Right,' she announced with a hoist of her bosom and a tug on her straps. 'He's not going to be talking to Hélène today!'

But even Janette's substantial cleavage was no distraction for the enraptured François, and Hélène received his full and undivided attention for the next three days. It was one of the many jokes that we shared during a fantastic four days when we hung out, chatted, drank wine and tried to nail down some very serious decisions about crossing the ocean.

Such as, what shall we put on our playlists? Janette rather eccentrically decided that she was only going to have Edith Piaf. If the boat was going to go down, all she wanted to hear was '*Je ne regrette rien*' reverberating in her earphones. Frances was opting for a load of old folk, while Helen, or Hélène, was putting forward the idea that some audiobooks would be a great way of whiling away the time.

Our other major decision was what to call ourselves. It is never a good idea to brainstorm after sinking the best part of a bottle of wine or two. Not that it stopped us. The terrible ideas came thick and fast.

M.A.A. was one – *Mums' Atlantic Adventure*. Awful. *The Awesome Foursome*. Worse. *The Oarsome Foursome*. Downright shocking.

'I think our name should have something to do with Yorkshire,' suggested Janette.

'We don't want to be Yorkshire,' said Helen, who always disagreed with Janette if she possibly could, and, indeed, vice versa. 'That's not national enough. That's keeping it too local, and we're not going to get national sponsorship if we're just Yorkshire.'

'But we're from Yorkshire. We all live there. The lot of us. We should be Yorkshire. It's a great place to be from.' She looked at all our faces. 'It is! Yorkshire people get stuck in. We call a spade a spade. If it's green, it's green. It's not lime. You know what I mean? It's very much our culture to be very direct and straight and just say it how it is. Just do it how it is. I think there is probably a very different culture about Yorkshire. And we celebrate it! And it's not the wine talking!'

'Much,' replied Helen.

'We're real workers. Nobody pretends to be posh… Well, they do, but it's not a county that pretends to be posh. If you look at it as a county, you'd never say it's a posh county, whereas if you looked at Sussex or somewhere you'd go, "Oh, that's quite posh," wouldn't you? You wouldn't say that about Birmingham. You'd never say it about Liverpool and you'd never say it about Yorkshire.'

'There is something very special about people from Yorkshire. We are different. We should celebrate it. There is a steely toughness about us. It must be the cold breeze off the North Sea!' declared Frances.

'Anyway, I don't know why we're bothering; we're only a three at the moment,' pointed out Helen as we all looked at Niki and Caroline. One of them had to come with us. One of them really was going to have to push extra hard to make it happen. We couldn't row as a three – there wasn't a three category. It was solos, pairs or fours, and we needed to be a four.

And on we went, into the night, discussing the pros and cons of Yorkshire and what sort of name we wanted for the boat and the team. It was clearly important that we got the crucial things sorted first! The fact was that we still had neither a boat, nor a team.

Then, almost as soon as we got back to York, Caroline called Janette, sending her apologies. It was just too complicated for her to make the crossing; she had a lot going on at home and she had her prison GP work. So she offered her services as our in-house/on-the-Atlantic doctor and she could also give us some general help with all the paperwork. It was an offer we very gratefully accepted.

So all eyes fell on Niki. Could she persuade Gareth that her rowing an ocean was a good idea after all?

She and Gareth had planned to spend a long weekend in the Lake District as a family treat for them and the children, and Niki's parents had come along as well. They were going to look after the two boys while Niki and Gareth went on long walks. It was on these walks that they started to talk about the race, looking at it from all angles.

'It was a very hot topic of discussion!' said Niki. 'Our circumstances were very different from the others. My family was younger and I was in business with my husband. For me to leave was a very large wrench. Both Janette and Frances are the main breadwinners in the house, so both their husbands look after their children anyway. Apart from the fact that Janette is incorrigible and Mark would never stop Frances from doing what she really wants to do. He might be unhappy about her wanting to row the Atlantic, but he was never going to tell her she was not allowed to go.'

And despite the confident declaration to Frances that she was definitely on the team, Helen's position was still not that clear either. Rather than workshopping the idea like Niki and Gareth, she and Richard had simply not talked about it. And yet, by his silence, Helen was fairly sure that he might have just about given his tacit approval and she might have won the argument. Or non-argument. The race guide and registration form were, after all, still on the kitchen table; they hadn't been binned or burned. So there was still hope, even though the actual words 'you can go' had not come out of Richard's mouth. Nor, indeed, had Helen paid her 500-euro registration fee. But then quite a lot was going on in their household at the time.

'It was weird, but I think the idea of the challenge was already beginning to change me,' said Helen. 'I was in Leeds one afternoon, totally by chance – I had been sent there for a meeting as a replacement for a colleague – and I suddenly decided to pop in and see Richard in his chambers. It was about half-past four and I thought it would be nice to have a cup of tea. He wasn't expecting me and I wasn't really expecting to find him there, as he is always in court, but I went anyway. I walked into his office and instead of him being delighted, he was extremely downcast and miserable, surrounded by legal briefs and pink ribbon. I had caught him at a bad moment. He was just sitting there, staring.

'"I hate this," he said, looking up at me. "I really hate this."

'Normally I would have told him to keep buggering on, like I have done for the last 16 years – life's tough and dull and no one ever said it should be fun – but this time I didn't. I said, "Look, you can do anything!" I was feeling incredibly positive.

'"You've got transferable skills," I said. "Change it all now. Go and join a recruitment agency and make a leap. I don't know, you could do something like Director of Public Prosecutions. You're clever, you are talented, you can do anything!"

'He wasn't really listening to me. "Don't be stupid. Those jobs never come up. There's a DPP in London, one in Scotland…"

'"I don't mean that job particularly, but I'm giving you an example of your transferable skills. There are loads of things you can do! You don't have to do what you don't want to. You're in control of your destiny. You can change things if you want to."

'I walked out of his office and got in my car. As I was driving home, my phone rang – it was Richard. "You'll never guess," he said, sounding a lot different than a few minutes earlier.

'"What?"

'"As soon as you left, I went on the legal website, and the first job that came up? Director of Public Prosecutions, Isle of Man."

'I just said, "Oh my God, it's fate." Because I hadn't meant that job in particular, just any job… Absolute fate.

'"I've just phoned them up," he said, sounding slightly in shock. "They're sending me an application form." So that weekend he did the application form and sent it off, but I just knew it would happen – *we* knew it would happen. We knew he'd get it. It was just a matter of when.'

Meanwhile, Frances started attending night school, qualifying for her RYA Day Skipper licence. Janette and Ben booked to go to La Gomera for the start of the 2013 Talisker Challenge to see if they could pick up any tips, advice or crucial information that might help us. And Niki? She just bided her time…

And not long before Christmas, Gareth came round. It was not a sudden, overnight road-to-Damascus conversion. He didn't see the light or hear a choir! It was a gentle percolation. He'd begun to appreciate that Niki was truly committed to the plan and, as ground crew, she was already spending nights at Janette's house at meetings, helping out, trying to work out how to raise money, get sponsorship – helping to get the project off the ground. What was the point of all that hard work and commitment, he'd reasoned, if you don't actually ever get to row the race? Niki was doing all the donkeywork already, without any of the joy of the adventure.

And once Gareth had said yes, Niki was anxious to get the approval of her parents.

'I told my mother first in the kitchen,' said Niki. 'I wanted to be absolutely sure I was going before I said anything. She was a little bit shocked to begin with. She definitely went pale. It is not every day your daughter tells you she is going to row the Atlantic, she wasn't exactly jumping around, but she was extremely positive. She offered all sorts of help with Gareth and the kids. I was relieved. But I was worried about telling Dad. I asked her if she thought Dad would be all right about it. And she said she thought it would be better if I told him myself.

'"I'll tell him you want to pop over later and have a chat," she suggested.

'My poor dad. She told him I wanted to have a chat in the morning, but she refused to tell him what I wanted to talk about. The poor bloke. He'd been worrying and worrying all day. So when I finally told him, some four or five hours later, he was SO relieved. He'd been through all the options. He thought I was either dying of a terrible disease or I was divorcing Gareth, so when I told him I was rowing the Atlantic, he couldn't have been more overjoyed! He was absolutely delighted! He just stared at me to start off with. And then a large grin slowly spread across his face.

'"That's amazing!" he said. "Just amazing!"

'And he hugged me.

'He later told me he wrote in his journal that night that my telling him I was going to row the Atlantic was one of the best days of his life.'

Niki was on board! We were a four, at last. Now there was a real possibility of the race actually happening. We could row as a team. We *were* a team. Four totally different women, from very different backgrounds, united in one task – to get across the Atlantic. To get this far felt like an achievement in itself.

'It felt great!' said Janette. 'I remember feeling really pleased when I heard the news. Niki had been doing a lot of work and it just would have been a shame had she not been able to go the whole hog, so to speak. Also, Niki is a wonderful, kind person and very caring and I thought to myself, "We need that on the boat. She will look after us when we need looking after and she will get the job done." You can ask her to do anything, and she does it straight away. You can rely on her for sure. I used to think, "Bloody hell, how does she manage to fit that into her day?" Sometimes I would secretly try to beat her to it (I think she knew that), but there was no getting ahead of Niki.'

Telling our children that we were going to do the challenge was something we were all extremely worried about. Concerned about the unsettling effect of our 'trip', we approached the idea with as much excitement and enthusiasm as possible. There was a huge amount of emphasis placed on travelling to Antigua for the finish, and going to the Canaries for the start. The truth that we were going to be away for Christmas was slightly glossed over, and all the positive, up-beat ideas about their mums crossing the Atlantic were expressed.

As it turned out, the kids were all remarkably sanguine.

Janette's children Safiya and James were very relaxed about it. 'They didn't really bat an eyelid when I told them I was going to row an ocean,' she says. 'They just said "Cool!" as if it was some kind of everyday occurrence! Like, "OK, Mum, that sounds fun - when are you going?"'

'I'm fine with my mum being away,' said Jack, Frances's youngest son. 'But will Dad cope? I worry about him, and him being able to find my tie.'

Corby, Niki's eldest, was delighted. 'Takeaway every night!' he cheered. 'My clothes might not be washed, but it'll be KFC every night!'

Her youngest, Aiden, was a little more cheeky: 'Four random mums rowing an ocean – they must be drunk!'

It was 14-year-old Lucy, Helen's daughter, who seemed to understand the idea better than most. 'It's a once-in-a-lifetime opportunity and it can never be taken away from you once you've done it. When you are really old and grey, you will still have the story about how you once rowed the Atlantic. And you will probably never stop telling it!'

SHIP'S LOG:

'Communication is key. We all have dreams, hopes and goals, and sometimes by sharing them with others we can start to see them happen. The more people you share your dreams with, the more likely it is they will happen. Let the world know your dreams. Telling someone motivates you – it acts like an incentive.'

(JANETTE/SKIPPER)

CHAPTER 6

One Step Forward

'Ask for what you want, and be prepared to get it.'
MAYA ANGELOU

Down at the boat club it was Janette who broke the news. She and Frances had been discussing telling the coach for a while, but now that the team was finalised (albeit with Richard's not-quite-really-there-yet approval) it felt like the right time. And she chose a rain-soaked Saturday morning to do it. She, Niki, Frances and a woman whom Janette had christened 'Perfect Pam' (due to the exemplary way she took instructions – unlike us!) were entered as a quad, and with the boredom setting in as they hung around waiting for the race to start, Janette thought she would liven things up a bit by telling the coach their new and exciting plan.

'Hey, coach!' she said. 'Guess what? You'll never guess what we're going to do.'

'No idea.'

'It's a challenge – one of those physical challenges…'

'Um…' He looked at us, a little nonplussed. 'Row in the Boston Marathon?'

'No,' beamed Janette, waving an oar at him by way of a handy hint. 'Bigger than that. A bit further away than Lincolnshire.'

'Rowing in the Mediterranean?'

'Think bigger seas, like oceans! Big oceans!'

'You're rowing an ocean?' Now he was very much paying attention.

'The Atlantic. We're doing the Talisker Atlantic Challenge.'

He looked from Janette to Niki to Frances, clearly calculating our combined age of just over 188 years old. Then he looked at us all carefully again, obviously waiting for the punchline of this strange joke.

'Wow! That *is* a challenge,' he finally replied.

'I know!' Janette grinned. 'The idea is to inspire ordinary women to do extraordinary things.'

'Well, you are certainly doing that,' he nodded.

'Helen Butters is doing it with us,' Janette enthused.

'Helen?' he replied. 'Princess Helen who does nothing but complain when she is out on the river? Surely not? How is she going to last an afternoon on the Atlantic?'

'Oh, she'll be different on the ocean,' insisted Janette, feeling very much compelled to stick up for Helen. 'I guarantee she will.'

'Maybe,' he replied.

'What's this?' smiled Perfect Pam, joining the group.

'We're rowing the Atlantic Ocean,' Janette blurted, mainly to see the expected negative reaction on Perfect Pam's face. But she just looked puzzled.

'They want to inspire ordinary women to do extraordinary things,' repeated the coach.

'Oh, that's fantastic!' exclaimed Perfect Pam, smiling at all three of us. 'Very impressive. Very impressive indeed. Are you doing it for charity? You must do it for charity. How about the Prince's Trust? They do lots of good stuff with children. I am going to get a coffee, does anyone want one?'

We all politely declined. 'Well, she was nice and positive,' said Niki as we watched Pam walk up the riverbank.

'I know!' nodded Janette. 'Lesson one in life. It's a basic. Never judge a book by its cover and always give people a chance. Don't underestimate someone and don't be quick to jump to conclusions.'

Word quickly got around about our plan. We received an email from Julie, the captain of the Guy Fawkes' ladies team, wishing us well. Apparently a little bird had told her and she was bowled over by our bravery and couldn't believe we were doing such a thing. Did we have a website, she wondered?

A website? That would perhaps be a good idea. Helen and Janette were, perhaps unwisely, charged to get this off the ground. Helen said she'd seen somewhere on Facebook someone who did this sort of thing. Someone called Andy? Who lived in her village, Cawood? Armed with the address and, having lived in the area for the past 15 years, supposedly some local knowledge, they set off together on foot to find him. It took a while – about an hour of trampling around in the dark, with various detours up and down the pavement, sloshing up various muddy driveways and searching fruitless cul-de-sacs. They knocked on some eight or nine doors (most of the village, in fact), interrupting people's supper, or in one case their rapt enjoyment of *Coronation Street*, before they finally found Andy. They said they knew they'd found the right house when an earnest-looking chap with long hair and pale skin answered the door. And he was lovely. He immediately embraced the idea and offered to get a website up and running as soon as possible. Helen promptly produced a list of things we needed for the website, while Janette did a double-take. She had never known Helen to be so efficient! So as Helen went through the list, Janette enthused about the adventure and the list of charities we were looking at.

There are so many good causes out there; it was hard to know which charities we wanted to support, but Perfect Pam was right. We did need to choose one or two. It seemed like madness to go to all the trouble of rowing an ocean if we didn't raise money while we were doing it. We had a meeting at Janette's house. And it was probably a lot more emotional than any of us intended.

Both Helen and Frances had had a parent die of cancer. Frances's mother died when Frances was just 28 years old.

'She'd first been diagnosed with breast cancer when I was 10 and when, after a long, weary battle, she eventually died on the oncology ward of Huddersfield Royal Infirmary, there was nowhere for me to go,' explained Frances. 'There wasn't any real support and no one talked about it. My dad did his best but he was grieving himself, and although I was 28 years old I was not really a grown-up. So when I met a woman from cancer support charity Maggie's at a breakfast seminar through work, I thought their story was so powerful. I really wish they had been around during that period. It would have been so helpful. I find it so odd that she has missed so much of my life. She never met Mark or my children. My father remarried two years after my mother died and that was also a great shock at the time. I was still feeling the hole that my mother had left, but my father had been able to move on. He rang me one day at work and said: "Great news! I'm getting married." I had not met Audrey at that point. It really struck me that day that a spouse is replaceable, but a mother is not. My stepmother Audrey is lovely. She has always been very supportive and encouraging and has been a wonderful grandmother to my children. And she is fabulous with my father, who was naturally quite lonely when my mother died. It was a relief to know that he was not going to be on his own any more. I still feel my mother's spirit is close to me – and I felt that more than ever while we were out on the ocean.'

Helen's situation was similar. Her father also died of cancer. 'It was a big shock,' she said. 'One day he was there, decorating my sitting room, and then six months later he was dead. I remember him being at my house and me thinking, "God, you look very pale," and he went to his GP because he felt tired all the time. They sent him for a scan and he was diagnosed with pancreatic cancer. It's one of the worst ones. I don't think my mum and dad really knew that, so it was just a torturous six months. It would be my birthday and they'd come round and I knew that it'd be the last time he'd be there for my birthday, so I'd be crying at the sink and then trying not to cry when I turned round. It was just awful. Luckily, I wasn't working at that point, so I could spend all my time with them. That's what I did. Then I remember the day that Mum phoned me up and said, "He's really not well." I went round. The communication between the hospital, the GP and us was really confusing, so nobody knew who we were supposed to ring, what we were supposed to do. Which is why Maggie's is so important to me, because if we'd had Maggie's, our experience of his end-of-life would have been so much better. I always remember the last time we were all together as a family. It just happened to be me, my sister, my brother and my mum, all at home before we took him into hospital, and he never came back out. But I was fine with it, because I'd done everything I possibly could and I'd been there by his bedside, so I felt okay about it, actually. What I couldn't deal with was the funeral bit, which is when my brother Paul and my sister Clare were brilliant. They organised the funeral, they did all of that stuff. I couldn't even go to the graveside. I went to the church, but I couldn't go to the grave. But I thought, "Well, Dad wouldn't care." I was there when he needed me and I'm there at the church. I found he'd done this thing – a "What's the meaning of life?" document on his computer. Just his thoughts about why we were here.

"'The following few pages are just some of my thoughts,' it said. "Questionings and ramblings over more years than I care to remember. Everyone will ponder these basic questions from time to time throughout their lives… I also believe that the utopia of finding all the answers will never happen, although the searching is all very interesting and keeps us busy."

'I printed it off and gave it out at the funeral for people to take away. I think during that period I learnt some serious coping strategies – trying not to cry in front of him and just dealing with everything. He was definitely around me on the boat, kicking me up the arse at times when I was scared and needed a boost!'

In fact, we'd all been touched by cancer. Niki's mum had also fought and survived breast cancer, as had Janette's mother, who had cancer of the throat, so Maggie's was our first choice, and a charity very close to all our hearts.

We continued to sit at Janette's kitchen table, discussing whether we should simply raise money for one charity or if we should add another.

'Why not do two?' asked Niki.

'Spread the love,' agreed Helen.

'It will make us work harder,' added Frances.

'Then we should definitely do something to do with Yorkshire,' declared Janette.

We sat and debated and researched, going through the pros and cons of various worthy causes.

'Yorkshire Air Ambulance?' suggested Janette. 'It's Yorkshire and us two have worked and still work for the NHS.' She nodded towards Helen. 'And I have a friend who was rescued by them once.'

'It's a popular charity,' added Helen, who, as a communications officer for the NHS, knows her stuff. 'And it's close to our roots and is well worth supporting.'

It was decided. We'd write letters to Maggie's and Yorkshire Air Ambulance and announce our intention to support them on our challenge, and we'd also sit down and go through the list of contacts we had to set about raising money. Rowing the Atlantic is an expensive business; we had to find ourselves a boat and supplies, and get as much sponsorship as we could, so that none of the money we raised by donations would be used at all on the trip. Everything we raised would go to the charities, of that much we were all agreed. Where the rest of it would come from, though, would be anyone's guess.

In the meantime, Janette and Ben went to La Gomera to see the start of the 2013 race – the one that Janette had originally thought she'd signed up for just six months before! They booked themselves into the same hotel, the Parador, that we were to stay in two years later (with our plastic bags of chafe-free pants and toothbrushes), and spent four days meeting the rowers and checking over the boats. Although she and Ben principally went for a nice long weekend, their trip did prove invaluable. Not only was it useful in terms of finding accommodation and working out the lie of the land for our arrival two years later, but also Janette came back brimming with confidence.

Firstly, all the rowers they'd met had taken her proposal to row the Atlantic seriously.

'No one laughed in my face. A couple looked me up and down, but you know, I wasn't looking very healthy. I was 13 stone and not remotely athletic. But they hadn't laughed. Not even smirked.'

Secondly, she had been encouraged by the diversity of teams – the fact that not all of them were professional rowers or adventurers. In fact, there was one team who had apparently almost never rowed before. They were a team of handsome young polo players who, by all accounts, just turned up, grabbed their headphones from their digs 10 minutes before the starter klaxon and got into their boat, splashing off into the sunshine, practically still holding a glass of champagne. (Extraordinarily, Atlantic Polo not only finished the Talisker Challenge Race; they were winners in their class and the second team to reach Antigua.)

And thirdly, Janette and Ben came back with the realisation that the hardest part of the race was actually going to be getting to La Gomera in the first place. We had so many things to buy, so many things to organise. The costs, the budget and the amount of energy we would need was a huge undertaking in itself.

By now we were telling anyone and everyone we met about our plan. In the run-up to Christmas, you could give any one of us a glass of wine or a flute of fizz and we would share our story with the room. We needed support and we needed to drum up as much interest in our quest as possible. People were mostly positive when we mentioned the madness of our idea. They couldn't believe that we were attempting to do such a thing. At our age! With all our responsibilities! What were we thinking? A couple of people weren't very kind – mostly florid old men in tight shirts with champagne breath who would insist that we were mad.

'There's no way you'll do that,' one bloke said. 'You've only rowed on the river. What do you know about the sea?'

And on the school run, there was a little bit of attitude. Mark was asked by a fellow dog-walker friend how Frances could possibly leave her children for that long, as *she* simply would not be able to do such a thing. To which he replied that she was leaving them with their father, which was possibly an all right thing to do.

Frances said that it takes all sorts to make a world. Some people will never understand. They feel uneasy when other people try and break the mould, rock the boat, and do something a little different; when they stop treading the same path as everyone else.

'Even my dad said I was bloody mad,' said Janette. 'But I think he'd always wanted to do something like that – not row but sail an ocean. And he was worried. He's sailed a lot himself, and he'd been in some bad weather, so he knew what bad weather could do and he'd been frightened by it many a time! So he had an idea of what I was in for.'

Janette invited her parents and sisters over for Sunday lunch in order to tell them the idea, before they heard it on the grapevine from someone else.

'You're mad!' pronounced Maria.

'Insane,' agreed Jane.

'It's crazy,' added Joanne. 'But then that's you.'

Janette's mum was quite worried. 'What if you need to be rescued?'

'As far as I know, most boats make it across,' declared Janette helpfully.

Her mum didn't seem too pleased with this reply , but nevertheless seemed resigned to the fact that Janette would do it anyhow.

'Since you were a young child, Janette,' she said, 'I have been waiting for news like this. I expected it earlier, if I'm honest. By the time you got to 40 I thought maybe we'd got away with it. You were always determined as a child. You'd never give up. You were bossy, always jumping in with two feet. And NO ONE can tell you what to do! Not ever. Because you'd go and do it anyway!'

'Mums know their daughters,' agreed Janette. 'Warts and all!'

By the end of lunch, they were all onside. Janette's dad was interested in the route, and all of them concerned that she came back safely.

'I could understand their reservations,' said Janette. 'If it were my children telling me that, I'd be the same. I'd encourage them and support them, but I'd also worry a lot.'

There were a few others who were less keen to come round and made it clear they didn't share the same ambition. There were some older women who looked at our adventure as a flight of fancy. The idea that we had not settled for our lot, that we still wanted to do something else beyond our careers, bringing up children or being good wives was something they found quite difficult to comprehend. There weren't that many of them, but those who disagreed with what we were planning were actually quite vocal. Maybe it was an age thing. They had never been allowed to express dissatisfaction; they had never been allowed to dream about doing anything else. They had not been allowed to go on their own journey. Perhaps it was jealousy that we were trying to do something new, something for ourselves. One thing is for sure, we would often get accused of being selfish. Sometimes it was expressed as concern. More often it was simply a bald statement: this was not a trip a mother should do. We should leave it to the men and be satisfied with what we already had.

But what if what we've got is not enough? Marriage, jobs, children – we were all incredibly lucky, that much we knew. We'd all worked extremely hard to get where we were, but… but… Was there something else? The wind in our hair? The rain on our face? Deep, intimate friendship? A challenge? Risk? Adventure? An opportunity to test ourselves to the absolute limit? To stretch ourselves and see just how far we could go? And, most crucial of all, to see what, or who, comes out the other side. The idea that there is a bigger, more inspiring world out there, crammed with opportunities, excitement and experiences, was too great to resist. It was all for the taking.

In the words of the American endurance swimmer Diana Nyad, whom Frances was fond of quoting: 'What you get by achieving your goals is not as important as what you become by achieving them.'

Or as Helen would say: 'It's only three months! In a lifetime, that is nothing. Three months to be out of an office, out of a nine-to-five, Monday-to-Friday, month after month, year after year job. Who would not give anyone three months? Look at the bigger picture, not the three months. Who doesn't benefit? The children get to see a different part of life that is steeped in positivity, something they would never experience anywhere else. They absorb it and it's in them forever. The idea that they can do anything will stay with them all their lives. Just three months, that's all. And if I listened to the naysayers and said, "Oh, I can't do that. That's three whole months. I'll just stay at home at the kitchen sink," what an opportunity missed for everyone!'

With Dr Caroline Lennox for our rowing weekend in Perpignan, France in September 2013.

Meeting *Rose* for the first time in Burnham-on-Crouch.

Our first outing with *Rose*, trying to tip her over.

With Greg Maud, Ross Johnson, Oliver Bailey, Jason Fox and Perfecto Sanchez who also rowed across the North Sea in May 2015.

On *BBC Breakfast* with Naga Munchetty and Jon Kay after our North Sea crossing.

Helen's children Lucy and Henry, and Niki's children Aiden and Corby, waiting to wave us off in Southwold before we set off across the North Sea.

With the BBC's Mike Bushell after our first stint on the red sofa where Helen grabbed Mike and told him she loved him!

Janette at Caroline's house learning how to stitch up wounds on her birthday.

Ladies in Yellow: Doing our Survival at Sea training down in Hull.

Frances learning all about raft tipping!

With Reverend Kate Bottley when *Rose* was blessed.

The team switching on the Burn Christmas lights on the village green in November 2015 before we set off.

ur fundraising ball at York Racecourse. L to R: Lucy Butters, Mark Davies, Frances Davies, Henry Butters (in front), Richard Butters, Gareth Doeg, Helen Butters, Niki Doeg, Ben Benaddi, Janette Benaddi.

Janette with her children James and Safiya and husband Ben on the boat at San Sebastián Marina, La Gomera, before we set off.

Niki, Helen and Frances having some downtime in La Gomera.

Giving it some welly as we train for the Talisker race.

Some seriously deep waves in La Gomera as we practise for the journey of a lifetime.

Christmas Day at sea, 5 days and 318 nautical miles into the row.

Frances tucking into lunch.

Janette pretending to be excited about the prospect of yet more Ultrafuel, 2000 miles into our journey.

January 2014

By the time the boat club dinner came around in January we were all quite excited. It was the one-year anniversary of our decision to enter the race and the four of us were now committed to entering and rowing those 3,000 miles. Niki and Helen had yet to pay their registration fees, but Gareth was on board now and Richard could see that Helen was going whether he liked it or not, so he'd decided he was beginning to like it.

Dressed in our finery, we settled down at what now appeared to be our usual table towards the back of the room. This time it was just the eight of us and everyone was in a good mood. It was also the anniversary of our husbands actually meeting, and so much had gone on, so much had happened in those last 12 months, that it seemed right that we were all here together again.

Ben poured the wine, Janette regaled the table with stories of the handsome polo-playing boys in La Gomera, Frances and Helen talked training, Richard and Mark chatted about their Christmases, while Niki and Gareth were just enjoying their first rowing dinner experience.

We were all slightly on tenterhooks. At the drinks beforehand we'd been talking to other parents, telling them a little about our trip, spreading the word, hoping that we might pick up some sponsors or donations or just some encouragement. Which we did. Everyone was so enthusiastic about the idea, and obviously the boat club people there already knew about us.

So during the dinner we waited for the speeches. We listened attentively to the rundown of the school's sporting achievements. We were waiting, our hearts pumping slightly, riding a small wave of adrenaline and expectation. We were going to row an ocean – would they say anything? Would they salute us? Toast us, even? Wish us bon voyage and say that they were delighted and proud of our intention? We held our breath, straining our necks, peering over from the back of the room. And then, suddenly, the speeches were all over.

We looked at each other.

No one had said anything at all. No one had mentioned us. No one had said a word about our challenge. But then, why on earth should they? It was a school boat club dinner, where all matters to do with the school and the boat club were discussed. Our adventure and our plans had very little to do with them. It was our trip and our obsession. And the Guy Fawkes' Boat Club is only a satellite of the main rowing club itself.

But… And then it suddenly dawned on us as we sat there, nursing our glasses of wine, that perhaps no one actually took our idea seriously. Or worse, they didn't want to make a big fuss of us or mention it just in case we failed. Maybe they thought we'd never make it to the start line in the first place.

We didn't win any raffle prizes that year, and the night ended rather soberly. It was a harsh reminder about how hard we were going to have to work that coming year – about how far we still had to go.

SHIP'S LOG:

'Don't get discouraged; there will be doubters. There is risk in pursuing a dream or a goal. Each step forward is a step in the right direction. Don't let anyone stop you from taking the step.'

(JANETTE/SKIPPER)

CHAPTER 7

Rose

> 'Start by doing what's necessary, then do what's possible, and suddenly you're doing the impossible.'
> ST FRANCIS OF ASSISI

It was the beginning of 2014 and we had precisely zero funds in our Atlantic bank account. We had attracted lots of interest. Everyone (well, almost everyone) was enthusiastic for us. But we did not have a single sponsor. Not one. Helen, as our communications director, had come up with some great ideas for attracting sponsorship deals. There were myriad options to choose from, starting with the £250 Club, which meant you could have your name plastered (6 x 4 inches in size) on the boat for £250, plus a profile on the still-to-be-built website. Then there was the Platinum Sponsorship deal at £10,000, for which you received kit branding, logo and brand recognition on all media, promotion and a 2 x 4 foot logo on the boat. Plus there was the ultimate 'bespoke' package that was available by negotiation, with more branding and profiling than you could shake an oar at. But there was one major problem with all of this.

'We need the boat,' said Janette one evening as she ponderously played with her pencil and sipped her coffee. 'There's no getting away from it. We're nothing without a boat.'

'She's right,' nodded Frances, leaning back in her chair.

'No one is going to give us any money without one,' confirmed Helen, leafing through all the sponsorship forms and ideas that Niki had just printed out.

'Well then,' said Janette, rubbing her hands together. 'Let's get one.'

'How?'

'I'll buy one.'

We all looked at Janette. Was she seriously offering to buy an ocean rowing boat single-handedly? We all knew she was impetuous. She and Ben had once gone to the Boat Show in London only to come away with an order for a 40ft yacht (apparently it was the offer of six free cushions that sealed the deal), which they worked out how to pay for as they drove back up the M1. Janette is renowned for being a positive risk-taker; she weighs up the pros and cons and then moves. And once she moves, she moves swiftly. She is dynamic, kind and very, very generous. The ultimate yes person. She always says she works out the worst-case scenario and usually the worst case is nowhere near as bad as you think. It's all about gut instinct – the sixth sense, as she calls it. She thinks we should listen to it and trust it more often.

'What?' she said, looking from one shocked face to another. 'You're paying me back. I'm not giving you a boat! What do you take me for? It's an investment. We want to row the Atlantic, we need sponsorship, and for that we need a boat. It's simple. No boat means no sponsorship, and no sponsorship means no rowing across the Atlantic. So let's get the boat and you lot can pay me back later.'

The going price for an ocean-going rowing boat starts at £33,000, and the only reason Janette had that amount of money to donate – sorry, loan – to our cause was because over the years of building the business she and Ben had been squirrelling away some money for a rainy day. And today was a rainy day indeed – bloody pouring!

Ben backed her decision, but there were a few who thought she was completely mad to put so much money into what looked like such a precarious project.

'The coach at the boat club took me aside. He was very concerned. He said he'd heard that I was putting a lot of money into this. I don't know how he got to know about it, but they talk, don't they, at boat clubs? He said he was worried that the project wasn't going to take off and I'd be left with this boat. He was worried that we weren't even going to get to the start line and he thought I'd have this useless thing and the others would just walk off into the sunset, leaving me to it. He was mostly worried about Helen. Poor Helen. In his eyes, she was clearly rubbish. She did make a huge fuss when she was rowing in the river, squealing if a wave came along. But I told him not to worry. "She looks like a princess and she acts like a princess, but deep down she's not. When the going gets tough she gets going," I reassured him. Although the going has to get *very* tough for her to get going.'

We bought the boat from Charlie Pitcher, the world's fastest Atlantic solo rower, who has a boat workshop called Rannoch Adventure in Burnham-on-Crouch, Essex. Bizarrely, we had first met Charlie at a lunch at the finance company Brewin Dolphin, in London, just before Christmas. It was something that Frances had organised after a chance meeting in the sandwich queue one lunchtime. She bumped into an old work contact, Martin, whom she chatted to about the row and he very charmingly invited all four of us to a lunch in London to meet the brilliant Sally Kettle – who'd rowed the Atlantic with her mum, Sarah.

It was one of those days when everything went drastically wrong and then suddenly very right. We were supposed to meet Frances in London, but for some reason we got on the wrong train and ended up in Hull. None of us was paying attention and we were all looking the other way, relying on someone else. Never a good thing. It didn't matter, we said, if we were a bit late. It'll be one of those big lunches with loads of people in a big room and we can just slip in at the back and no one will notice. We might have taken the wrong train, but we'd be fine.

Come 1.40 p.m., we crept into a private dining room on the top floor of the building to find lunch set for 12, our names on our plates and some very empty chairs. It was mortifying, made all the more so by the fact that the stunning Sally Kettle was waiting for us to arrive to start her talk about her experience on the Atlantic. We, of course, apologised profusely and took our seats as speedily as we could, before listening to her amazing story and her incredibly inspirational words. After the lunch we gathered around her, asking her all sorts of questions.

'How cold was it?'

'How big were the waves?'

'How mad did the whole experience send you?'

It was extraordinary to meet a woman who had actually done what we were so desperate to do. And she was fantastic. She was reassuring, positive and motivating. She said how her mum (she was our age group, after all) had struggled and shared what she had found difficult, and then she asked us if we had a boat yet.

'You should talk to Charlie.' She nodded towards a blondish bloke standing in the corner. 'He's a world-record-holding rower and he builds boats.'

So at the beginning of February a group of us woke up unreasonably early and set off in convoy to Essex, arriving just before midday.

Charlie was there to meet us all. Frances and Mark were there with their two children, Jay and Jack. Helen and Richard brought Lucy and Henry, and Janette and Ben came along too. It was a sunny morning and we were all extremely excited as we looked around the marina and were introduced to the rest of his Rannoch Adventure team in Charlie's workshop. Just before lunch, we gathered in his office as he talked us through the plans for building the boat.

All of Charlie's boats are handmade and bespoke, taking into consideration exactly who is going to be rowing them, and for what purpose.

It was the first time any of us had been confronted with the reality of what we were actually planning to do as Charlie talked us through the possibilities – we would need GPS here, a watermaker there, cabins for us to sleep in that had to be sealed at all times to guard against capsizing, though the boat was self-righting so we needn't worry about that. We could all see the idea beginning to take hold.

Oddly, the person who was most enthusiastic at the Rannoch Adventure boat yard was Richard.

'Then and there, he completely changed his mind about the whole thing!' said Helen. 'He went from being the most negative about the project to being the most positive. It was one of the quickest, most abrupt turnarounds in history. I couldn't believe it. One minute he thought the idea was ridiculous and the next it was positively brilliant! But he likes facts and here was something that he could see. A boat. I also think that before he was scared for me, and of what could happen, because the whole thing was so very dangerous. But when he spoke to Charlie, he began to understand how the boat works, how it self-rights. He was reassured and he suddenly became really supportive, suggesting ideas and coming up with plans, offering to help raise some money through sponsorship. Also, at no point during our meeting did Charlie ever question our ability to row the Atlantic. Obviously he wanted to sell us a boat, so he wasn't about to say, "What? You lot? What do you know about rowing an ocean?" But he made it seem perfectly possible: of course we could do the Talisker Challenge. Why ever would we not be able to?'

By the end of the morning we had a basic plan. We'd decided on a boat of just over 28 feet long, with two cabins with four of what would very generously be described as berths (known in the trade as 'coffins' – we couldn't actually lie down flat in them with our legs outstretched, and it would be a tight, intimate, on-top-of-each-other squeeze to fit two of us in at any one time). We'd have an in-built watermaker, a GPS system, navigation lights, batteries, electrics, and as many bits of modern safety equipment as were available to make her as safe as we could and as easy to navigate and steer as possible. It was a lot of 'bespoke' for such a small boat, but we were going to say goodbye to eight children in La Gomera, and the conclusion was that if we scrimped on something now, we might seriously regret it later.

And the grand total? It was going to cost £67,000. Janette very gamely signed off on the down payment right then and there before she and Ben disappeared off back up to York, while the rest of us had lunch at the marina feeling, frankly, a little bit sick. The mood was very sombre as Frances, Mark, Jay and Jack sat down with Helen, Richard, Henry and Lucy.

'It was a lot of money and it was hanging over us like a cloud,' said Helen. 'I remember sitting there, playing with my salad, thinking, "We've got to raise £100,000 from sponsors to cover the boat, the equipment and the 22,000-euro entry free for the race itself. How are we going to raise that sort of money for the trip, and then raise money for charity on top of that?" I don't think Ben was so enamoured with the idea any more either, having just watched his wife write out an enormous cheque! I genuinely felt very anxious and stressed. It was a lot of responsibility. Frances was very cool about it, but then she always is. She kept saying it would be fine, that she knew lots of people who would be falling over themselves to support us. I remember crossing my fingers under the table and praying that she was right.'

But now at least we had a boat. Well, it was being built. We looked a little more like we meant business. It made us look a lot more credible than just walking into an office in our tracksuits saying: 'Hi, we're four mums and we are going to do this challenge. Can you give us £2,000, please?' If we had a boat, we looked like we were a 'possible' to make it to La Gomera and, at the very least, during a tricky pause during the sponsorship pitch, they could always ask us a few questions about the watermaker.

With Janette so drastically out of pocket, we really had to start making some money. She insisted she was fine about it, saying if she played golf she'd be paying fees to join a club, but she rowed so she needed a boat. But we were so anxious not to let her down. Our increasingly worked-out behinds were up against the wall. We spent night after night sitting around Niki's kitchen table or drinking coffee at Helen's, writing endless letters to corporations, big businesses and anyone who had any connection with the rowing community, anyone who supplied transatlantic rowing boats for any sort of money, support or free supplies. But it was all fruitless. Mostly no one replied or even acknowledged our letters, and the cheques most certainly did not come pouring in.

By April we only had one member of the £250 Club: his name was Geoff, and Helen and Janette had a meeting with him in a very posh hotel near Wakefield. We were introduced to him through a friend of Helen's, one of the mums at St Peter's, and he ran a company called Involved and was a semi-professional adventurer.

'We were nervous about meeting him because we had never met a real adventurer before,' said Janette. 'We were only there to pick his brains and ask him all sorts of questions about adventuring and how to make an adventure happen, and that's when he offered to be our first sponsor. He said he'd like to join our £250 Club. It was extremely kind of him. I have a feeling he felt a little bit sorry for us.'

It was a start, we determined. All we needed to do was find a lot more Geoffs.

Meanwhile, the boat was coming along. She had been moulded and finished in carbon, and while we were waiting for her to be fitted out, Charlie invited us all down to an open day at Rannoch Adventure. It was the first time we really dipped our toes into the ocean-going rowing community, and they were a radically different bunch from the river rowers we were used to. They were a much wilder bunch. There is some snobbery between the river rowers and the ocean rowers. River rowers think ocean rowers can't row; they think they have zero technique. Apparently, you don't need to be able to row to cross the ocean; you just need to be able to keep going. Although none of us would fancy sharing that point of view with any of the blokes at the open day. But ocean rowers are certainly different. They were much more international, much more adventurous-looking, with salt-stiffened hair and sun-blasted skin, and they had all done something a little bit out of the ordinary. Some of the guests were old customers of Charlie or rowers from previous Atlantic races, and Angus, Charlie's nephew, was talking about entering the race that we were already signed up for. We milled around the workshop, checking on the progress of our boat and talking to as many of the guests as we could, hoping to glean as much helpful information as possible.

At around midday they held a raffle and embarrassingly, again, we started to win almost everything. It got to the point where we no longer wanted to go up to collect our prizes. The atmosphere in the room was becoming a little frosty to say the least, as people started to turn around and stare at our increasingly uncomfortable faces. We won a day out with Charlie training on a boat, which was useful. We also won a Raymarine autohelm. Having never rowed further than the pub, we had little comprehension of its importance. It was only when Charlie asked to buy it back from us for £400 that we realised quite what a prize it was. His daughter, Lottie, kept telling us to keep it, saying we'd need it out there on the ocean, but we sold it back to Charlie, only for us to buy it back from him six months later! That was a hugely important day for us.

Initially, our ocean-crossing meetings were held at The Grange. We'd row the river on Saturday morning as usual and then retire to the sitting room, by the fire, with our cups of coffee and reviving biscuits. But by this stage, we were meeting more often at each other's houses in the evening with our piles of paperwork spread out on kitchen tables, laptops out, and maybe sometimes some wine too. We'd trawl through the lists of things we were supposed to have done or achieved since the last meeting. Queen of Admin was Niki. She was uber-organised and would make a list for absolutely everything. If any of us wanted anything done, sorted, sourced, checked, double-checked, placed into a Dropbox file, the person to ask was Niki. Though her arch-rival in Dropbox was Janette, for we soon learnt that there was nothing Janette liked more than making a bullet-point list and popping things into a brand-new file of her very own making. The logic of the file and indeed the list was not of paramount importance. But Janette is a woman who defies logic.

Helen was in charge of all communications and PR. She was the one who was always trying to work out how we could raise our profile in order to raise more money. She was the one who decided we should get ourselves out there a little more; we should start meeting people, talking about our project and our plans and be a bit more… inspiring.

But for that we needed the boat.

'Rose.'

We decided to call her *Rose*. We needed a girl's name, obviously, and we were from Yorkshire and we'd already started to use the Yorkshire rose symbol on some of our marketing and sponsorship forms, so to call our boat *Rose* seemed like a good idea. Our team name, despite over a year of brainstorming, was eventually cracked by Mark. He suggested Yorkshire Rows to Frances over dinner one evening. It was a simple, clever play on words that required little or no explanation and, more importantly, we all liked it. Even Helen.

Eventually, in October, we received the phone call from Charlie that we had all been waiting for. *Rose* was ready for collection and Charlie was offering to take us out on her for the day, as a way of honouring one of our many Rannoch open day prizes.

Together, in Janette's husband's van, we all drove down to Burnham-on-Crouch full of excitement laced with anxiety. We couldn't stop talking, discussing what *Rose* might look like. This was the first time we would get to see *Rose* and row in her. What would she feel like? Would we be able to handle her? After all, none of us had ever been in an ocean-going rowing boat. What if we couldn't manage her? What if we weren't good enough? What if we had made some terrible mistake and couldn't actually row her at all?

There was also a lot of money at stake. Mainly Janette's. But, houses aside, none of us had ever spent so much on a single item in our lives. It was enough to makes us all feel a little queasy.

We were silent as we drove into the yard outside Charlie's workshop. Turning the corner, we suddenly saw her. There she was, all shiny and white, sitting on a trailer behind Charlie's car. Her lines were sleek, her curves were smooth.

'Oh my God! Look at her!' declared Janette, clutching her chest as she opened the car door. 'She is beautiful.'

And she really was. She was bigger than we thought and so very streamlined, like she could cut through those huge waves like a hot knife through butter. There were three seats on runners, should we need to row three up at a time, and there was one double cabin at one end of the boat and another smaller cabin at the other. One was full of navigational equipment and was loosely referred to as an office, and at the other end was the 'luxury' double suite.

We all fell in love at first sight; it was a very emotional moment. She felt plucky, determined, cute yet tough. She was so full of character that it was like we had discovered another person.

'Hello, *Rose*,' said Helen, patting her on the backside/stern. 'Welcome to the team.'

'So, do you like her?' asked Charlie as he came bounding out of the office towards us, a large smile on his face.

'She is lovely,' nodded Frances.

'So lovely,' agreed Niki.

'She is more than we hoped for,' added Janette, looking a little teary.

'I expect you're keen to take her out onto the water,' he said.

We all stared at each other a little nervously. Take her out? Now? That was the reason we'd driven all this way, but it felt a little sudden. What if we damaged her? Rowed her into something? Ran her aground? She looked so box-fresh; we didn't want to scratch her anywhere.

'Hop in,' said Charlie, oblivious to our reticence.

We all squeezed into Charlie's car as he drove very confidently and surprisingly quickly, towing *Rose* through the narrow streets of Burnham-on-Crouch, straight to the Co-op car park.

'Out you get,' he said, nodding towards the shop. 'A trolley each should do it.'

'Do what?' asked Janette.

'A trolley of water each,' he said. 'That should be enough ballast.'

'Ballast?' asked Helen.

'She's made of carbon fibre so she's as light as a feather. You put her on the water without any ballast and it'll be like trying to control a paper cup in a hurricane. She'll bounce and fly everywhere; you'd be straight into the side of a yacht before you know it. Plastic bottles of water are really heavy – a trolley each should do it.'

'I'm at least one trolley on my own,' piped up Janette.

Charlie looked at her. 'We'll need a few more than that!'

Perhaps the Co-op in Burnham is used to girl gangs with an apparent desperate thirst for Highland Spring, because no one batted an eyelid as we cleaned them out of nearly every case of mineral water going. Wheeling our trolleys out, we met Charlie back in the car park; by now he was standing in the middle of *Rose*, ready to stash pack after pack of mineral water in the bottom of the boat.

'Keep going!' he shouted as we hurled them up at him. 'We've got to make sure she sits nicely on the water.'

About half an hour later, we were in the slips, dressed in our waders, about to launch her out into the water. Niki (of course!) produced a bottle of champagne from her exceptionally deep handbag and we proceeded to christen our girl.

'May God bless her and all who row in her!' declared Frances, popping the cork loudly across the water and baptising our baby in a fizzy foam bath.

We clapped and cheered. 'To *Rose*!' we repeated. 'And all who row in her!'

On the river, *Rose* felt much bigger than anything else we had ever rowed. It was a distinctly odd feeling, sitting down at the oars and taking them in each hand, ready to set off on our journey. Here we were – Yorkshire Rows – finally aboard our boat that was going to take us across the Atlantic. But the sky was darkening overhead and it was beginning to rain and Charlie was bawling in our ears, warning us not to bump into a nearby yacht and to set a proper course out of the marina towards the River Crouch and the wider estuary.

Thankfully Charlie took the helm, as none of us wanted the responsibility of getting *Rose* out into the open water. She was pulling right and left as we pulled left and right, and it took all of Charlie's energy and expertise to keep her on a steady course.

Once we reached the middle of the estuary he told us to stop rowing. At first we thought it was a comment on our skills, or lack thereof, but he wanted us to rock the boat. He wanted us to see just how much we could push her, just how much she could take. Under his instructions, we all stood on one side of the boat and tried as hard as we could to turn her over. It was impossible. Even with all our weights combined, we couldn't get her over. It was a far cry from the skinny riverboats we were used to, where all you had to do was itch your nose, lose concentration, think about what you might have for lunch, and you were straight in the water. But *Rose* was solid. Rock solid. Despite her incredibly light frame, she was sturdy, dependable, someone we could rely on.

On out into the estuary we rowed. We were all trying very hard to keep a rhythm, to keep together, in the hope that we might impress Charlie. But he remained unmoved. It was pouring with rain and his eyes were on the horizon, straining to see the pub where he was planning to stop for lunch. As the wind got up, so the waves on the estuary grew bigger and, despite all our ballast, we still bobbed around on the water, like a ping-pong ball. We'd experienced a few breezy days on the river, but nothing compared to this.

'Keep going!' said Charlie as he pointed our bow towards a pretty white Georgian pub close to the shore. 'Not much longer.'

The fish and chips and scampi in a basket were all the more delicious after the two-hour row, as was the half pint of shandy.

'Right, I'll see you later then,' announced Charlie as he accompanied us back to *Rose*. 'I'll walk back.'

'Really?' There was a note of panic in Helen's voice.

'You'll be fine,' he shrugged.

'Walk?' questioned Janette, who clearly felt she'd rowed half-way to France by now.

'Yeah,' he said. 'It's only a couple of miles. You'll be okay. You know where you're going.'

We were about to row an ocean; surely we could find our way back to Burnham-on-Crouch?

'Yeah, yeah,' said Frances, who was looking forward to having *Rose* all to ourselves.

'Of course,' nodded Niki. 'We'll be fine,' she added as we very confidently pushed off.

Dressed in our mismatching bobble hats, baggy leggings and granny cardigans, we must have looked quite a sight as we boarded *Rose*. But with Janette at the helm, we launched, our oars moving in perfect unison. It felt fantastic to be in charge of *Rose*. The freezing wind might have been blasting our scarlet cheeks, our noses might have been running slightly, but we were at last working in harmony. Our oars dipping in and out of the water as if powered by one person. Not a glitch, not a crab, not a clash. We were smooth. Focused. *Rose* was part of our team. And although she was the fifth member and the last to join, she completed us.

'Hey – you ladies can row!' he shouted at us over the slate-grey sea. 'You can really row!'

'Yes, we can!' replied Janette. 'Yes, we bloody well can!'

SHIP'S LOG:

'It's those little steps in the right direction that get you to the next place in your journey. Sometimes you want to give in, and it's tempting to do so, but you keep going because you know that for all the bumps in the road, there will certainly be some smooth parts, and when you hit them you will feel so good.'

(JANETTE/SKIPPER)

CHAPTER 8

Back Home

'It had long since come to my attention that people of
accomplishment rarely sat back and let things happen,
they went out and happened to things.'

LEONARDO DA VINCI

If our rowing skills were not in doubt, our orienteering most certainly should have been. For within half an hour we were completely lost. How it is possible to get lost on a straight piece of river when you are travelling simply from A to B, who knows? But we did. And then, of course, we made the fatal mistake of taking out our mobile phones and searching on Google Maps, which is never a good idea in the pouring rain in the middle of a busy estuary. Added to which, we were all convinced that we knew exactly where we were going. Only none of us could agree where.

'I definitely remember that house over there,' pointed Helen.

'Well, that doesn't tally with Google Maps,' said Frances, looking down at her screen.

And on and on we went, rowing in circles, trying to work out which little marina off the big, fast-flowing estuary we were supposed to be aiming for. In the end, as the rain turned horizontal and the light began to fade we decided that any marina was better than no marina at all and we opted for the one closest to where we thought we should be, in the hope that it was the right place. It wasn't. But it wasn't terrible. It was the right marina, just the wrong mooring, but we had little choice by then as it was getting dark, so we found the closest available spot and went for it.

'Careful!' said Janette as we edged ourselves in. 'That looks like a very posh boat ahead.'

'Ahoy there!' came a shout in the darkness. We all turned around. 'Up here!' We looked up.

On the deck of the posh boat, waving a bottle, was a rather jovial-looking chap. 'Come on board!' he suggested. 'Have a drink.'

So we did. Turned out the jovial chap supplied paint to the Queen, and quite a lot of wine and crisps to us. We were joined in his cabin by another couple who lived in Burnham and, after a few drinks, everyone had promised to sponsor us. In our relief at finding a berth and a few much-needed glasses of wine, we'd forgotten about Charlie who, judging by the number of missed calls we each had on our phones, had been frantically trying to ring us, fearing we were lost at sea.

'Where the hell are you?' he shouted when Janette finally called him back.

'We're in a bay, somewhere near…' Janette tried to explain to a relieved, if slightly irate, Charlie exactly where we were.

He tried to be annoyed even when he finally found us on the posh yacht, but it was impossible to resist the convivial hospitality of Mr Paint, who soon had Charlie sitting on his rather pleasant sofa, sipping a large glass of wine too.

As the evening wore on, we decamped from the yacht to the pub where we were staying that night. Mr Paint and his pals joined us and insisted we drank another bottle of champagne. His stories were as generous as he was, and eventually, after a lot of exhausted yawning, we thanked him profusely and said we must go to bed. How he made it back to his yacht without tumbling into the water, we never knew!

Upstairs in the pub, Niki was checking her bedroom door. She loves a gadget almost as much as she loves a list, and her Amazon addiction really should be treated. Along with a new toothbrush, pots of face cream and a travel brush, she'd brought with her a special laser security device that throws a beam across the door that sets off an alarm if tripped by an intruder.

'Niki,' said Janette, a little puzzled. 'We're in Burnham-on-Crouch, not Chicago, Washington or New York.'

'You can never be too careful,' replied Niki, glancing up and down the corridor before securing the room.

This was our first night sleeping together – in two separate twin rooms – and we were quick to work out how to split ourselves up. Janette and Niki shared together on the grounds that they both slept naked and snored, whereas Helen and Frances both wore pyjamas and did not. It was a simple equation that we stuck to while on land.

The following morning, we were grateful to see Mr Paint up and about, having clearly made it back to his boat in one piece, but we were sad to leave *Rose*. Charlie wanted some time with her to iron out a few teething problems he'd felt when we'd taken her out on the water, and we also needed to find somewhere to put her and somewhere to launch her from to practise before she could come home to Yorkshire.

Janette offered to have *Rose* on her farm, so we knew she had somewhere to go when we arrived in York. The only real problem was finding somewhere to practise. She is quite a lot larger than any of our usual rowing boats, so the Guy Fawkes' Boat Club was out of the question, as there was no slip (or boat ramp) to launch her from. We needed proper 'slipways' where she could be launched into the water from her trailer, plus a substantial stretch of water to practise in, as *Rose* was a lot more difficult to handle and not a terribly agile boat. She is built for the open sea, for 40-foot waves, not a pootle up and down the Ouse between York and Poppleton.

Helen and Janette were placed in charge of finding the slips. 'We had not thought it through,' said Janette. 'We had not thought of where we might be able to practise. So we drew up a list of marinas and places where you could launch a boat in the York and Hull areas.'

The first place they found was an old boatyard just outside Goole, not far from Hull. Quite apart from it looking like the sort of place where crafts came to die, it was too small and too tight to get *Rose* into the water there, plus it gave out onto the Humber estuary, which is very tidal and, we thought, quite dangerous. It was an accident waiting to happen. The next place was even more obscure. As Helen and Janette twisted and turned along the narrow roads, they ended up in what appeared to be a housing estate.

'But we're miles from the sea, or any bit of river,' said Janette, straining to look out of the window.

'Are you sure you put the correct address into the satnav?' asked Helen, equally puzzled.

'Of course I have.'

'Where are we going to launch a boat from here? We're in the middle of a housing estate.'

'Maybe there's a secret stretch of water round here,' suggested Janette, eyeing the rows of houses. 'Through a back gate…'

'Or maybe…' said Helen, looking back at the website, 'this is not the address of the slips, but actually, if you look properly… the home of the club secretary.'

We decided not to bother the club secretary over lunch and returned to York, where after a few more weeks of negotiation we managed to find a place for *Rose* in York Marina itself, which was something of a coup. It was close enough for us all to get to and deep enough for *Rose* without too many obstacles between us and the river.

All we had to do now was collect her.

In one of our many meetings we had decided in our unending wisdom to have a fundraiser party for Yorkshire Rows at York Racecourse. We'd put the word out far and wide, and sold some 350 tickets, and we desperately needed *Rose* to be there. She was the main attraction, along with local BBC news presenter Harry Gration MBE, from *Look North*, whom we had managed to persuade to do the auction (his children go to the same school as ours and his wife was one of our supportive book-club friends). Handsome and talented as he is, we did not have a party unless we had the boat.

Janette wanted us all to go and collect her – after all, it was her first trip home – but neither Frances nor Helen could make it, so it was left to her and Niki to do the honours.

The journey down was without incident and we took possession of *Rose* easily enough, signing all the final papers and cheques. It was only as Janette turned out of the boatyard that things got tricky.

'I ended up driving down the narrowest street in Burnham-on-Crouch!' said Janette. 'I thought I was going the right way. That's the satnav for you. It was the worst street you could ever go down for your first time driving a boat on a trailer like that. Literally, the wheels were touching the doorsteps. I had to go really, really slowly. It was so stressful. I was sweating profusely, but I was being very calm and saying, "It's fine. It's fine. It's absolutely fine. We're taking it slow. She's not going to get damaged. It's fine. Just let me do this. It's fine" – as I gently drove over everyone's front doorstep, taking out their milk bottles!'

And it didn't stop there. Two hours further up the motorway we needed some petrol. This was not an operation that any of us had thought through. How would we get the van and the boat in and out of a petrol station? But the gauge was flashing red and we had no choice. We had to pull in to the next services. Why didn't we think of that before we collected the boat? Which entrance should we use? Lorries or cars?

The lorry pumps are taller, so we opted for the cars. Janette drove at an agonisingly slow speed into the forecourt – the last thing she wanted was to overshoot and have to reverse the boat/car. She got out of the car and started filling up, and within seconds we'd drawn a crowd.

'What is that?'

'Where are you taking that thing?'

'What are you up to?'

We'd thought *Rose* was very obviously a boat, but everyone else thought otherwise. The crowd grew, the petrol station became blocked and then everyone started honking their horns. While the crowd all chatted among themselves, Janette managed to edge out to pay the bill before slowly but surely, now with a huge audience, dragging *Rose* back out onto the motorway.

It was evening by the time they all arrived at the farm. 'I parked her very carefully and put a big blue cover over her to protect her,' said Janette. 'I was so worried that somebody might steal her that we pulled her into the back garden and parked her in front of the kitchen so that I could see her. I was checking out of the bedroom window before I went to bed, and as soon as I woke up, to see if she was still there.'

Over the next few weeks *Rose* was stored in a barn belonging to a local farmer while Ben was enjoined to build her a shed. 'We were so worried about her,' said Janette. 'About her being outside and having to cover her up, and the wind kept blowing her covers off. We wanted to keep her out of the rain, because we got her in October and it was coming up to winter time, so Ben built a shed. The problem with the shed was that it wasn't high enough for the aerial on top of the boat, so we had to take the aerial off to get her into the shed. And it was slightly too short, so her bum stuck out. It wasn't ideal, but at least she had her own little shed to keep her out of the wind and rain.'

Rose left the shed to come to the ball at York Racecourse, and after a lot more shouting and reversing and people sharing their uninvited opinions, she finally took pride of place at the entrance.

As it turned out, we may not have been able to navigate our way back from the pub to Burnham-on-Crouch, but we could certainly organise a very good party. We drafted in a lot of help. Our friend Leigh, who works for an events company, sorted out all the logistics for sponsorship and ticket sales. We were inundated with donations for the raffle. Charlie and his nephew Angus came up from Essex to lend their support. Niki's sister-in-law, Sharon, did the table decorations; her brother, Steven, took the photos and her parents sold tickets like there was no tomorrow. Frances raided her contacts book, selling tables and gathering prizes. Helen drummed up PR and support, and Janette put it all in some giant Dropbox folder.

It was such a fun night. It felt a little like we were all getting married again – at the same time! Our friends and family, relatives and kids, all in the same place. The atmosphere was great.

We had dinner first, at tables with comedy names such as 'Sore Behinds', 'Three Sheets to the Wind' and 'Gone Overboard'. We had angel readings with Helen's friend Dawn. We had a rowing machine that you could pit yourself against, and a photo booth where everyone could record their level of jolliness in a take-home snap. We'd issued 'boarding passes' instead of tickets, and upon presentation of said passes you were allowed to board the beautiful *Rose* – just so long as you took off your shoes first.

It was the first time we had really had to work together as a team. We'd done a few races, clung on to a couple of trees at the head of the river, but it had never been just us four organising something together before. In the lead-up to the party it was obvious that we each had very different strengths: some had an eye for detail, and others the big picture. Niki did a lot of sorting. Frances did a lot of advising, saying, 'It'll be fine.' Helen did a lot of befriending people and making them help us, and Janette did a lot of profuse thanking.

But actually it was a team effort from all of us and all our friends and family.

Just as everyone sat down to dinner, all the lights went out and loud ocean noises of the winds and the waves were played into the room. The idea was to make everyone feel like they were there with us on the boat. Then we played the short film about the Talisker Challenge, shot the year before, which was terrifying and showed the level of danger faced by every competitor. There were plenty of oohs and aahs in the room, but just in case anyone thought we were taking ourselves too seriously, we suddenly arrived, pretending to row onto the stage to the tune of 'Rock the Boat' in our ball gowns.

Niki kicked us off to a dynamic start, thanking everyone for coming. Frances introduced the delights of the communal toilet bucket and invited our fellow guests to test-drive it. Helen graciously thanked everyone for helping to put the whole thing together and Janette asked us all to 'capture some magical moments, create happy memories and surround ourselves with laughter and friendship. Have fun, go on... dance a little... like no one is watching!'

Having danced a little too much, and perhaps enjoyed a little too much of our own hospitality, we said goodbye to our guests and then realised we had to get *Rose* out of the building before we locked up. With Ben at the wheel, we all lined up behind *Rose*, our husbands in their tuxedos and us in our ball gowns, to give her a push. Left a bit, right a bit, heave! Manoeuvring a heavy vessel through a hall and up a ramp and out through some narrow double doors is not something we would recommend to anyone in their best sequins and high heels. But out she came into the moonlight, with one final push. A real test of teamwork!

At the end of it all, we had raised over £25,000, which is not bad for four mums with zero fundraising experience, and to do it together with the support of all our families and friends, with *Rose* as the star of the show, was hugely important to us.

The next morning, there were quite a few of us who wished we'd been a little more abstemious.

But there was not much time to sit around drinking tea and taking it easy. After our slightly disastrous outing in Burnham, we decided that we should get as much experience handling *Rose* as possible. We were not strapping Olympic rowers who would be able to power ourselves out of trouble should a giant wave or storm hit us in the middle of the ocean. Confidence in our boat and our ability on the water would be everything come the Atlantic.

In the second week of December, we all turned up at Janette's to pick up *Rose* and headed off to Hornsea Mere, the largest freshwater lake in Yorkshire. Niki was driving us, so it was the first time we had not used Ben and Janette's van to tow *Rose*. She punched the address of the rowing club into the TomTom and we set off. It was a cold, icy morning, but we were all looking forward to getting her in the water again. We were talking about the party and how surprisingly successful it had been and how incredibly relieved we were to finally be on our way in terms of sponsorship, when Janette piped up.

'Are you sure this is the right way?'

'That's what the satnav says,' replied Niki, carrying on ahead.

'It must be right,' nodded Janette. 'Only I'm sure I don't remember these roads being so narrow.'

Just as she spoke, the road slimmed down to a very tight lane, with unforgiving walls rather than hedges bearing in on us. It was impossible to turn or reverse, so we had no choice but to continue. The walls on either side grew tighter and higher as the road narrowed again. Time and again one of us had to squeeze out of the car to help Niki. 'Why is it taking us this way?' she said, her voice about three octaves higher in panic.

Then suddenly we crossed a cattle grid and the next thing we knew we appeared to be driving across a golf course.

'This is a golf course!' said someone, stating the bleeding obvious. The rest of us tried to look ahead, not at each other.

'Oh crap!' yelled Niki as she drove us down the icy hill ahead, picking up speed now that we certainly had more space around us. There were golf buggies scattering to the left and right, and some rather astonished looking gentlemen stared as if they'd never seen a car full of middle-aged women dragging a large boat behind them on the eighth green before. Clubs poised in mid-swing, mouths hanging open, they watched us bounce over the grass to another cattle grid at the bottom of the hill. Niki tried to pump the brakes to stop us, but the ice and the smooth golf-buggy path were not a great combination and we skidded towards the main road we were surely supposed to be on.

'Shiiiiiit!' Niki screeched. And together we all just closed our eyes and hoped for the best as we slowly slid across the main – and thankfully traffic-free – road and over to the other side. Finally the car and the boat came to a halt.

'That was not supposed to happen,' stated Niki, in case we had been in any doubt.

'Umm,' said Janette, leaning over from the back seat, the first of us to manage speech. She squinted at the TomTom. 'Have you got that thing set to HGV?'

It was minus four degrees when we arrived at Hornsea Mere and the water looked particularly uninviting. As we slowly edged *Rose* towards the shore on the trailer, we realised that we had something of an audience.

There was a group of four elderly men watching our rather poor progress with a slight smile on their faces. This was the first time we'd launched *Rose* ourselves and without Charlie to help it was something of a process. 'Do you want some help?' one of them asked.

'No, thanks!' replied Frances. 'We're fine.'

'It's like being asked if you want help from the cast of *Last of the Summer Wine*,' hissed Helen as her wellingtons slipped in the mud.

'Careful!' declared another.

'Yes. Thank you.' Helen's smile was tight.

'At least let us clean the pontoon for you – all that goose muck over it, it's worse than an ice rink,' said one of the old men.

And before we could say anything, they'd grabbed some brushes and scrapers and were shifting all the goose shit off the decking. Of course, it wasn't us they were interested in at all, it was *Rose*, and after a few minutes of scrubbing the questions came thick and fast. Where was she from? How old was she? Where was she going? She clearly had the allure of a well-preserved Bond Girl. As we lowered her into the water, they were bowled over by her curves and her sleek lines.

'She's a beauty,' one of them whispered.

If it was below zero outside, we could only imagine how cold the water was. It wasn't so much frozen as a little crisp around the edges, with a hardened layer of shining ice across the mud. It was certainly cold enough to give us all a case of dragon breath every time we spoke, and it nipped the ends of our fingers.

'Right,' said Frances as she rubbed her hands together. 'Does anyone know exactly how this works?'

She nodded towards the rudder that had to be attached to *Rose* while she was in the water. This was not a job for someone in waders. It required a drysuit. And out of all of us, Frances was the most game. In fact, she wanted to do it and, more importantly, she was the only one who owned a drysuit. After all, who in their right mind would want to scuba dive off the frozen shores of the UK?

As Frances slipped into something distinctly less comfortable, the elder chaps quizzed us a little more about why we – four middle-aged women – were the proud owners of such a beautiful boat. We told them our story and our plans and they were full of enthusiasm and advice. They were all keen sailors and one of them had been a diver in the Marines. So when Frances arrived in her suit, he was extremely helpful, handing her the rudder as she submerged herself into the freezing water. Attaching a rudder in the water is a difficult skill to master; add an audience and sub-zero temperatures and the prognosis is not good. After about five minutes, Frances's hands were scarlet and so cold she could not move them. The rudder was proving more difficult than we'd thought.

'Give me a minute,' said the diving Marine as he disappeared off into the boathouse. A few minutes later he was dressed in a drysuit and up to his neck in the freezing water, attaching the rudder. 'There you go!' he said, giving *Rose* a pat. 'Enjoy yourselves.'

Attempting to channel the panache of the ladies we'd seen in France, we thanked them and leaped into *Rose*, as one, before taking hold of the oars and setting off. Unfortunately, we had not been to the local Co-op and had a minimal amount of ballast, which in the gusty conditions was not nearly enough. Within minutes of setting off we found ourselves being blown back to shore with such speed and force it was impossible to row against. The ex-Marine watched our speedy approach and jumped into the water just before we crashed into the pontoon.

'It's a bit gusty today, ladies,' he said, giving us an almighty push. 'I'd try to get yourselves away from the shore.'

'Yes, yes,' agreed Janette as she pulled in the oar. 'Thank you very much!'

Off we went again, this time really putting our backs into it. Niki was at the helm, urging us on. We had a point to prove now, so we all grimaced and pulled together. But *Rose* was like an ice skater; with every breath of wind she gently floated in another direction. No matter how hard we rowed we could not keep her going in a straight line. After about 20 minutes, we sat back in our seats for a well-deserved break.

'Cup of coffee?' suggested Niki, pulling out a thermos from the bag that just keeps on giving. 'Jelly Baby?' she added.

We sat in the middle of the lake, drinking our coffee, munching slowly on our Jelly Babies, enjoying our brief picnic, just as another strong gust of wind took hold of *Rose* and we began to drift slowly towards a forest of bulrushes. We all looked at each other and then over to the shore, hoping we might be rescued by our knights in shining armour again. We scanned the shore. They'd gone. Damn it! One of us was going to have to put the drysuit on again.

We had exactly a year before we set off from La Gomera – we only had 12 months to really nail this thing!

SHIP'S LOG:

'We were starting to really form a team. We were becoming more cohesive and working out which of our strengths we could rely on. We had many challenges early on. It was not an easy ride, as we mostly learnt by our mistakes. It's good to make mistakes – it's a great way to learn, even if sometimes it can be a little bit dangerous. The moment you stop making mistakes is the moment you stop learning.'

(JANETTE/SKIPPER)

CHAPTER 9

The North Sea

'Nothing is impossible: the word itself says "I'm possible".'

AUDREY HEPBURN

After Christmas, Frances handed in her notice at work.

Her *Groundhog Day* life had proved too much. 'It was time,' she said. 'It actually got so bad at work that I just wanted a change.' So instead of staying where she was and putting up with it, fearful of starting from scratch and worried that she would never find any clients, she and a few like-minded friends left and set up a new company on their own. 'It felt as if I was on a treadmill, and I needed to break that.'

But setting up on her own only a year before the row was a huge gamble for Frances. 'I have always had a really independent streak. I am not scared easily. Maybe it's because my mother died when I was young, but I have always looked after myself; I have never been financially dependent on anyone. All the way through I have always earned enough so that if Mark ever left me or if he died, I would be okay. It is really important to me that I am self-sufficient. I have a lot of respect for Mark, giving up his job to look after our family, because I could not do it. I am dependent on him emotionally, but I just could not be financially.'

So she took the plunge along with her friends and colleagues Suzie, Martin and Simon. They set up Progeny Private Law in Leeds, a law firm specialising in private client work. And she crossed her fingers and hoped her self-confidence was not misplaced. 'Maybe I'd drunk too much Yorkshire Rows Kool-Aid.'

She did, however, have a back-up plan. 'I had been saving £150 a month into a bank account for the past five years – it was sort of my running-away money, although I had no intention of actually running away! So I thought if I only got paid half my wages while I was away rowing, then at least we had something we could dip into to help us out. Or, if all else failed, I had a tiny bit put away.'

Helen was also squirrelling away as much cash as she could to cover her leave of absence. She opened a 'Rowing' account and upped her hours at the NHS, working every day that was available. 'Obviously I wasn't going to get paid while I was away, so for that year I had no holiday whatsoever, and I agreed with work that I could basically work through the whole year, not take any holiday and then take it all when I left in November. It meant that I'd only lose maybe two months' salary. Everyone else went on holiday, all three of them, to France and stayed with some friends of ours while I stayed at home, working. I just didn't take any time off at all. Then, at the end of November, I was left with about eight weeks' holiday. I told work that I would work all the extra time they had, and they said, "That's fine, but if it becomes a health and safety problem then you have to stop." They made me take two days off in the whole year. I'd be sitting at my desk and pretending not to yawn, going, "I feel so fine!" I worked solidly for 12 months.'

It's no wonder, then, that Helen fell asleep in the middle of the Royal Yachting Association's first aid course at the Railway Institute in York. One minute she was staring into space and the next her forehead was firmly planted on the desk and she was snuffling away very gently.

Although at the Survival at Sea course a few weeks later, it wasn't quite so easy to slack off...

It was 8.30 a.m. on a cold February morning when we arrived at HOTA, a specialist training facility on an industrial estate in Hull – as Helen quipped, ironically,: 'UK City of Culture 2017.'

At first we couldn't find the room, so we ended up walking late into the classroom, to be met by rows of male faces. They varied in age, height and girth, but there was a heavy preponderance of tattoos. Some were bald, others were less follicly challenged, but they all stared at us as we walked in, as if to say, 'You lot are in the wrong classroom.' We sat down as quietly as we could and the teacher, another ex-Marine, started by going round the class, asking how many years' experience we'd all had at sea, and when was the last time we'd done a Survival at Sea course.

The first to answer was a bald bloke at the front who'd been a rigger for 20 years. He'd done the course every three or four years, and didn't know why on earth he had to be back here again. Then there was a bloke who worked on the ferries, and was only coming to tick a box so he could get back to work. And so it carried on around the room. Each of them saltier than a seadog, and each of them equally surly and only there begrudgingly. And then it came to us. Janette was first up.

'So?' asked the ex-Marine, sounding more than a little bored. 'How much sea experience have you got?'

'None,' replied Janette.

'Okay…' He looked puzzled, and the whole room turned around to look at us again. 'Why are you doing the course?'

'Because we are rowing an ocean and we need to have the certificate,' she mumbled.

'You're what?'

'We're rowing an ocean…'

'You're doing what?' He looked at each of us in turn as if he had not seen a more deluded group of females in his life.

'We are rowing the Atlantic and we need to get this certificate to be able to do it.'

'Seriously?' he asked.

'Have you ever been to sea, love?' piped up the rigger at the front. Everyone laughed.

'Yeah, yeah,' said Janette. 'I have been out on a boat.' Everyone laughed again.

'It's a rough old sea, you know, the Atlantic,' he continued.

'We've been practising a lot on the river,' retorted Niki, much to the amusement of everyone.

The first part of the morning was not that useful for a team on an Atlantic crossing. There was a lot of explaining about muster points, and how to call people to a muster station, which of course we had no idea about, and which the ferry boys could answer in their sleep. We went on to learn about seasickness and the rules of engagement on the sea – who gives way to whom. Eventually there was a break for coffee and some less than enticing biscuits, during which time we were approached by about five or six blokes, checking that our story was true and not just a ruse to cover the fact that we were chambermaids on cruise ships or something much less auspicious.

'You're really brave,' said one bloke, chewing a Rich Tea.

'I can't believe you're doing it,' added another.

'You're fucking mad,' said a third.

There was a lot of swearing that day. They were a group who seemed to specialise in fruity language, which only got worse when we had to throw ourselves into a giant cold tank of water.

We spent the best part of the afternoon simulating various crises at sea. The first step was to practise getting on the sea survival suits, which sounds a lot easier than it actually was. Yellow and made of heavy rubber-coated material, they are loaded with zips and clips and are nigh-on impossible to slip into in a panic. And then we had to jump into the 'sea', just as someone switched off the lights.

Janette is not very keen on deep water, especially if it's a freezing cold tank being stirred up by a spirited wave machine. So she held her nose as she leapt in, only to be barked at by the instructor who said she'd held her nose incorrectly. But Janette didn't care; she was more worried about actually drowning. 'It was really hard work, treading water in a heavy suit, while they chucked water at you in the dark. I couldn't get my breath. I thought, "I am not going to get through this."'

Once we were all in the water, we had to inflate the life raft, flip it over and form a human chain to get everyone into the boat. There were about 15 of us all bobbing around in the water, being sprayed in the face, shouting at each other, while trying to haul one another into the boat. 'Some of the bigger blokes were finding it hard to cope,' said Janette. 'They were really struggling. They were wearing all this gear and I guessed some of them possibly hadn't done any exercise since the last time they were on the course! It is very hard work trying to get into a life raft when you've got a bit of a gut and your shoes are full of water!'

Although Niki and Frances seemed to love the whole experience, as we all stood huffing and puffing and drenched by the side of the tank, attempting to take off the sodden wet-weather gear, Frances had a suggestion.

'I think they should do this for children's parties. It would be a great laugh.'

Fortunately, the rigger standing next to her couldn't deck her; he only had enough breath left in him for a wheezy, stifled laugh.

Come 6 p.m. we all had our certificates as we staggered out of the building. An afternoon of jumping in and out of a tank and trying to scramble onto a raft was absolutely shattering. Judging by the way we collapsed into the car to drive back to York, we all needed to do some serious fitness training. Clearly, the weekly CrossFit classes that we were attending were not cutting it.

And we still had so much more money to raise. We were desperate to increase our profile, so we were thrilled when Helen managed to get a small amount of publicity on BBC Radio York. Naturally we were introduced to the listening public to the tune of 'Rock the Boat', but we were just pleased to be there. Jonathan Cowap, the presenter of the show, was charming and asked Frances and Janette loads of questions, and all we could think, as they laughed and chattered their way through the interview, was: 'We've put it out there now. We are going to have to row this ocean. There is no way we're getting out of it now.'

Apart from money, of course, what we also desperately needed was some ocean-rowing experience. It is all very well pootling up and down to Poppleton on a Saturday and being blown across Hornsea Mere once a week, but what we really needed was to get *Rose* out on the sea, put her through her paces and work out exactly what we didn't know.

So when Charlie invited us back down to Burnham-on-Crouch, to what was grandly titled the European Off-shore Ocean Rowing Series, we leapt at the chance. We packed up *Rose*, our Lycra onesies and our overnight bags and headed back down to the familiar salubrious pub on the quay. Helen and Frances, being the pyjama-wearing silent sleepers, checked in together, opposite Janette and Niki, the naked snorers, and Niki set up her laser security system before we headed off out for dinner at the Yacht Club, where Charlie had gathered together all the teams who were going to be racing the next day.

Walking in, a glass of warm white wine in hand, we recognised some of the rowers from the Rannoch open day where we'd ingratiated ourselves by cleaning up in the raffle. But there were others who'd come from much further afield. Team Beyond – Philip and Daley – had flown in from

America, and Greg Maud, an adventurer (who we later found out could nail the theme from *Frozen*) had come all the way from South Africa. Charlie's nephew, Angus, was competing as part of Ocean Reunion (with an as-yet undiscovered fondness for peanut butter served in a bag) along with a group of old friends – Joe, Jack and Gus – all from Uppingham School. But the beefiest, butchest specimens by far were a group of five, who included Jason Fox, an ex-SAS Marine who was then on the Channel 4 TV show *SAS*. They were called Team Essence. Essence of pure testosterone. They towered over us and were rippling with muscles. It was hard to believe that we could possibly be in the same race. (Amazingly, we were to meet all of these teams again in La Gomera, except Team Essence who were not allowed to enter the Talisker Challenge as they were not a quad but a group of five.)

The following day, everyone crammed into Charlie's office to listen to him explain the rules of the three different races.

This first race was short, like an obstacle course, round and round the harbour where you had to hit various buoys and waypoints in a certain order to win. It would be a test of the agility and handling of the boat. Having had very little experience with *Rose* in open water, we didn't fancy ourselves for that one. Or indeed for any of the other two races, which were a three- to four-hour row around a buoy and back, and a much longer eight-hour push the following day.

On the first race, the obstacle course, we all refused to be at the helm. We had all had a go the last time we were on the estuary and none of us had acquitted ourselves with any sort of aplomb. The least awful of all of us was Janette but she was loath to do it, as she really wanted to row. But needs must and there was no one else, and no choice. 'Them three were bloody useless,' said Janette. 'I wasn't great, but at least I had a feel for the wind and the waves, so I ended up doing the steering for the whole bloody weekend.'

With Janette at the helm, we headed off, determined to prove ourselves against such stiff competition. But sadly it was not to be. Despite a whole supermarket shelf of fizzy water stashed in the bottom of the boat, we were still blown about on the waves like some sort of rogue inflatable. If we weren't bumping into other boats, we were colliding with buoys. There was one moment towards the end of the race when Janette was actually convinced a buoy was moving.

'It's coming towards us!' she yelled. 'Why isn't it chained to something? What's happening? It's actually moving!'

Of course, we were the ones moving, and eventually we crashed slap bang into the thing. But there was not very much we could do; the wind was up and Janette had not yet worked out how to handle the boat.

The second race thankfully required a little more rowing and a little less steering, although there was a certain amount of orienteering required. This was the three- to four-hour row up the estuary, around one buoy and back again. The first leg of the journey was difficult as it was against the tide and we really had to push ourselves to get anywhere, but after the morning's debacle, we were keen to show that we weren't just a bunch of housewives playing around on the water. Janette found the right buoy using her splendid map-reading skills and by the time we turned, we were not very far behind the rest of the other crews. However, on the way back something happened. Perhaps it was because Janette had finally worked out how to steer the boat. Or perhaps we got lucky riding the current, or maybe we just read the waves better. Or maybe it was because, in comparison to all the others, we could actually row. Two years of pootling to Poppleton may not make you the strongest rowers in the world, but it certainly gives you some technique. And we had enough technique to get past Team Beyond, the two American boys. Even more amazingly, Team Essence were still behind us. If we turned and looked over our shoulders we could see their huge burly frames pumping away on the oars. We were getting really excited. Janette was giving us a running commentary.

'Come on, girls,' she urged.

Suddenly we realised, 'Bloody hell, we could smash this race.' So Janette took up her Queen Boadicea position and started loudly encouraging us to row harder.

'Come on, girls! We've got a chance! Give it all you've got! Give me 20 hard strokes – one, two, three…'

We mustered up every ounce of energy we had and rowed like we had never rowed before. We edged closer and closer. We could hear Team Essence huffing and puffing and straining at the oars.

'Come on!' yelled Janette. 'One last effort!'

Every muscle was burning, our thighs were screaming, our hands were yelling, our lungs were on fire. We closed in and, as we edged past, we saw their exhausted, furious faces as they were suddenly left bouncing around in our wake! We'd done it! We'd got them. We could see the finish line. All we needed now was for Janette to get the boat swiftly around the last buoy, which she managed with grace and aplomb. Unbelievable! We'd done it! We'd won!

Well, it felt like we had as we collapsed, exhausted and panting, over our oars. In fact, we'd come second after Ocean Reunion, which was not bad, considering Angus not only helps his uncle build all the Rannoch boats, but also spends a lot of his time on this particular stretch of water. Second! Second! A group of middle-aged mums from Yorkshire! We were quietly, not-showing-it, tickled right-bright pink. We were not so useless after all!

And the reaction of Team Essence made our small victory even more pleasurable.

'Well done, boys!' exclaimed Niki as they rowed in to finish a few minutes later.

Her tone sounded a lot more patronising than she intended. And they were livid. They moored up, got off their boat, marched straight to their cars and, slamming their doors, drove off. They didn't speak to anyone or make eye contact, and were only seen again when they turned up the next morning, teeth firmly gritted, focused on winning the next race.

It was a tough one – an eight-hour row into the North Sea and back. We were feeling pretty confident when we set out. Could we make them eat our wake for a second time? Perhaps that was too much to ask for. We matched them on the way out – not stroke for stroke, but not far off. However, the return trip was not so good. The water was choppy and Helen announced that she felt a little sick.

'What, seasick?' asked Niki, sliding back and forth in her seat. 'D'you get carsick?' Helen shook her head.

'Seasick?' repeated Janette from the helm. 'That's not very helpful when you're planning to row an ocean.'

'I'll be fine,' said Helen, with a firm nod.

'I bloody hope so,' said Janette, exuding little sympathy. 'We can't afford to carry dead weight.'

Not that we could ever really have caught the SAS boys again. We were rowing against the current, which is like trying to haul a giant spoon through treacle, and they were simply much stronger than us. In the end, they hammered us, frankly, which seemed to make their day and go some way to repairing their battered pride. But we didn't mind; we'd had a fantastic couple of days and we'd had a laugh, taken our girl out on the water and hadn't come last. In fact, we'd done okay.

'D'you fancy rowing the North Sea? I'm organising some off-shore training races for this year's transatlantic crews,' Charlie asked as we were packing up *Rose*, preparing for the long, slow drive back up to York. We all stopped what we were doing.

'The North Sea?' asked Frances.

'It would be good training for the Atlantic,' he suggested.

'It'll be cold,' said Helen.

'You'd be the first women to do it...'

'Oh, don't say that to Janette!' said Niki, slowly shaking her head. 'She's incorrigible!'

'The first?' Janette looked at him. He nodded. 'Ever?' He nodded again.

'We won't hear the end of it now,' said Helen with a smile as she got into the back of the van. 'All the way up the bloody M1.'

And we didn't. The idea went back and forth across the seats of the van as we drove.

'We do need more practice in *Rose*,' began Janette.

'But on the North Sea?' replied Helen.

'We need to spend the night on board,' said Frances.

'We need to row in the dark,' agreed Niki.

'We need to row and not be able to see land. We need a proper run at it before setting off from La Gomera,' declared Janette.

'And this would be the perfect opportunity,' agreed Frances.

By the time we reached the Midlands we were all sold on the idea. All it would really require was a little organisation.

Actually, quite a lot of organisation was required, particularly for Helen. Richard announced that he had got the job as Director of Public Prosecutions on the Isle of Man, as everyone – most of all Helen – knew he would. She had seen more Manx signs in the past four months than she'd seen in her (and possibly Richard's) entire lifetime. The only problem was that he had to move. He couldn't be DPP of the Isle of Man if he didn't actually live on the island. So not only was Helen going to be on the Atlantic for three months rowing an ocean, Richard was not going to be at home either. What was going to happen to Lucy and Henry? Who was going to look after the children? And the dog? Should they all move to the Isle of Man together? Should they stay? What was already a difficult situation suddenly became a whole lot more complicated.

But Helen was not going to give up. Having got this far, it didn't seem fair to be thwarted by mere logistics. Lucy and Henry didn't want her to give up either. Even Richard, who had been so reluctant, was now adamant that a solution had to be found. Then Grandma Pat, Richard's mother, stepped forward. She had originally been less than keen on the idea of her daughter-in-law rowing the Atlantic. But she had found herself swayed when she'd listened to a speech given by Sally Kettle at the end of the summer term at St Olave's School. Sally had spoken about her experience crossing the Atlantic, along with her mum, and had finished up by telling the school that she knew of four mothers in the audience who were preparing to do the same. She had invited all of us to stand up, which we did, to a faint ripple of applause. And Grandma Pat suddenly felt herself a bit proud of Helen and her hare-brained scheme, and now she was offering, very kindly, for Henry, Lucy and the dog to live with her while Helen was on the Atlantic. It seemed like a solution and Helen was extremely grateful, but in the end Richard was concerned that looking after two teenagers and a Labrador would be too much for his mother, so they managed to persuade St Peter's to let the children flexi-board, going to stay with their granny at the weekends, and with their father coming backwards and forwards to see them. It was a very big sacrifice. They had turned their lives upside down so their mum could follow her dream. And they had done it without complaint or fuss. It was a move that humbled Helen. If everyone was going to put themselves out for her this much, she'd better make it across!

But first we were going to row the North Sea.

Perhaps we had not taken the idea of crossing the North Sea seriously. After all, in comparison to crossing the Atlantic, it was only a little bit further than

Poppleton. Like rowing across a pond. It looked easy. In fact, we were so completely underprepared when we arrived at Southwold in Suffolk that we turned up in our onesies. Well, not quite in our Guy Fawkes' onesies, but certainly the sort of Lycra workout gear more associated with getting in touch with your pelvic floor in your local village hall. It was May, the sun was out – this would be like a stroll in the park, we thought.

'Where's your wet-weather gear?' asked Charlie as we stood on the beach in our leggings at 6 a.m. We looked at each other. Surely one of us had a few jackets in the car?

'To be fair, we didn't get a list like in the Talisker, which is very strict on what you have to have,' explained Niki. 'Charlie sent us a few emails saying we need this and that, but nothing was actually stipulated. It was something of an awakening in many ways. We'd been really busy and we hadn't really thought about it. Then all of a sudden it was like, "Oh crap, we've got to have a life raft, we've got to have an anchor." All these things that we didn't have, and couldn't afford to buy, because we were still quite far from the start line and we were still trying to raise money. We borrowed some essentials from Angus and Charlie. I think they lent us a life raft and an anchor and various bits, but we didn't have any of it till we got to Southwold. And, crucially, we didn't know how to use it.'

So with only a few hours before we set off, we launched ourselves at the local chandlery. 'We had the wrong map, the wrong chart. We needed some netting,' said Frances. 'We spent so much time trying to raise money, which was really important, but we could've ditched a few of the Saturdays taking *Rose* fundraising in Leeds or York, to whichever craft fair we'd decided to show up to for a couple of hundred pounds at the most, and had a proper day just understanding more about the equipment. But as it was, we didn't know very much at all.'

The more we panicked, the more undiscerning we became. So we loaded *Rose* up with lifejackets, survival suits, head torches, sleeping bags, an almanac of tides, snack packs, dehydrated food and enough water to take us to Gibraltar. She was so heavy and low in the water by the time we'd finished. The trip was only supposed to take about 48 hours at the most. We could have left over half of it on the beach and gone to the local takeaway and simply ordered a few pizzas. But we had not thought anything through, which is never a good place to start.

'We'd talked about it a lot, saying we were going to row the North Sea. It looked like a quick jaunt. What was there to discuss?' said Niki. 'But no one had done it before. Perhaps there was a reason.'

Turns out, the North Sea is incredibly unpredictable. There are two ways to cross: one is straight from Southwold to Scheveningen in Holland; the other is to zigzag with the tides, as they rise and fall every six hours. And no matter where you think you might be going, there is nearly always something in your way.

'It's like bumper boats,' said Niki. The North Sea/Dover Strait is the busiest shipping lane in the world with some 500 to 600 boats passing through it every day, and we were the smallest craft on the ocean. Only the week before, Team Beyond – Philip and Daley – had abandoned their boat in the middle of the Strait (while doing a timed crossing as part of our race) and had called up Janette the following day to tell her that we should absolutely not do the trip. Their experience was enough to make the rest of us panic.

'They had terrible weather and were very seasick and surrounded by huge tankers,' explained Janette. 'They sent me a picture of their GPS and there were loads and loads of boats. You could see them, little dots all over the screen, like a bad case of chicken pox. And they said, "Look at this! Look how crowded it is out there. They're everywhere, these ships, and they're big. You guys need to think seriously about whether you should do this." So they abandoned their new boat in the middle of the North Sea and got a lift with a fishing boat. I said, "It's not a problem." They had rough weather and were very sick, and don't forget, they'd never been out on a sea before. I called all three of them to say, "I've been out to sea. We'll be fine." The fact that I had only pottered around the South of France with a gin and tonic in my hand was neither here nor there. I had been to sea – that was my story, and I was sticking to it!'

Come 7 a.m., all our families were there to see us off. All except Niki's dad, Pete, who had volunteered to drive the trailer over to Scheveningen in Holland to meet us when we arrived at the other side, and Janette's sister, Jane, who had taken one look at her accommodation in the nearby holiday camp and announced that she was not staying the night and had driven straight back to York. It was a bank holiday and we were by the seaside, so the options were limited at such short notice.

In fact, even at that hour of the day the beach was busy. We spent so long answering everyone's questions about what we were doing there and what sort of boat *Rose* was that by the time we set off we'd forgotten to put all the coordinates of our waypoints in the autohelm. But worse than that, we also hadn't had time to eat. Our pub was obviously not serving breakfast before we'd left as it was so early, so we decided to use it as an opportunity to try out some of the dehydrated food we planned to take with us across the Atlantic. We had also yet to have a go on the Jetboil – the stove – something we needed practice with. So after our brief meeting with Charlie, we sat down to a bowl of tepid, strawberry-flavoured porridge, which proved to be inedible. Sickly sweet, it was pale pink in colour and was the consistency of wallpaper paste.

'It makes you want to throw up right here and now!' declared Niki, putting hers straight in the bin.

'We are *not* taking this with us,' stated Frances.

'I'd rather go to sea on an empty stomach,' said Helen, placing her packet on top of Niki's.

Which, given what was to happen later, was perhaps her problem.

'Hang on!' Janette suddenly said as we walked towards *Rose*. 'A moment… if you please.'

We all looked at her rather quizzically as she pulled a fistful of black beads from her anorak pocket.

'Really?' asked Frances, looking down and raising an eyebrow.

'Rosary beads?' asked Helen, clutching at her stomach a little, still feeling the effects of the strawberry-flavoured porridge.

'They belonged to my godmother, Great-Aunty Rose,' said Janette, swinging them in front of us. 'Mum's given them to me for good luck.'

'Right,' nodded Frances, with a look that indicated she didn't do rosary beads.

'I think we should all touch them,' said Janette, 'and say a little something.'

'What? Out loud?' asked Frances.

'Anything that'll help,' said Niki, tapping the beads with her fingers and closing her eyes.

'Absolutely,' agreed Helen. 'Dear Great-Aunty Rose, please look after us on this crossing…' began Helen, closing her eyes and praying away. 'Please keep us safe… so… thank you very much, Amen.'

'Amen,' agreed Niki and Janette.

Helen opened one eye to look at Frances. 'Amen?'

'Amen,' sighed Frances, touching the beads briefly with her fingertips.

'There,' declared Helen, opening both her eyes again. 'Sorted.'

'We should be all right now,' concluded Janette, popping the beads back into her pocket.

'Absolutely,' said Frances. 'What could possibly go wrong?'

We set off with a staggered start. The other transatlantic teams, Ocean Reunion, Team Essence and Greg Maud (who was rowing with Perfecto Sanchez, as it was deemed too dangerous to row the North Sea in a solo boat), all went out before us. In contrast to our Lycra leggings and fleeces, Team Essence were bizarrely dressed for a storm in the Falklands in full heavy-weather gear plus life jackets, and in front of an audience made up mostly of our families, they proceeded to make a complete mess of their exit. Not only did they smash into our boat, but they also took out the BBC TV cameras that were filming the start of the race, before finally heading out to sea. Somehow we managed not to let our families down. We were in and off in one swift movement (just like our inspiration – those French gazelles). Even the current was making us look good. The sea was choppy, but the tide was very much in our favour and we appeared to fly out of the harbour, with Boadicea at the helm.

Almost as soon as we hit the open sea, though, Helen started to feel sick. The boat was going up and down on the waves, up and down, up and down, and slowly but surely she became silent and then she turned a pale shade of green and then that was it. She couldn't row, she couldn't speak, and the only way she could cope was to retire to the tiny cabin below. She wasn't the only one. Frances was also feeling the motion of the boat.

'With Frances, she'd be out on the oars and then every so often you'd hear a quick scramble, the blades would go down, she'd retch over the side and then a minute later she'd wipe her mouth and get back on the blades,' explained Niki. 'But when Helen started being sick a few hours into the row she just went into the cabin. She did come out occasionally and try, but would end up back in the cabin. She was so ill. She had just a seasickness patch behind her ear and she'd had nothing to eat. She'd already been feeling sick because of the stupid porridge that we'd eaten and she hadn't taken any medication. She chucked a whole lot of that back later, but you need to take it before you set sail. It was a bit of a shock for us all. We were all sitting there, quietly worrying about her, about how she would cope on the Atlantic. Even Helen, I think, had real doubts at that point. She couldn't be like that for the whole trip: a) she wouldn't be able to row, and b) she'd die.'

Our plan had been to row two hours on, two hours off, which we had been told was the minimum required for the body to recuperate, but with land still in sight we had to abandon the idea. So with only three of us rowing we changed to an hour on, and a half-an-hour rest period.

Needless to say, Janette was not terribly sympathetic. 'I kept asking her if she wanted to eat anything or if she wanted to come out of the cabin and have a little try on the oars. It was like trying to coax a small child out of its room.'

But as the day wore on, we had much bigger problems.

'There were boats everywhere. As soon as we left the harbour they started,' said Niki. 'There were hundreds of smaller pleasure boats, and then further out there were fishing boats, and then the tankers.' Obviously we had been expecting the North Sea to be busy and we knew it was dangerous and terrifying – we'd seen Team Beyond's GPS – but nothing could prepare us for quite how quick and just how enormous the tankers were. Once we reached the open sea, and the two massive shipping lanes that bisect the North Sea, it became like a game of chicken.'

There are rights-of-way laws on the water – a more manoeuvrable boat must not impede a less manoeuvrable boat, so smaller boats with engines give way to yachts under sail, tankers and people like us – but tankers are so huge and so fast that for them to shift course is a big deal. We were just rowing – going 2 knots to their 14–16 knots. So actually, for us, moving quickly wasn't really feasible. That's why it was so dangerous. They could plough us down and not even notice, like a little matchstick in the water. However, the situation was worse than that. It turned out that our biggest problem wasn't the big ships, because we could see them on the radar; it was the fishing vessels.

They didn't stick to the deep channels. The deep channels are helpful – you know you're going to cross them, it's going to take about four hours and you're going to have to be alert, to keep your eyes open at all times. But the fishing vessels could be anywhere. And although we had an AIS (automatic identification system), a lot of fishing boats don't. So that meant they couldn't see us and we couldn't see them. It's okay in daylight hours, but come nightfall it's terrifying. We began to see quite why those chaps in Team Beyond had abandoned their boat.

We decided that the only way to stay safe was for someone to be on watch the whole time and look for the lights and any other sign of incoming traffic.

But Helen couldn't go on deck. Despite all of Janette's powers of persuasion and Niki's kindness, encouraging her to eat or drink, she remained in the cabin. So it was just the three of us as we rowed on into the night.

'Weirdly, I quite like a crisis,' said Frances. 'So in a way, having Helen out of action meant the three of us had to work out a different routine and be so strict with our timings.'

On we rowed – 1 hour on, 30 minutes off. 'We were making good progress,' said Frances. 'Being out there at night and seeing the lights of the ships, it was such a novel experience. I was really enjoying myself.'

Although none of us enjoyed the moment when Frances came out of the cabin at around 3 a.m. to discover a huge fishing boat bearing down on us.

'How long has that been there?' she asked, staring at the massive nets hanging off either side of the boat.

Niki and Janette had been so busy chatting as they rowed that neither of them had noticed. We even had a rear-view mirror attached to *Rose* so that we could see where we were going, but none of us had bothered to look in it.

It was so dark out there and the lights were so confusing, it was also hard to keep an eye on each other. Niki tripped at one point and fell over the side of the boat.

'I was hanging upside down off the side of the boat with my hair in the water, my knees hooked over the safety line. My heart was in my mouth as I managed to scramble up and drag myself back on deck. It had happened so quickly no one had even noticed. "God bless safety lines," was all I could think!'

That wasn't the first time she nearly went over. With Helen monopolising the bucket, the others were forced to use other forms of toilet facility. They had brought along two other methods of going to the loo, to test drive for the Atlantic. The first was a plastic bedpan and the second was a sort of Shewee device. The first was so shallow and our backsides ended up so close to our pee, dipping into it, that we just ended up sodden and covered in the stuff. And with the second it proved completely impractical to stand up with your pants down on a bobbing boat while straddling a plastic funnelled cup. So Niki opted for the third way.

'We had been told to just stick our arses over the side of the boat and go for it. But when I did that I nearly turned the whole thing over! Maybe it works better if you are a bloke, but for us the only way it would work was if we peed in tandem, one on either side of the boat. Otherwise we were in danger of capsizing the thing!'

Another thing that kept us entertained during the crossing was the radio.

'We were on it the whole time,' said Niki. 'Janette was the only one who'd actually done her radio exams at that point, so she knew what we were meant to say. But us two were just chatting away to people. I was surprised we didn't get arrested when we got to Holland actually, because we were using the main channel for just chatting to people. "Oooh, there's a boat over there, let's give them a call." We'd get on the radio: "Hello! We're an ocean-rowing boat…" Janette had even written out the protocol for us, but we ignored it. It's not until you go on the course that you understand why you have to keep the channel clear, instead of tying it up with general conversation. I was the naughty one because I like to talk. But they don't like to acknowledge you, because for bigger boats it's a protocol issue. They have to do their paperwork – anything on Channel 16 (the main channel) has to go in the log. But we were also making sure they knew we were there and they'd seen us. But there probably is a better way to do it than how we did it. Apparently everyone could hear us flirting with other boats. When we got to the other side they picked up all the transmissions. They could've given us a bollocking for not using the correct protocols. God knows why they didn't.'

But after a while even flirting with passing ships began to pall, and the exhaustion of continuous rowing and no sleep combined to create a very odd cocktail. 'The sea plays tricks on you,' said Niki. 'I started to hallucinate. A light would rush towards me and then I would see men working. They were from the turn of the century. They'd have flat caps, like you'd see on people rolling beer barrels in those old pictures. They were working on a boat or a very big buoy. Then eventually the light would shoot back and I'd be able to get an idea of the distance again, but I saw it a few times. I think it was just the lack of sleep, the sensory deprivation at night. My brain doesn't deal well with monotony. It needs to be stimulated. And there just wasn't anything there.'

By now the row was beginning to really take its toll: our backs were agony, our hands were blistered and the initial adrenaline had all but run out. And we still had another eight or so hours to go. Rowing for an hour, resting for 30 minutes. By now the shipping lanes were rammed, and by the time we passed the Hook of Holland and the entrance to Rotterdam, there were some 10 tankers lining up waiting for their opportunity to come into the channel and head for the harbour. We had to time our crossing of the shipping lane to perfection for fear of being run down.

Finally, having already spent one night at sea, we were at last heading towards the Scheveningen harbour in the pitch black. It was gone midnight, we could not see a thing and the tide was very firmly against us.

'It was really, really hard and we didn't know where the hell the port was. And when you're exhausted, you can't concentrate. Frances and I were looking at the navigation screen, thinking, "What have we done wrong? Where have we gone wrong? Why aren't we going to the port?"' said Janette. 'There were boats all around us, my heart was beating like crazy and we had no idea where we were. It was impossible to tell if we were going one way or another.'

It became clear that amid the mad scramble to leave Southwold and all the questions we'd answered on the beach, we had forgotten to put the last waypoint into the GPS and we were heading not for the port of Scheveningen, but directly into the harbour wall.

'We were heading straight for it and we had no idea,' said Niki.

'I suddenly realised what we'd done,' said Janette. 'And I yelled to Helen, "I know you're sick but you have to get out of there, out of the cabin, and help us. We're close to the harbour wall and the tide's pushing against us, the wind's pushing against us and we need three people up rowing and the rest of us are knackered. We're not going to get into the port unless you get out of there." And to be fair to her, she did get out and row.'

And we rowed hard. Harder than any of us has ever rowed before. Every muscle was screaming, every sinew straining. 'I could feel them all losing confidence,' said Janette. 'It was like they doubted we were ever going to get there. I said, "Right, let's get this fucking boat into that port now, girls! Come on. We can do it. We can get there."'

And we absolutely rowed our hearts out. Janette was shouting, we were swearing, we had reached the pain barrier and we were going beyond it.

'I was completely out of it because I'd OD'd on seasickness tablets,' said

Helen. 'I'd been throwing everything down me in the hope that something would work. And then Janette yelled that I was needed on deck. I crawled to the oars. I felt terrible and we rowed and rowed against the current, trying to get into that harbour. I basically rowed for two hours non-stop without anything inside me. I was absolutely determined to get there.'

'For the last hour Janette and I swapped and I steered us into the harbour and she took over the rowing, but it was literally like you were rowing for your life against the tide, hour after hour. More and more. Again and again. You went forward two metres, back a metre and a half, and then forward two metres. It was awful,' said Niki.

'All of a sudden I saw the boys, Team Essence, going into the port and I could see the lights on their boat just in the moonlight and I thought, "Bastards! They've got there before us." They must have been a mile or so, maybe a bit more, away from us. If only we had not messed up our navigation we might have beaten them, but as it was we were the last in,' said Janette.

Crawling into the harbour, we were totally exhausted. We'd been rowing solidly for 45 hours on the world's most congested sea, but we had made it.

'Congratulations!' shouted Charlie, applauding along with the small crowd and the TV crew who had gathered in the port at about ten past four in the morning. 'That's amazing!' he repeated as we scrambled ashore. 'You are the first women to ever row across the North Sea. It's a record! You've got a world record! Hip hip hooray!' he declared, just as Janette teetered towards him, collapsed on the floor and threw up at his feet.

'When we moored up there wasn't enough room for us to have a separate mooring,' said Frances. 'There were four other boats ahead of us that we had to climb over to the pontoon, and as we did so we realised they were all covered in vomit – the smell was absolutely disgusting. Now, Janette and the smell of somebody else's sick – she can't cope with it at all, which is reassuring for someone who was a full-time nurse! So she just smelt that, saw it and then just went completely.'

'To be fair to Janette, it really was awful,' said Niki. 'Honestly, those Marines, Team Essence, were just sick everywhere. Although, in a way, that was quite reassuring, because I thought, "Actually, do you know what? Obviously everyone's sick. It's not just Helen and Frances."'

But the following day, after we'd crawled out of bed and, by way of congratulating ourselves, gorged on hot baths and room service, including several mugs of hot chocolate, we sat down to a meeting. 'We had quite a frank conversation in the hotel in Holland with Helen about her seasickness, where we sort of said, "We need to fix this and we need to see that we *can* get it fixed,"' said Niki. 'It was never mentioned that Helen wouldn't row. But it was obvious that this was serious.'

'They were completely right,' said Helen. 'But I learnt a few things on the North Sea. Firstly, if I lay down I'd feel okay, so I knew I could get some kind of respite. It wasn't going to be continuously terrible. If I lay down and ate something I'd feel better still. But it was certainly a cause for concern. Actually, a massive cause for concern!'

And then, just as we'd finished our cups of coffee, Helen turned around and spotted a little old lady in a scarf in a nearby café.

'Do you know what?' she said. 'Last night, when I was rowing my heart out, I saw this little old woman just sitting on the boat with her headscarf on. She was just like that one over there. I was hallucinating, but I wasn't scared or anything. I'm not sure if it was the rowing or the seasickness drugs, but actually she was quite comforting, just sitting there.'

'What did she look like?' asked Janette.

'Little, with a scarf,' said Helen.

'Really small?'

'Tiny.'

'Oh my God, that's Great-Aunty Rose!' declared Janette, searching in her pocket for the rosary. 'She used to wear headscarves and she was tiny.'

'Well,' said Helen, 'I think Great-Aunty Rose was actually with us.'

'My mum prayed for her to help us on the boat,' said Janette.

'And I saw her, sitting on the deck of our boat!'

Later that day, as we prepared to leave the hotel and return to the UK, we had another conversation in the lobby. As we walked with our suitcases, our muscles so tense and exhausted that it was actually hard to move, we discussed who was going to captain us across the ocean. After what had happened on the North Sea, and our failure to put the waypoints in, plus the confusion of how to get into the port, it was clear we needed someone in charge. We had always thought we could manage to cross the Atlantic without a skipper, but less than 48 hours on the North Sea had made us realise our mistake.

'We all said why we didn't think we should be it,' said Frances, 'because I think none of us wanted to be in charge. I certainly didn't because I was the boss at work and I didn't want to be the boss outside of work as well. We all decided it couldn't be Helen – including Helen herself. Helen is very confident about things she knows, but when she is out of her comfort zone she's not so sure of herself.'

'We couldn't have Niki as skipper,' said Janette, 'because even though she does like to be in control and she's a very good manager in the area that she works in, at sea she was very worried and anxious. She would say things like, "Oh my God, this is going to happen," or "This isn't going to work." Which you can't do when you're skipper. You've got to have someone who is positive. Helen didn't want to do it anyway; she didn't feel that she knew the sea enough to be able to take command. And I think Frances was a bit too relaxed. And she didn't want that sort of responsibility. She was doing this to get away from all that.'

So in the end the decision was unanimous. The woman to take us across the Atlantic would be Janette. It was Frances who asked her and Frances who insisted. She was the only one who had any knowledge on the water and she had really proved herself on the North Sea. She'd managed to get us into that harbour against all the odds. She'd rallied us and got Helen back on the oars. She'd flogged her guts out to get us in. She was the natural choice.

That night, as Janette lay on her bunk in the cabin that we all shared on the P&O Ferry bringing *Rose* back from Holland, she stared up at the ceiling, unable to sleep. 'I knew that it was the right decision,' she said. 'I absolutely knew it was the right decision, but I wasn't happy about it because I knew what a responsibility it was. I absolutely knew before we set off that it would be the most massive burden. I was the one who had to make sure that three mums actually got across the Atlantic. They had families, children. I felt sick.'

SHIP'S LOG:

'If you see a problem or a challenge heading your way, look at it as one big adventure. That's how we saw the North Sea. We just did not see it as a problem; we thought of it as something that could be easily done. It would be fun and great practice for our real adventure. It really helped to put a different perspective on it, even though we didn't do that intentionally. Embrace the challenge. Look at it as an adventure.'

(JANETTE/SKIPPER)

CHAPTER 10

The Final Countdown

'Failure will never overtake me if my determination to succeed is strong enough.'

OG MANDINO

There is nothing like rowing a sea to make everyone realise you're serious about rowing an ocean. When we finally got back to the UK, the reaction to our North Sea record was extraordinary. 'We weren't just four women who were thinking about doing something. We'd actually *done* something,' said Helen. 'And it did raise our profile.'

We went from doing small amounts of local newspaper press to *Look North, Calendar* and then finally *BBC Breakfast*. We were so excited about being on the show. This would be a game-changer for us and the charities we were supporting. And we couldn't believe that out of all the crews who were now preparing to row the Talisker Challenge, they had picked us to interview. Niki had received an email the day before asking us if we were free. It was apparently Women's Sport Week and fortuitously we were women, doing sport, and we were available, which is often all that is important when you are doing media interviews, apparently! We leapt onto the train and stayed the night in MediaCityUK in our own rooms – which made an extremely pleasant change from the hovels we were used to – and barely slept the whole night.

The next morning, in hair and make-up, dressed in our Yorkshire

Rows tracksuits and trainers, we decided who would talk about what so that we didn't end gabbling over each other in our enthusiasm. Firstly, Frances would explain how it all began, Niki would add that we had husbands and children so were good at compromising, Janette would say she was skipper and Helen would talk about rowing the North Sea and how violently sick she was.

It was over in a flash. They used some dynamic footage of the Talisker race with some seriously dramatic music, which frankly looked terrifying, and some photos of us in our onesies, which were equally terrifying and not something any of us were particularly keen on seeing again. But we didn't make fools of ourselves. The presenters, Naga Munchetty and Bill Turnbull, were extremely charming. We talked about wanting to inspire our children, to get mothers to think of themselves in a different way and challenge their perceptions, to break out of their comfort zones and stretch themselves, and suddenly it all felt very real. Not only that, but the phone did begin to ring. At last. After a period of truly struggling to get anywhere in terms of sponsorship or offers of help, the wind had changed.

'I think people didn't want to back what they thought was a sure-fire loser,' explained Frances. 'And we had no track record of anything. No one for one minute thought we were plausible. We were some women who had a dream, an idea, a plan that had been hatched after a few glasses of wine and that was it. We'd sent out so many emails and so many letters and had received very little in return. In the beginning, it was clear we needed personal introductions, as they were the only ones that got us anywhere. The only people who really gave us money were friends and family. But after the *BBC Breakfast* interview, not only did people take us a little more seriously, but we also had a few more offers of help.'

The sponsorship offers didn't exactly fly in, but we were given multiple pairs of chafe-free pants, Holland & Barrett offered to help with our snack packs, and Helen was sent numerous pills and patches and devices

to conquer her chronic seasickness. It was such a relief to finally be getting somewhere – anywhere. It had been a little like trying to row into
Scheveningen harbour.

We had spent months touring *Rose* all over Yorkshire and beyond for
little or no return. 'It was heartbreaking sometimes,' said Janette. 'We'd
look in the newspaper to try to work out what events and shows were
happening – a car show in Harewood, Selby Rugby Club, Toulston Polo
Club, a shopping centre, a racecourse. And then we'd call them up and
ask if we could come along and fundraise. Mostly, places were full or they
were going to charge us a fortune to be there.'

'It was hard work taking the boat out because you had to get her
there, and only Janette or I could drive her,' said Niki. 'But we'd try to get
as many of the rest of us there as possible. Sometimes there would be all
four of us, and often one or more of the husbands would come down and
help out, just to talk to people and shake buckets. Or the children would
come – they were quite happy going out, talking to people and giving
buckets a shake in front of people. Actually, people gave money to the kids
more easily, especially the younger ones. It is quite hard to say no when
a child under 10 tells you they are raising money for an air ambulance.'

But a lot of the time it was fairly depressing pickings. We'd make £40
here, £120 there. And we were very specific about what the money was
for. Cash raised from the public was always going to the charities. Anything
that we raised for the row was from sponsorship alone.

On outings where we had been invited to show *Rose* by various
sponsors, we found other things to keep us amused. Naturally, Helen
kept seeing feathers everywhere. Even the waiter who served her coffee
at one point in Leeds Commercial District added a feather motif to her
cappuccino and was genuinely called Cherub: she screamed, he screamed,
they both screamed.

Meanwhile outside, Janette was chatting to a lovely old lady who made little metal angels, and she gave us hers, which she was wearing, to wish us good luck on the Atlantic. We carried Angel Isabella all the way across the ocean – along with our rich collection of crucifixes, crystals, St Christophers, rosary beads and, of course, the Holy Mary we received in La Gomera – mainly because we were too scared not to!

A week later, on another outing to a holiday-home park where we were invited by one of our sponsors, we were busy shaking buckets and raising money when a woman caught Helen's eye. 'She had this tiny little dog and I just felt I wanted to talk to her. There was something about her that drew me to her. And as she was chatting away I realised she was probably a little bit psychic. She said something to Gareth first, which he disagreed with, and then she said to me that "great things were going to happen". She told Richard, "You're going to have to be strong." To which Gareth laughed and joked, "Well, that's you two getting divorced then!" Which really upset my son, Henry. And then she said to Janette that being the skipper was going to be "very tough" for her. We hadn't even told her that Janette *was* the skipper! It was all very odd. She said, "You will have some decisions to make, and they'll be tough decisions, but you need to be firm. Firmer than you've ever been." It was like she really did know something that we didn't. She promised to think about us on our trip.'

But frankly it was meeting people like Isabella and the spiritual woman during our days out fundraising that made it more bearable. Although some of us were better at meeting and greeting than others. Niki was perhaps the most gifted. 'I was terrible at it,' said Frances. 'The worst fundraisers were the ones that went on all day, because by the end of it I was bored of people asking the same old questions and I wasn't interested in the answers at all. Niki had endless enthusiasm. She never, ever ran out of enthusiasm for answering questions about the boat. Often, by the end of the day, Helen or Janette and I would be sitting round the corner having a coffee and Niki would still be going, chatting away. If we started at 10 a.m., I would have been completely through with it by four and just desperate to go home. But Niki would be going, "No, there's at least another £50 out there." It was admirable.'

And Helen was always keen to turn a defeat into a victory. When we spent the day at Leeds Rhinos for an open day, we strategically placed *Rose* next to one of their top rugby players, and as the queue built up for him (we naturally had no one!) Helen took a whole load of photos of people "queuing to meet *Rose*" and put them on Facebook.'

In the end, we realised that it was really going to be up to us and our immediate, fantastically supportive families. 'We paid for ourselves,' said Janette. 'We had donations of equipment and some reduced prices, but we did put a lot of money into it personally. We had to pay for all our training, our courses, all our trips everywhere, the ferry for the North Sea, all that kind of stuff. From time to time we were able to pay for big kit purchases using sponsorship, but the majority of it, the day-to-day stuff, the smaller items, we paid for out of our own funding.'

Of one thing we were absolutely sure: any money that was raised specifically for either of our charities was untouchable. It would, of course, go directly to them. Anything that was collected in our rattling buckets went to them, and anything that was pledged went straight to them. And the other thing we were all adamant about was that one day, eventually, hand on heart, we would all pay Janette back. It was just a matter of when.

Time was ticking on and we had just over six months to get ourselves fit and ready for the ocean. For some of us it was a little easier than others. Janette is probably the least inclined towards any form of exercise. Given the choice between taking the lift or the stairs, she's a lift woman if ever there was one.

'I was lent one of those water rowing machines, so I'd sit in front of the telly, watching the news and rowing while Ben was cooking dinner,' said Janette. 'The only problem is that those machines are so noisy I could only row on my own, with the subtitles on. Ben used to tell me that he thought I needed to do more training. I used to say I was hard at it. I travel a lot and I'd always pack my swimming costume when I was on a conference, fully intending to do some lengths if there was a pool in the hotel that I was staying at, but honestly I'd never take it out of my suitcase. I also had one of those stretchy bands that you're supposed to tie to a doorknob. I'd have a glass of wine and think, "I should really do 20 minutes on the band," and then I'd end up doing emails and staring at the thing. I did have a go at a few Boxercise classes too. I didn't like them, and I was rubbish. I did them with Helen and she was very hard on me. She kept shouting, "You're not even sweating, Janette!" I didn't last long there. In fact, if I'm honest, I did very little physical training at all, until the race got a little closer and I succumbed. I got myself a personal trainer. He came twice a week. God, I wish I hadn't. I remember thinking, "Why the heck does anyone pay to have someone put them through 20 thousand bloody burpees and a million more bloody jumping jacks?" I did persevere with the trainer, but I have to admit on a few occasions he was cancelled due to some terrible migraine or a chronic cold, or any other pathetic excuse I could conjure up at short notice. I was the skipper and if the rest of the crew knew quite how unfit I was, they probably wouldn't have got into the boat with me at all!'

Fortunately, the rest of us were a lot more conscientious.

Frances was already quite fit before she'd even had three glasses of wine and persuaded us to row an ocean. And she actually enjoys exercising. She used to go to British Military Fitness classes twice a week, mainly because they were just across the road from her office, but she did go for a whole year and didn't miss a single class. Her favourite thing to do is clip an iPod shuffle to her bra strap and listen to Queen on a long run along the river, but as the prospect of the race drew closer she concentrated on rowing. 'I stopped going for a run in the end, but I would do my weights – just my weights – probably five times a week, and I did try to do the rowing machine four or five times a week as well. I'd watch TV while I was rowing. I got very obsessed with *Lewis*, with the sound off, fervently reading the subtitles.'

Helen worked out constantly. As she was working all the hours the NHS allowed, and the rest of the time she was looking after Henry and Lucy, it was almost impossible for her to find the time to go to a class or take time out of her day to run around the park. So she worked out, all the time: in her kitchen while cooking, while checking homework or doing the ironing – her motto was something along the lines of 'there's always time for a quick plank'. So while making the supper she would do sit-ups; while waiting for the kids' pasta to boil, she'd knock out a few star jumps; at breakfast she'd squat while buttering the toast. And on Sundays she'd throw a quick plank while checking the chicken in the oven. 'I was multitasking – something mums have done for centuries. If you don't have time, you make time. It is extraordinary what you can actually fit into a day.'

Meanwhile, Niki removed herself to the garage. Ever tactful, she wanted to make the training and the courses – such as the RYA Yachtmaster Ocean Theory – impact as little as possible on the family's lives. So she would do all the admin for the boat if Gareth was out for the evening, and when she needed to train she'd take herself off to the small gym that she'd set up in the garage. 'I would do it when he wasn't around, just so that he didn't think it was taking over my life.' Although Niki was perhaps a little too successful.

'He kept on saying that I wasn't doing enough exercise! He was of the mind-set, like a lot of people are, that if you're going to row the ocean you need to be some superhuman athlete, whereas actually that's not as important. The key is getting to the start line in the first place, so having to do all the admin to get the money. And the mental side of things is way more important than the physical side. We'd never heard stories of anyone who hadn't done it because of the physical side. You see loads of people giving up because it's shit and because mentally it drives you mad, but nobody seems to give up from a physical point of view. Everyone who'd done it had said to us that you don't have to be superhuman unless you want to go for a real speed record, which was never our aim. So most people ask you, "How's your weight training?", "How's your stroke rate?" Well, you don't need to do as much of that as you think.'

With that in mind we stopped going to the rowing club. It was sad, but we had to be ruthless. We had so little time left to prepare for the race, and indeed so little time during the week, that anything that was not going to directly help us was kicked into touch. Any spare moment was better spent on *Rose* than it was on the river.

And there was still so much to do.

Niki organised a behavioural profiling session for us with a friend of hers and Frances's, Catherine Baker, who runs a training and consultancy company and who had very kindly offered to help mentally prepare us for the challenge.

The idea was to find out how each of us would react under pressure and how we could get the best out of one another in a moment of crisis. It was a fascinating process, using multiple-choice questions about our feelings in certain day-to-day situations, which would then help us to understand how we would react in more stressful times.

The results were useful.

Niki found out that she doesn't like to antagonise people and doesn't like conflict. She also hankers after freedom from control. She is apparently reliable under pressure, but under extreme pressure she is likely to stick the rules and rebel!

Helen, on the other hand, had already been Myers–Briggsed to the max. 'It was not as earth shattering for me as it might have been, as I have been profiled many times before. I know I think on my feet and I always look for a solution to a problem, although it was extremely useful to have a few indicators of how the others would perform under pressure.'

Frances, somewhat unsurprisingly, doesn't like being told what to do. If you bark orders at her, all that will happen is she will either refuse to do what you demand or she will retaliate. Her back will firmly go up, and the situation will deteriorate. The best way to deal with her, apparently, is to ask for her help. So don't bark at Frances; plead with her instead and she'll be only too delighted to assist! Janette, on the other hand, loves a crisis. Her test results indicated that she was bored, flat-lining and listless without the stress of running her company. She needs a challenge, pressure and lots of decisions to make. She likes to run at 500 miles an hour (metaphorically, obviously), which is why she is so successful. She doesn't like a safety net and prefers to jump in with two feet rather than one. In short, she was perfect transatlantic material. Why hadn't she done the thing before?

Having tested that we were mentally capable, we also underwent a full medical, courtesy of a friend of Niki's called Maurice. Actually, he was quite insistent that we had one, peppering his sentences with charming phrases such as 'at your age' and 'dropped-down dead'. A heart specialist at Leeds and York hospital, he had us in for the day, putting us through stress tests, ECGs and cardiograms. He kept helpfully citing examples of footballers who'd keeled over on the pitch with undetected health problems. He said that it was better we know now if we had anything wrong with us, rather than 1,500 miles away from Antigua. Helen was worried. She had been diagnosed with a heart murmur when pregnant with Henry and was terrified that she would be prevented from rowing. It would be so disappointing to have got this far, only to be told she wasn't fit for the challenge. Thankfully, we all passed and went sent letters informing us: 'Nothing abnormal found. Except their heads need seeing to.' We're not sure what the life insurance people made of our letters when they received them.

But the medical profession are renowned for their warped sense of humour, as the wonderful Dr Caroline so artfully demonstrated when she held a birthday party for Janette at the end of October, only to produce a plate of raw pork chops.

'It was my birthday and Ben was away, so she invited us all over, although only Frances and I could come,' said Janette. 'When we arrived the table was laid with a pink pork chop in each place, with a whole load of surgical instruments. All the dressing packs with the gauze swabs were there, and all the material you'd use for suturing. She'd also baked an enormous, amazing chocolate cake and she'd got a bottle of sparkly.'

Caroline thought we needed to know how to stitch ourselves back up again in the event of an accident. So she taught the two of us how to suture, while we ate cake and drank champagne. She taught us to put the gloves on, which Janette vividly remembered from her nursing days. Frances was a little less enamoured with the task, seeing as it was something else she had to learn to do, and kept on saying that come the time and the injury, she'd leave the stitching down to Janette, as she was a trained nurse and Frances didn't have the patience.

As well as learning to put a pork chop back together, Caroline taught us how to administer sub cutaneous fluids. 'I remember phoning up Helen as I was going home,' said Janette. 'I said, "Helen, it's fine. I've got a saline drip and all the stuff from Caroline, so if you're dehydrated we can just hydrate you back again. All I need to do is put a needle in your stomach!" I don't think she felt very confident!'

But Caroline's generosity did not stop at a chocolate cake worthy of *The Great British Bake Off* and a packet of pork chops. She also trawled through the medical kits that we were supposed to take with us, deeming them not good enough or fit for purpose, so she proceeded to scrawl off a whole pad of prescriptions, providing detailed instructions on how to use them.

'She looked at the medical kits that the race had put together and said they were "woefully inadequate",' remembered Frances. 'She warned us: "You're on your own out there, girls." So we ended up with an enormous shopping list at Boots, which I stuck on our credit card. Our medical kit cost £800. What the guy behind the counter must have thought as he was putting all these drugs together, I don't know. But Caroline was a hero. She did little index cards, all in wonderful order: this is your pain relief, this is your seasickness, this is your infection stuff, these are your antibiotics. She did little notes for us for everything. She spent hours of her time researching, preparing these notes for us, numbering our painkillers from one to four – from paracetamol to tramadol – depending on how bad the pain was.'

Her help and patience were invaluable, although how dextrous and adept any of us would be at stitching each other up while being battered by a force-12 hurricane was another point altogether.

Another vital member of our support team was Paul Cheung, who was our team chiropractor for almost two years, and helped us more than most physically in our preparations. As well as crick-cracking us into shape every two to three weeks, and offering advice, he came to see us off before our North Sea crossing and at La Gomera (where he also treated half the other teams, on the harbour walls next to the boats).

But we were not leaving everything to science.

Cue God. Previously, at an event in Leeds, we'd had the celestial good fortune to be placed on the same table as the Reverend Kate Bottley, the delightful, entertaining vicar who wears comedy slippers while sharing her views with the nation on *Gogglebox*.

During the event in Leeds she'd asked us quite possibly the rudest question we'd ever been asked: how were we going to pleasure ourselves in such a teeny tiny boat in the middle of Atlantic? We naturally responded by suggesting she might like to come and bless the good ship *Rose* before our voyage. She was delighted and on a crisp October morning, just after Janette's birthday, we all turned up in white T-shirts and trainers, accompanied by more friends, family and supporters than you can shake holy water at, for the baptism of *Rose*.

The Reverend Bottley arrived, bringing along her pal and fellow vicar Alicia, who did the actual religious honours, splashing a few drops here and there. We gave them both a Yorkshire Rows mug and Alicia named *Rose* and gave us another St Christopher to add to our burgeoning collection. And Anne, Helen's mum, cried.

One of the upsides of gracing the *BBC Breakfast* sofa was that Talisker invited us up to their distillery on the Isle of Skye to film part of the promotional video for the Atlantic Race Challenge. It was an extraordinary offer. They had chosen us out of all the handsome, youthful, photogenic crews to film on the loch just next to where they made their whisky. We'd seen their films before and were genuinely shocked that they'd asked us. It was two months before the start of the race and it was another great excuse for a weekend of practice rowing on *Rose* and, of course, an all-girls road trip.

However, it was after about eight hours on the road up to Skye that we realised just what a long road trip it was. The bends were tight and we were running out of petrol – seriously running out of petrol. We'd tried freewheeling down the hills in order to save fuel and were now really only running on vapour.

'There has to be a petrol station somewhere,' declared Janette for the eighteenth time, staring out of the window.

'Did you say petrol?' asked Helen, suddenly waking up. 'I saw one about five minutes ago, just off the road.'

'That's so you!' said Niki, clinging onto the steering wheel fiercely, peering into the darkness. 'Why don't you ever speak up?'

Fortunately, we managed to make it to our destination, and when we arrived at the small B&B where we were staying for the two days of filming, our team bonding improved. Well, it had to — there was only one bathroom for the four of us. And at 6 p.m., Helen took to the pink bath, computer in hand, attempting to do some Yorkshire Rows emails. The first to come and use the loo was Niki, rapidly followed by Janette.

'I think you should all come in!' announced Helen from the small pink bath. 'I think you should all come and see me starkers and you all need to be able to go to the toilet in front of me.'

'I have no desire to see your ropy old fanny!' declared Janette from the loo.

'Why not?' asked Helen, moving her computer to one side and flashing her boobs. 'We've got to get used to it. When we're on the boat, we'll mostly be naked.'

'Speak for yourself,' muttered Janette, standing up.

'She's right,' agreed Frances, joining the bathroom gang. 'I think it's a good thing to do. I think we should go to the toilet in front of each other as much as possible.'

'I've just been,' announced Niki from the next-door bedroom.

So as well as filming for the Talisker promo, our tacit stated aim for the two-day stay on Skye was sufficient public urination to render us immune to all bodily functions. The result was a lot of laughing and a lot of seeing Helen naked as she monopolised the bath.

'I can't live without baths!' she'd declare, leaping in.

'You're going to have to on the Atlantic,' Janette would reply.

Filming the video was hard work. Firstly, we were shown around the Talisker factory and given a history of distilling, along with an extensive tasting session! Secondly, we had to perform out on the loch in the freezing-cold, icy wind for hours. Back and forth they sent us, up and down in the choppy waves. Simon and Ollie, the director and producer, ordered us about while the drone handlers, Stef and Pete, tried to get footage of us rowing through the water from above. The sky was blue and the sun was out but it was still biting cold out there and the temptation to so much as glance up at the drone as it slowly crept past was extremely hard to resist. All we could mumble to ourselves was: 'Don't look at the drone, don't look at the drone,' as it hovered right in front of our faces.

One of the great advantages of doing the video was that we met a lot of the Talisker team. So when we turned up two months later in La Gomera for the start of the race, they greeted us as old friends, which, when you are severely out of your depth and on the point of expiring with nerves, was a great help indeed. We'd been out to the pub with race organiser Carsten, we'd met Simon and Ollie who'd be filming in La Gomera, and they'd all heard about Helen naked in the bath.

By the time we got back down to York and our families, we were raring to go. All we could really think and talk about was the row. And eating. We had to eat like we had never eaten before – although when we say 'we', it was all of us except Janette. We'd been advised that we needed to put down fat before crossing the ocean, as we would end up losing quite a lot of weight. As none of us was particularly well endowed in the first place, we needed to eat as many crisps, chips, cakes, buns, bakes and chocolate as we could before going to La Gomera.

'I would shovel it in on the sofa while watching TV,' said Helen. 'And then feel quite sick afterwards. It is an odd, counterintuitive thing to try to put on weight. I didn't really enjoy it very much.'

'I found it hard,' said Niki. 'I have more or less been the same weight all my life. I found it quite difficult to pile on the pounds.'

'It was just another one of those things we had to do,' said Frances. 'I didn't really enjoy how it made me feel, with all my clothes being tight. But we had to be practical. We were told we'd lose up to two stone on the Atlantic, which is not great if you don't have it to lose.'

By now the pressure was on, and with our departure approaching Niki set about 'Yorkshire Rows proofing' her house.

'I went into full OCD overdrive. I held back from giving Gareth a full list of absolutely everything, but I did try to make a lot of stuff a whole lot easier for him. The first thing I did was stock the freezer. It was easy for Janette; Ben was used to looking after the children, so all she really needed to do was to pack her bags and shut the front door, but I was aware that Gareth was working long hours. So I bulk-cooked stew, lamb tagine and bolognese, filling the freezer until it could take no more. Then I moved on to the children's clothes, raiding the second-hand uniform shop, piling up extra football kits, more rugby shirts, socks, shorts and spare boots, and laid them all out in the guest room. It was just so that if he came home late from work he didn't need to wash their clothes – he had a spare set waiting, so he could pack their bags rather than sitting there till 2 a.m. watching the tumble dryer. I wrote lists of telephone numbers and schedules, with after-school clubs, and a homework schedule. Nothing would be left to chance.

'I knew Gareth would be fine. I told everyone that he'd be fine. He'd probably be inundated with ready-cooked meals from concerned neighbours and friends. I think I was doing things I thought I should be doing, rather than saying, "Do you know what, Gareth? Good luck. See you the other side." But I was worried. Then again, perhaps I thought I was indispensable. You like to think you contribute, that you are needed.'

With the house covered in Post-its, the freezer full of cooked meals and the spare room decked out in enough school uniform to clothe an entire other family, Niki set about organising Christmas.

'I put the Christmas tree up two days before we left, which was at the end of November, but the kids really like doing the Christmas tree with me. It's my thing. I'd put the tree up, but I couldn't find the star for the top that Corby had made with Gareth when he was three. It's misshapen, covered in foil, with just the tiniest bit of glitter left on it. It's the most ugly-looking star you've ever seen, on a skewer stick, but it goes on our Christmas tree every year and I couldn't find it before I went. I was so upset; the tree isn't complete without it. I looked for it everywhere, but I was in a rush. I thought that maybe all the stuff hadn't been brought down from the loft and that's why I couldn't find it. I had to leave the tree with no star on it.'

Helen shopped like she'd never shopped before. 'I did all the Christmas presents, the stockings, the cards, as well as Lucy's sixteenth birthday present for 20 January. I bought her a silver bangle with a secret engraved message. But other than that, I didn't really do a huge amount. I didn't do a list, or sort out a whole load of phone numbers, or buy any school kit. I just closed the door and went, which is actually, I think, a testament to how well I thought they'd all cope without me. I didn't feel like I needed to do much, other than sort out the presents.'

Janette and Frances did nothing.

'No. I did a bit of Christmas shopping,' said Frances. 'I bought some family Christmas presents. I didn't manage to buy any presents for my friends. I also bought some "Santa" presents for the boys, which Mark then proceeded to give to other people. Romantically, I signed a power of attorney so that Mark could deal with my tax return and pay my January tax bill while I was away. I put the Christmas tree up, but I didn't need to do any cooking and no one needed new clothes or anything like that.'

'I didn't even do that,' said Janette. 'I didn't do anything. I left it all to Ben. However, I did update my will. And, of course, I got Ben, Safiya and James one present each. They all got the same thing: an Apple Watch!'

As the days ticked by, we had to focus on getting everything we needed for the row. We had equipment to check, sort and pack. Fortunately, we were able to enlist the help of Lee Fudge, a former ocean rower himself. He was a safety officer for the Talisker Challenge, and he had also been helping us plan and train for the race. He'd spent numerous evenings in Niki's kitchen going over tactics. He'd helped us plan our route and given us various tips on how to survive whatever the Atlantic decided to throw at us. But more fortunately than that, he was the only one who noticed that our survival suits were not quite up to scratch.

'We'd borrowed them from HOTA,' said Janette. 'They are very expensive to buy, so as a cost-saving measure we asked the centre if they wouldn't mind lending them to us for a couple of months and we promised to bring them back. Unfortunately, or fortunately, when Lee was checking them over he found a label inside them saying: FOR POOL USE ONLY. They were only demonstration suits; they were full of holes and would not save our lives at sea. At all.' Realising our mistake, Niki was dispatched at the last minute to purchase four fully ocean-worthy outfits. 'They cost a fortune, about £800, but there was nothing else we could do.' Luckily, Gareth's firm, Stanford Rhodes Wealth Management, were one of our sponsors and bought the outfits for us.

A few days later, Helen organised an all-important preparation for the race: an angel reading for us all at her house with her friend Dawn. Although none of us particularly believed in angels, the apparition of Great-Aunty Rose on the boat in the middle of the North Sea and our growing anxiety about the row made us all decide it was a truly excellent idea. After all, when you're in the middle of an ocean, thousands of miles from anywhere in an 8.5-metre boat, who would turn down a bit of divine intervention? Although, as Frances pointed out, knowing that you're rowing to a certain death on day 23 of the voyage would probably put us all off from turning up at La Gomera in the first place. But, thankfully, Dawn had no such news for us. Over shepherd's pie and Prosecco, we each chose a crystal from a collection she'd brought and then went into Helen's candle-lit dining room for our reading. We were going to make it, she said. Phew! It was going to be tough on all of us, there would be moments when we would be miserable, moments when we'd miss our families, moments when we'd be desperate to get off the boat, but we would all pull through. We'd all be fine and we'd all make it to Antigua! Suitably fortified by her positive predictions, we had another glass of Prosecco and toasted our sure-fire future success.

With two weeks to go before we left from La Gomera, we had one of our final, final Yorkshire Rows meetings at Janette's house and it was decided that not only should we assign roles on board ship, but we should also agree on some communal visions and values. If we were going to work together as a successful team during what was bound to be a testing experience, we felt we should come to some sort of agreement. This is what we wrote:

ROSE – Our on-board values

- We will always look after our other team members, thinking of their needs before our own.
- We will share our feelings and thoughts with the rest of the team.
- We will speak out in a positive manner if we feel we need to.
- We will be sympathetic to other team members when they are having a tough time.
- We will always do our share of duties and helping out.

- We will listen to each other and respect each other's views, even if they are different to our own.
- We will celebrate together our successes along our journey.
- We will enjoy our journey and have fun.
- We will do our best in whatever we do on board.
- We will always be on time for our shifts.

And remember: the strength of our team is each individual member. The strength of each member is our team. There is no 'I' in 'team'. We = power.

Our safety word to be used when needed is 'PEANUTS'.

'Peanuts'? We're not sure why we chose 'peanuts', or who it was who chose 'peanuts' (no one will take responsibility for it), or even why we actually needed a safety word in the first place. Clearly one of us had been reading *Fifty Shades of Grey*… Anyway, 'peanuts' it was. We all just hoped none of us would ever have to use it (and, in fact, we never did use it).

As part of our final preparation we made a hugely important trip to see a Maggie's Centre in Newcastle. Unfortunately, given that it had been Frances's wonderful idea to choose the charity as one of the causes we were hoping to benefit from our row, it was sad that she wasn't able to go that day and see what amazing work they do.

For the rest of us, it was humbling and uplifting to meet all the staff and see them in action. And as we were given a tour of the building where they offer practical and emotional 'kitchen-table' and 'peer' support, we were lucky enough to meet a lovely chap called Matt, who had lost his leg through cancer. He was a positive and inspiring young man who seemed to be so taken by our story that he, too, wanted to row the Atlantic. We loved meeting him and spending time in his company; he was a shining example of the power of positive thinking and his extraordinary energy was something we will never forget.

Just as we were leaving the centre Janette received a phone call that stopped her in her tracks. It was her mum calling with bad news. She asked Janette to sit down and take a breath. Her Aunty Kay had been diagnosed with advanced lung cancer.

'It was like I had been kicked in the stomach,' said Janette. 'I sat down on a wall and listened to my mum, but my brain was whirring, the world was spinning. She was so full of life and she'd only just got remarried. It was a huge shock.'

'She should come here,' said Helen, giving Janette a hug.

'Yes,' said Janette, fighting back the tears. 'Now we know why we're trying to get a place opened in Leeds. Everyone who needs it should have a Maggie's on their doorstep.'

With less than a week to go, we held a farewell party – or 'Bon Voyage Barn Dance', as Janette decided to call it (being married to a Frenchman) – at Barmbyfields Barns, just outside York. It was not so much a fundraiser as a thank-you to all our friends and families who had supported us over the last two years.

Just before arriving at the party, we went to Janette's local village, Burn, where they had given us the honour of switching on their Christmas lights. Not only was it touching to be asked, we were also following in the footsteps of Yorkshire legend, *Coronation Street*'s Hilda Ogden (the late Jean Alexander), Mr Yorkshire, Harry Gration and York Theatre Royal's panto dame and author Berwick Kayler. They also gave us a giant golden key and scroll to share. They bestowed upon us the honour of Sports Ambassadors for the village. They presented us with a golden oar and said they were planning on keeping the lights on until we returned safely home. Whenever that might be…

As we got into the car to leave Burn for the party, we sat in silence as it suddenly dawned on us all that we were really going.

The barn dance was a mad, emotional night full of toasts and hot dogs and heartfelt speeches. Corby, Aiden, Henry, Lucy and Helen's niece and nephew, Ella and James, all got together and gathered round a rather crackling microphone and made a speech about how proud they were of their mothers going to row an ocean, and it went something like this:

Aiden: 'As you all know we are here to support Yorkshire Rows before they depart on an amazing journey, that is the Atlantic Ocean.'

Lucy: 'We are all going to miss them so much but are so proud of what they have already done and are going to achieve in the near future.'

Corby: 'Seeing my mum do this is so inspiring and makes me feel like I can achieve anything.'

Henry: 'I never thought my mum would be rowing the Atlantic, but I will always support her 100 per cent and can't wait to see her when she comes back.'

'It was so very sweet to see them all up there, I did actually cry,' said Helen.

Everyone danced and mingled and drank wine and bought raffle tickets. Mark Brocklehurst (a friend of Frances's), who was a competitor in a previous Atlantic challenge, cornered each of us to tell us what an appallingly brilliant journey it was. It was the best and worst thing he had ever done.

'You'll love it,' he said. 'And you'll hate it. You'll never be indifferent. It will take you to the edge and beyond.'

Janette chatted away to Aunty Kay, who was there with her husband, Tony. Despite her diagnosis she was being very funny about Janette's journey, making her laugh as they wished her all the best. They said they were very proud of her for doing such an extraordinary thing. Little did Janette know, as she hugged her aunt goodbye, that this was to be the last time she would see Kay. Sadly, she died two weeks later.

At 2 a.m., when the four of us finally sat down together with our husbands, we toasted (not for the first time): 'To *Rose* and all who row in her!'

'Good luck and bon voyage. I have to admit that I never thought you'd get this far,' said Richard. 'I am so very proud of you. We all live such short lives, and most people do normal things like work–sleep–work–sleep–work–sleep, and what our wives are doing is something supreme and I am very proud of that.'

'You are all complete lunatics,' added Ben. 'But I believe you can do it. There is nothing you girls can't do together.'

'Four mothers, rowing 24 hours a day. It is a spectacular achievement, a huge feat. There isn't a weak link among you,' said Richard, raising his glass.

Gareth smiled warmly at Niki. 'I know you can do it. I will be with you every step of the way. I will be thinking of you every night.'

'I'm not worried about you, you'll be fine,' said Mark, looking at Frances, sitting on the other side of the table. 'I'm just worried that you're going off on an adventure without me. We've always done things together. And now you're going to say, "Remember this? Remember that? Remember the dolphins? The whale?" And I won't have seen any of it. You'll come back changed.' And he smiled at her.

'She'll definitely come back different,' said Richard.

'You're hoping?' said Gareth.

'She'll come back better,' said Richard.

'What? Blonde?' laughed Gareth.

'Just better,' repeated Richard. 'I think we will all be… better.'

SHIP'S LOG:

'Attaining your dreams and goals does not come easy; it takes perseverance, hard work, learning, sacrifice and the passion to succeed.'

(JANETTE/SKIPPER)

CHAPTER II

The Row

'I can't change the direction of the wind, but I can
adjust my sails to always reach my destination.'

JAMES DEAN

We were three days into the row and Niki had fractured her coccyx. Not that any of us knew it was that badly damaged at the time or we might have been a little more sympathetic. She was knocking back the 'diclofuckits' every four hours and was thankfully unable to see the vastly increasing bruise that was slowly but surely engulfing her backside. Her bum was actually black, and there were various hues of purple, blue and yellow spreading like a Turner sunset up her spine. But she refused to acknowledge it. In fact, she blanked it out, and all the while she continued to row her shifts, sitting on one buttock, with her leg hoicked up, a bit like a frog. It was obvious she was in agony. She was barely capable of talking. We all kept on saying she didn't need to row, she should have a rest, lie down, but all she did was ignore us, swallow a couple more 'fuckits' and get back on the oars.

'I never said how much my coccyx hurt because I didn't want them to think that I wasn't pulling my weight,' said Niki. 'I didn't want to be "the one who was injured on day three". And I don't make a fuss generally about anything anyway. It's not in my nature. But I think I coped with the pain by keeping quiet. When I'm at home I can gripe on to Gareth, because I talk to him about everything, but I will very rarely do that with anyone else, not even my parents. I would never say to them, "I'm having a rubbish time." I don't really share grievances. But I was in terrible pain, and I had nowhere to offload it, so I just tried to deal with it. I didn't want to put pressure on anyone else.'

Our adrenaline and our determination at the beginning was immense. We had, after all, spent over two years trying to get here – this was the dream, what we'd been aiming for during the dark days of trailing *Rose* around caravan parks, the hours spent writing letters, or clocking up miles on the water rowing machine while watching *Lewis* with the sound off. *No one* wanted to be the weak link. We were a team, and as a team we were going to get there.

Even Helen, who was crippled by chronic seasickness, doggedly continued to row.

For the first few days Helen didn't actually speak. Not a word. Just the rowing and the puking and the lying prone while trying to keep down the few little slurps of Ultra Fuel that Niki so kindly and diligently made for her. We had always known that the first few days would be terrible for Helen. We'd seen quite how debilitating her seasickness could be on the North Sea. We'd talked about it. We expected it. She'd stocked up on Stugeron and Queezibics, though she decided against the eye patches, which had not been so terribly successful in training. But we had no idea the sickness would carry on for so long.

'I felt so ill, throwing up every half-hour, but the Ultra Fuel kept me going. I was determined I was going to row after the North Sea debacle. And I did, I just kept going. I didn't change my clothes, I didn't brush my hair, I didn't clean my teeth; I just used to row and then collapse and then get up and row again. I didn't look after myself at all; I didn't have the energy. I just rowed and was sick. When it was my time to change shift I knocked on the hatch door, waited for Niki to come out and then

I'd throw up while I was waiting for her to come out, and then throw myself into the cabin and lie down. I knew I wouldn't feel sick then. And it gave me some comfort, knowing that I could get away from feeling sick if I lay down.'

Helen's seasickness lasted for four days. Before leaving she'd had a conversation with Ben, who had suffered such chronic seasickness on a voyage he'd done the year before that he'd ended up in hospital in Spain on a drip, until he was well enough to return to his boat and continue the voyage.

'I had Ben's voice in my head saying, "You'll be sick until you can't be sick any more. You'll be throwing up until you've got nothing inside you, and then slowly you'll start to feel hungry and then you'll start eating something and then you'll start eating something else and then you'll feel better again." And all I could think was, "Surely I've reached the nothing-inside-you bit by now? Surely I'm done now?" Not even Janette pointing to a couple of dolphins that were swimming alongside the boat could raise a smile. I couldn't even look at them. I could only look at the horizon. I remember thinking, "I don't give a shit about some sodding dolphins."'

But oddly, Ben's prediction came true. It was exactly what happened. I did start to feel a bit hungry and I fancied baked beans. Not the sausage and baked beans in the all-day breakfast packets that Niki had chosen, but just the baked beans. I started eating a few baked beans and I knew then that this was going to be fine. I could see the light at the end of the very long, dark tunnel. It was such a relief.'

It was a huge relief for the rest of us as well. As Helen stood at the bow of the boat, her hair all over the place, her T-shirt stiff with vomit, and quietly announced that she was 'a little bit peckish', Janette punched the air and Frances let out a cheer. Niki might have applauded had she heard above the sound of the crashing waves, and had she not been out of it on diclofenac.

Like an expert waitress, Janette ran through the list of culinary delights that were on offer on board ship, from chicken curry to beef stew, from macaroni cheese to shepherd's pie, but Helen was not tempted. She had her eye on the beans and only the beans would do. Cold or hot? Janette was only too keen to facilitate this miraculous recovery as she rushed around the boat, sparking up the Jetboil and sorting through the piles of packed food we had stored below deck. Eventually, cold beans it was.

'We had so much food,' said Janette. 'Charlie told us off for having our boat so low in the water when we left La Gomera. He said we must have a tonne of grub on there as our boat was only just above the water line. He reminded us that we had to row the thing across the Atlantic, but we were certainly over-stuffed. I was very keen to get rid of any of it.'

Meanwhile, at the other end of the boat, in what we glamorously called 'the office' – a 1.5-x-0.9-metre-square compartment with a ceiling height of 0.9 metres, which contained all the navigating and communication equipment we needed on our voyage, hence the rather self-aggrandising name – things were a little better, as neither Janette nor Frances had fractured their coccyx, nor were they suffering from chronic seasickness, although they could barely squeeze into 'the office' together at any one time.

'I was very relaxed,' said Frances. 'I'd had such a stressful couple of years at work before getting to the race; it felt totally stress-free on the boat. It felt like a huge weight had been lifted because all I had to do was eat, sleep, row and look after these three women. I didn't have to worry about my job or any decision-making. I didn't have to worry about Mark or the children. I was in a really peaceful place.'

Janette, as captain, was a little less relaxed and peaceful and was constantly checking the charts, making sure we were going in the right direction. We'd decided, like a few crews before us, to head south out of La Gomera before effectively taking a right, or rowing west, across the ocean to Antigua, hoping to pick up some helpful currents and handy trade winds to aid and abet our crossing. It would mean a longer journey in terms of miles, but hopefully we would find it a little easier to get there.

In the first few days, when Janette was not rowing she was hunched over all the equipment in the office. She was checking our speed, following our progress and talking on a daily basis to Ben who was watching the weather for us and seeing how well we were doing on Yellow Brick – a website that monitored all the Talisker boats, giving their longitude, latitude and speed, predicting exactly when they might arrive in Antigua.

'I was very conscious of being the only one talking to my husband,' said Janette. 'I would check in every day to see what the weather was doing and where we were in the race. I was very aware that I was the only one talking to their other half every day. I suppose the others could have done so, but they didn't. Ben was the linchpin in the land crew and he was the point of contact for everyone else. Everyone else's husbands, children and family. But I was also very conscious when talking to him. I was only ever upbeat and jolly; I didn't want to worry him. I was always positive. So the conversation was very brief; it was only about the weather and where we were in the race.'

Not that any of us really minded where we were in the race. By the end of the first day, our early advantage was waning fast, as indeed was our sight of land. Although not as quickly as we'd thought or hoped. Actually, it took two days for the land to disappear. We kept on spotting the volcano on Tenerife, which was a little annoying. It seemed that we'd rowed our behinds off for two whole days and nights and we apparently hadn't got very far. But when the land eventually did go, it went fast.

'It just disappeared,' said Janette. 'And it didn't really bother us. We'd been on our own before on the North Sea, so we were not overwhelmed by a sense of panic, like other people had been. What you worry about on the ocean, and what you don't worry about, is something you can't predict. What you think will be scary is not what you think. In fact, *nothing* is quite as you think.'

We thought we understood the water a little, having crossed the North Sea, but the wind and waves and the constant motion of the boat was something we were not expecting. We knew the Atlantic was big and we thought we might encounter a storm or two, but those first few days were relentless. The big waves didn't stop and the rocking of the boat was so much worse than we expected and our ability to achieve *anything* was extremely hampered.

'The first lesson we had to learn was patience,' said Niki. 'The idea that you could multitask, that you could make yourself a cup of tea while taking your wet-weather gear off and having a chat, plus keeping an eye on the speed of the boat, was a joke. You could only do one thing at a time and that would take three times longer than you'd thought. We all got used to walking like crabs, legs wide apart and holding onto the side, taking one baby step at a time.'

We spent most of the days attempting to row, but almost every time we put an oar in the ocean, it was ripped out of our hands or it would flip back with the brute force of the water and hit us in an extremely painful place. And on the worst night shifts, we did not even attempt to row, we'd sit out on watch, dressed head to foot in our wet-weather gear, teeth chattering, insides shivering, being consistently and persistently drenched by the freezing-cold sea.

'Everything was wet,' said Frances. 'We'd take off our damp clothes, get into our sleeping bags, naked, and then put our cold, damp clothes back on again two hours later. We would knock on the cabin door 10 minutes before the other person was due out on the blades, and there would be a terrible 10 minutes of transition, where I would lie there and think, "I don't want to get up, I don't want to row, I want to lie here and sleep."'

Not that we slept that much. By the time we'd managed to take our

wet-weather gear off, eat some sort of food and crawl into the claustrophobic cabin, it was almost time to wake up again. And we'd have some
very odd dreams.

'I used to have a regular dream about being in a car,' said Janette, 'going
along an extremely bumpy track, and every time I woke I was so deeply
disappointed to find myself on a cold, wet boat.'

But woe betide anyone who needed the toilet. We'd all had a pee on the
North Sea but had held on until we reached the hotel for anything else. So
the first time any of us had a poo on the bucket in front of the others was
on the Atlantic. The first couple of times were excruciatingly embarrassing,
mainly because the bucket was so close to the person rowing. The person
going to the loo was almost sitting on the lap of the person rowing. Add
in the huge waves and it was a recipe for disaster. Tipping, falling, spilling,
sloshing were all regular occurrences. Eventually, we would stop rowing
when anyone announced they wanted the lav. Frances would sit on the
bucket with her arms around the person next to her, trying to keep herself
steady. Helen, once she could talk, gave us a running commentary on
her business. Niki kept a firm eye on the horizon. And Janette? Well, the
less said about that the better. In short, it could not have been any more
intimate. And it was worse at night.

'I'd be in the office,' said Frances, 'in all my wet-weather gear,
desperate for a wee and knowing that I had to get down the length of
the boat, get covered in water by a huge wave, take off my salopettes,
sit down and hold on, with my bare arse out in the cold, then wee,
use one of my biodegradable wet wipes, hoping it didn't blow away
in the wind or I didn't get doused by another wave, before pulling my
salopettes back up again and making my way back to the other end of
the boat. It was no wonder I went to the loo as little as possible at night.'

And poor Niki had to do all that with her damaged coccyx. No
wonder she took so many painkillers.

But it wasn't long before we were all fighting her for them. It was just days before the sores and the blisters kicked in. We'd been warned: we had our chafe-free pants and pots and pots of nappy-rash cream. However, the combination of sitting down for two hours at a time and rowing and rubbing in clothes damp with seawater is a terrible combination for the skin.

Niki was the first to develop sores. She was sitting so oddly on her seat, she developed a pressure sore on her behind.

'I was only leaning on one cheek, so it didn't take long before the rubbing became unbearable and the whole thing opened up into a large wound that had to be dressed and padded every day.'

Which sounds fine when written down. But in reality, it was an undignified nightmare, which involved Niki (with a fractured coccyx) peeling off her pants, bending over, as one or other of us would attend to the wound while being rocked by the waves on what was effectively a giant seesaw. The rest of us were not long in joining her, and soon we developed a routine where we'd come off shift and douse our buttocks in surgical spirit, and then wait for it to dry before slathering on the Sudocrem. The only problem was that if the surgical spirit went anywhere else other than your backside, you'd soon hear about it on the boat.

'My fanny! My fanny!' would be screamed even louder than the sounds of the waves.

'I used to lie on my side, put surgical spirit on my bottom and then add on the Sudocrem. And then, with my arse out, I would chew my way through a Peperami and think, "This might look a little weird. You'd have to find a very specific website for this sort of picture!"' said Helen.

But it wasn't just our backsides (and frankly our fannies) that were beginning to really suffer; so were our hands and feet. We had blisters upon blisters on our hands, and our feet were always so soggy in the water and so cold it was difficult to stop the skin from splitting and cracking. And we'd been at sea for less than a week.

SHIP'S LOG:

'One thing that we were really good at on the boat was not beating ourselves up when things went wrong or we couldn't get something quite right or we couldn't get a piece of equipment fixed. We just thought maybe there is another way we haven't tried yet, and we kept trying. We were getting there a bit at a time and we were a work in progress. It was always okay to be a work in progress.'

(JANETTE/SKIPPER)

CHAPTER 12

Christmas

'When they first saw the star, they rejoiced exceedingly
with great joy.'

MATTHEW 2:10

24 December 2015

It was Christmas Eve, and we'd been told to expect a phone call from
BBC Breakfast. They had apparently planned for all our husbands and children to be on a sofa round at Niki's house to wish us 'Happy Christmas'
as a surprise. So when they did call on the morning of 24 December to
shout 'Surprise!' it was the loveliest thing in the world.

'Hi!' came all the children's voices down the satellite phone as we all
tried to cram into the office. There was only room for two at the very
most, so it was the tightest of squeezes.

'Hi!' their voices came again. 'Happy Christmas, Mum!'

We missed them all desperately. Niki's eyes immediately filled with
tears. How we wished we could have seen them all, sitting there, undoubt-
edly all dressed up, smiling on the sofa. It was an odd feeling to be so far
away from our families, all soggy and blistered, when we should have been
celebrating with them, stuffed fatter than Christmas geese with mince pies.

Poor Helen could not cope. She felt so sick in the cabin, her head was still swimming and her mouth was as dry as sandpaper as she tried to stop herself from hurling all over us.

'I've got to go,' she said, covering her mouth as she rushed out of the cabin, gasping onto deck.

The rest of us continued shouting out questions.

'How are you?' said Janette.

'What are you doing?' asked Frances.

'What are you eating tomorrow?' Niki wanted to know.

The replies were garbled and mixed, with everyone talking over each other, with plenty of time delays. Safe to say, there was much shouting of 'I love you,' 'I miss you, Mum!' and 'Happy Christmas!'

'I felt so awful,' said Helen. 'I was the only one who didn't speak to their children. Even now I find it very upsetting to think about them, sitting there, waiting to hear from me, and I just couldn't talk to them. I could barely speak. I was still ill, so all I wanted to do was be sick.'

We were all quite downcast after the phone call. What should have lifted our spirits had only really served to underline quite how lonely and isolated we were, sitting in the middle of this unforgiving ocean. All we knew was that Ocean Reunion were powering away from the rest of the fleet, while we were rowing flat out just to keep still.

Christmas Day was only day five of the journey and there wasn't necessarily an awful lot to celebrate. The sea was still being unkind, it was choppy and confused, and it was almost impossible for us to make headway. But Helen was eating some solids again and we were currently seventh in the race, apparently. What's not to celebrate? So celebrate we did.

On our packing list, along with the '1 spoon, 2 water bottles, 1 bikini, 1 head-torch, chafe-free pants x 2, personal hair accessories, i.e. hairbands…' we had been told by Janette to bring a Secret Santa gift, costing no more than £5 and weighing less than a feather, or thereabouts.

So as dawn broke on Christmas morning, what followed was an

exercise in delayed gratification. We carried on with our shifts, wishing
each other 'Happy Christmas' every two hours as we met on deck for
our changeovers.

'It's like New Year already!' said Frances, having wished Janette 'Happy
Christmas' about six times since 6 a.m. that morning. 'And still not a
present in sight!'

We'd decided that we'd wait until the afternoon before having our
'party' where we'd exchange our Secret Santa gifts. At 4 p.m. precisely,
we put down our oars and pulled on Santa hats, antlers or festive glasses
and handed around our secret Santa presents – a pair of socks from
Helen, National Geographic sea-life playing cards from Frances, a rowing
mug from Janette and a keep-yourself-cool towelette from Niki. Janette
got the playing cards and was so half-hearted in her thanks that we all
stopped and gave her a lesson in being grateful. Frances got the mug,
Helen received the towelette and Niki was given the socks. It transpired
that we'd given each other the present we really wanted ourselves.
Helen was desperate for the socks, Niki very much had her eye on the
towelette – so they swapped straight away. Janette blithely declared she
had no interest in anything, so Frances was the overall winner, bagging
the mug and the cards.

Then, just as we had run out of nice things to say about socks, cards
and towelettes and were contemplating getting back on the oars, Janette
told us all to sit down.

'Ooh,' she said, riffling through her deck bag. 'I think the postman
might have been.'

'The postman?' asked Niki. 'Out here?'

'Oh yes,' continued Janette. 'He has the same magical powers as Father
Christmas. There you are,' she said as she handed out envelopes to the
rest of us. 'Happy Christmas!'

'Before we set off I asked myself: when they're really low what am I going to do on the boat?' said Janette. 'When something bad happens, how am I going to lift them up? So I sent an email to all the husbands':

From: Janette Benaddi **Sent:** 11 September 2015 12:23
Subject: Something to start thinking about

Hi Mark and Gareth and Richard,
There's something I would like your help with, please, and you may have even already thought about it. You are going to help us get across the ocean, in those dark hours – and there may be some. Hopefully not, but it's always good to have contingency plans in place. I would like to take some surprise letters/notes with us on the boat from all of you and those who are close to the girls. When the going gets tough they can read a letter. We can do this any way you like – I can take all the letters and give them out when they really need them or, if you prefer, you can give them the letters. You know what will work best for your loved ones, so guide me on this. I think it might have more of an impact if there are some letters that are a complete surprise, if not all of them. You can always give them additional letters and leave some for surprises. I'm sure there are lots of things you want to send with them!

I have thought of a few situations when a bit of reassurance and a nice statement, phrase, letter from a loved one will really help. You could put their name on the envelope and also when they need to read it, for example:

Name – For when the shit hits the fan
Name – For when you hit rock bottom
Name – For when you are shit scared
Name – For when you're missing us
Name – For when you want to get off the boat

Name – For when you want to give up

You may think of some others, too, and you may ask other family members to do some too. What goes in the letters is down to you. This is you supporting your loved one and getting them across to Antigua; you will know which phrase or words will do it. You might need time to think about it or you might instantly know what should be said. Either way it's good to make a start soon if you can. If you prefer to do this a different way, that's great too. I just want to be sure we have everything we can have on that boat to get us to Antigua.

Atlantic Campaigns do a short family guide. I will be nudging the girls to share it with you so look out for it – it's quite helpful.

You lot are just as important as the crew in getting us there. If you want to talk to me at any time before we go to really fill me in on what you think will help, I can meet up with any of you before we go at any time. Also Atlantic Campaigns offer lots of support for families and friends. My job as skipper is to make sure we get across safely while enjoying the journey. I know that it's all our jobs, too, and we are the best team I have ever had the opportunity to be part of, so we will get there. We may even win!!! Especially with your help and support.

Thanks so much. Let me know your thoughts and what you think will work best for you and yours, also if there is something (small and light!) you want me to take for Christmas Day I will sneak it on board, so get it to me before 24 October if possible so it can go with the boat.

Janette Benaddi

What Janette found fascinating was the different ways in which the three men responded to her request. 'Helen's husband, Richard, wrote just one letter, and got his son to write a letter, and his daughter and Helen's mum to write a letter. They just had "Helen" on the outside. Mark, Frances's husband, had followed the instructions to a tee. He gave me a bunch of envelopes, marked on the outside: for when the shit hits the fan; for when you're missing your husband; for when you're missing the children. He did exactly what I'd asked. Gareth just did loads of letters. Niki had the most letters. He did so many. Got the kids to do letters. Got them to do pictures. It was really organised.

Janette's family, of course, were not party to the Postman Plan – but Janette did get a Christmas card from her family and a couple from some other close friends, and she did get a card from a friend of Niki and Frances who had written to all of us on the boat, which she also opened on Christmas Day. 'Even though she didn't know me, she'd done a letter for me,' said Janette. 'It was hilarious. She said, "I'm sure I met you at the tennis club in Poppleton." I'm sat on the boat going, "I've never met her! Never played tennis at Poppleton in my life!" But it did cheer me up!'

Helen was quite sanguine about her small postbag. 'I knew I had their support. I didn't need to read it. I was perfectly fine with only getting one letter from Lucy, Henry, Richard and my mum. That was fine. Richard and I don't have that kind of relationship. But Niki and Frances got amazing letters. And we voted Mark the most romantic husband on the boat.'

'There is one letter,' said Frances, 'that's absolutely lovely, where he says how proud he is and how it's as if the Frances he met has come back from all the stresses of having children, of careers, and how I was back to the kind of person I was when I was in my late twenties':

For Frances

Hello, sweetheart. By now you are thousands of miles away from me in the middle of a wild, wet desert. Just thinking about that makes me feel sick with worry for you and the other girls, but I know that doesn't help anyone, so I'm going to put those thoughts aside.

You know I'm not prone to romantic cards, love letters or the like. However, there is a first time for everything, and I can't think of a better situation to prompt me to write than this! When we first started dating, I thought you were a slightly crazy adventure chick, what with the diving, the paragliding, the mountaineering, the long-distance running, the holidays to exotic locations like Nepal. I remember thinking, 'Boy, life with her is going to be out of the ordinary: just take a deep breath and hang on for the ride!'

Well, in many ways that has been the case, what with us getting married and having the boys within just a few years of getting together, and the fun we've had along the way. Everyday life does, however, have a habit of getting in the way of personal aspirations, challenges and dreams, and somewhere down the line you had to prioritise your career and being a loving mother to Jay and Jack… However, there is a time and season for everything, and I am equally proud of you for taking the decision to enter the Talisker race. The commitment you have shown on the back of that decision has been incredible: how anyone can do the job you do, then come home and train while being a mother to the boys and a wife to me is beyond me, although I always knew that if anyone could pull it off, you could. You have reconnected with the Frances I first met: the crazy have-a-go chick who sets her mind on something and goes for it, overcoming obstacles along the way and always adopting the 'can-do' mindset.

I know you have it in you to do this. However hard the race is, however bleak conditions may be, and whatever challenges it throws at you, know this: you are loved beyond words. I love you,

I miss you, I am desperately proud of you, and I cannot wait to see you over that finish line. Stay safe.

All my love,

Mark

And for Niki it was all a little too much. Not only had Gareth written an emotional letter about how much he loved her and missed her, but he'd included photographs of the children and Christmas cards from her parents. And there was something else, too: a small parcel. Inside, in a plastic waterproof bag, she found the star she'd been frantically looking for the last night before she left. The star that Corby had made. The star that was always on the top of the family Christmas tree at home.

'That's where it was,' smiled Niki as she started to cry, turning the battered tin-foil-covered piece of cardboard over and over again in her hand. 'No wonder I couldn't find it.' She sobbed and sobbed and sobbed.

We all sat on the boat, in our Santa hats, a small rope of tinsel pinned around the door to each cabin, with most of us reading and rereading our letters (and Janette trying to recall her tennis-playing days), feeling extremely sorry for ourselves. It was not quite the morale-boosting exercise that Janette had planned.

Either we could all get back onto the oars and ignore the fact that it was Christmas or...

'Let's play some music,' suggested Janette. 'And crack open the mango gin!'

So we did. We had taken the mango gin (homemade by Rachel and Ruth – thank you) for emergencies, and this clearly was one. We rationed it to a very small glass, a thimbleful, each. It was delicious. Sweet and alcoholic, it slipped down a treat. Combined with *The Best Christmas Album in the World… Ever*, it was enough to put even Scrooge into the festive spirit! Slade. Wham! Wizard. Cliff. Bowie. Bing. And then ABBA

– always ABBA. (How many times did we listen to *Mamma Mia!* on the ocean? So many times even the fish probably knew the words!) We sang like no one could hear us and danced like no one could see us – because they couldn't. For the next hour and a half we laughed and crooned and warbled our hearts out. We also shared out a segment each of a Terry's Chocolate Orange that Niki's mum had sent us all. Never had anything tasted so delicious! It was divided up with great ceremony. One piece each. No more! Just one! To be sucked slowly on the tongue. The rest was to be saved for emergencies. It was, in the end, a Christmas that none of us will ever forget.

Boxing Day, however, was a different story. The wind picked up, as did the waves. The boat was listing and lurching all over the place. The antlers and festive specs were firmly stored in the hold and we were suddenly battling all the elements that the ocean could throw at us. It was pouring with rain and the tide was taking *Rose* in the wrong direction. Helen had been on the oars for two hours, rowing through heavy water, as thick as treacle, and was finally making her way to the bucket. She'd been desperate to go to the loo for the last hour and a half but she'd conscientiously held off until the end of her shift. But then, suddenly, as wave after wave pounded the boat, slamming into the side, *Rose* spun in the wrong direction and it looked as if she was about to roll or, at worst, capsize. Niki and Frances were battling at the oars, pulling hard to the right, and Janette was struggling at the helm.

'Helen!' she shouted. 'You have to get back to your seat! We have to turn this boat around!'

'I have just done two hours!' Helen barked back, pulling down her salopettes. 'I am not getting back on again.'

'Get back on there!'

'I need to wee.'

'I don't care!'

'I need a wee.'

'You're not fucking weeing, you're fucking rowing. Get back on your fucking seat!' Janette went puce with fury.

'I am WEEING!' she yelled back. 'And if you stop me I will piss all over this boat!'

'You need to get back on your seat now!' Janette shouted back. 'And you need to fucking row!'

Eventually Helen did finish her wee and staggered back to the oars and together all of us managed to turn *Rose* around and avoid what was potentially a very great disaster. But relations between Helen and Janette were frosty to say the least. Neither of them spoke to each other for the rest of the day, which was difficult in such a small space, especially as Janette had scheduled herself to row with Helen for that week. But when it comes to pig-headedness, they are perhaps on a par. They are both naturally combative and neither is prone to apologies. So Helen doggedly wore her earphones, listening avidly to Michael McIntyre's autobiography, *Life and Laughing*, on her iPod, while Janette stared fixedly at the horizon.

Finally, it was Janette who apologised. 'I shouldn't have shouted at you. I shouldn't have sworn at you. I could have done that in a much better way. I don't think you realised quite what danger we were in and I should have communicated that better. So I've been thinking about it, and when we're in a situation that is difficult again, I am going to shout: "All hands on deck!" And then everyone drops everything, whatever they are doing, whatever time of day.' Later, something occurred to Janette: 'I think that was the moment the old lady clairvoyant saw in the caravan park when she said I'll need to exert my authority right from the start so that I get everyone's cooperation in times of real need.'

'We learnt from that,' said Helen. 'I learnt I wouldn't rebel again. Probably I should have explained that once I start rowing I never get off my seat for anything, and that I had just done two hours and I was desperate to pee and the rowing had been really tough. I am quite tough and if you cross me, I fight back. When I was on the oars I did what I needed to do: no eating, no drinking, just rowing, getting the job done. Everyone thinks I am a princess, but I'm not. And I don't cry. Not that there is anything wrong with crying. But if you watch any of the YouTube videos of Ben Fogle and James Cracknell rowing the Atlantic, all they did was cry. They cried all the way across. Anyway, I thought, "I am not crying. At all." So I didn't.'

Our other problem, which was distinctly less sortable, was our increasing lack of power. It appeared that our little Christmas party – our hour and a half of singing and attempted dancing on a dramatically rocking dance floor, combined with the use of the autohelm while we were otherwise engaged – had seriously dented our batteries.

We'd spent hours with Charlie, when we first collected Rose, and then in La Gomera with Ben, learning how to maintain the batteries and keep them charged. They'd told us which systems were likely to use the most power. They warned us that if the battery charge dropped below a certain level, this would become an issue.

And it was a big problem. Once the batteries go below 12 volts, an alarm sounds very loudly and the monitor flashes 'Ship Battery Low' – the GPS, the autohelm and the watermaker need the batteries to be about 11 volts to work, otherwise they won't function and the alarm just keeps on sounding. And once that happens it is very difficult to get anything to work. Anything. So the alarm sounded and our autohelm stopped working, which meant that one of us had to steer the boat and, worse, our water-pump stopped working too.

This was the sort of disaster that had ruined other crews in the past. All the water we needed now had to be pumped by hand. And when you factor in that you have to hand-pump for 45 minutes for one litre of water, you realise what a nightmare it is.

Each of us needed 4 litres a day. So the pump had to be in action for 45 minutes, 16 times a day. Which meant that during the day we would row for two hours and then pump for 45 minutes and then flop down in the cabin for an hour before coming back on the oars.

'We just couldn't get enough power to make the pump work,' said Janette. 'The GPS was the same, as was the autohelm. We had no way of charging our telephones or our iPods when they ran out. I kept the phone switched off so we could carry on speaking to Ben and the race organisers, otherwise we'd have no idea where we were or where we were supposed to be going.'

As Boxing Day wore on, things became worse. Janette and Helen were not really speaking and the rest of us were exhausted and furious with ourselves that such a small thing like having some fun and a singsong could have so impacted our journey.

'The battery monitors were going down,' said Frances, 'so I sent Charlie a text to say that the battery monitors were showing really low. Should we ignore that because we'd tested the batteries and they seemed fine? Unfortunately for us, it turned out the battery monitors were not misreading. We had no power at all. I wanted to blame Charlie, but it was our fault.'

'I knew we could still make it across the ocean without power, but it was a desperate situation to be in. What was already difficult, just became doubly more so,' said Helen. 'I don't think I've ever felt so low in my life. I was miserable. This was really crap. Really crap indeed.'

So we spent the day eating, sleeping, pumping and rowing and going nowhere. It seemed like the ocean was punishing us for daring to enjoy ourselves. It was like it was trying to teach us a lesson. We'd not respected it. We'd been fooling around, dancing to ABBA and now we were going to pay.

It was early evening and the boat was being pushed back towards La Gomera, and no amount of us rowing was sending *Rose* in the right direction. So Janette rang Lee Fudge, who was one of the duty officers – on call 24/7 in case of emergencies – and he suggested we might put down our para-anchor, the giant parachute anchor that stops the boat from moving in any direction.

'Everyone else has,' he said. 'You're the last ones to still be going. The current and the wind are too strong. You may as well get the anchor out, otherwise you're just killing yourselves going nowhere.'

'So we put it down for the first time that night,' said Frances. 'It was the first time that the speed of the ocean had stopped and we were not moving.'

It was an odd feeling, being told we were allowed to stop. We dispatched the anchor and then just sat there, staring at each other. Not only was it very hard to get the thing out into the sea, with its complex combination of ropes and strings, but also it was an awful sensation, not going anywhere. It made us anxious and agitated, like we were wasting time. Hours. On a break. Being on para-anchor was a bit like being in a car park, where *Rose* was the only car and we were just sitting there in the middle of the ocean, bobbing up and down on the water. Except, of course, you don't bob. You feel every single roll of the wave as it takes you up in the air and smashes you straight back down again. It's like a very poorly balanced rollercoaster, and about as much fun.

'We were better in the office cabin,' said Frances. 'Because that end was closer to the para-anchor, but the bedroom cabin did bounce quite a lot.'

So with nothing to do except ride out the current and the poor wind and rolling swells, we passed out. All of us. We were supposed to wake up at 4 a.m. in time to check on the boat and our position, but we all overslept. It wasn't until Niki alerted us that the rest of us came crawling out of our hot, stuffy cabins at 4.30 a.m. We clearly all needed it, but Janette was not impressed and insisted that if we were ever on para-anchor again overnight then it was not an excuse to catch up on some kip; we should still keep watch as 'anything could happen!'

'But nothing did,' said Frances.

'But it could have,' replied Janette.

The rest of us bit our tongues. Of course she was right. We had just enough power to keep our navigation lights on and the See Me beacon flashing, but with no one on the bridge for 10 or 15 minutes, a huge tanker on autopilot, ploughing through the ocean on its way to Argentina or Brazil, could carve us up at any time.

'Or,' she added, 'we should be checking to see if the conditions have changed and if we need to bring the anchor in and get rowing.'

Now she was guilt-tripping us. Who on earth would pull up a para-anchor at 3 a.m. to get back on the blades? Janette, that's who. We kept even more schtum about how delighted we were to have had more than 90 minutes' sleep.

We had planned to come off the para-anchor at that point and get back to rowing, but then we realised that our power failure was now total and it would be impossible to steer the ship in the pitch dark, as without the GPS we wouldn't have any idea of where we were going. We could, in our rested enthusiasm, be powering back to the Canaries for all we knew. So we sat, eating a cold full English breakfast, riding the waves, waiting for the sun to come up.

We needed sun. We were desperate for the sun to recharge our solar panels, and we were desperate to conserve the tiny amount of power that we had. We were only allowed our cabin lights on when we were actually in the cabin and Janette shouted at us whenever anyone forgot.

In the meantime, we were hand-steering during the day, conserving enough solar power to use the autohelm at night. We used the hand-pump as much as possible, turning the watermaker on only briefly for a maximum of 40 minutes or so each day. But the batteries were almost as stubborn as Janette, and it took them over a week to become even 20 per cent charged while we were being so careful.

'After one phone call with Charlie he suggested we switch off our navigation lights to save energy. The thought of being in the pitch black horrified me for the first few nights,' said Frances. 'But then we all just got used to it and, actually, we didn't need the lights any more. We had the moon and the stars. We were fine.'

And despite our lack of power and the constant need to pump for water, we settled into some sort of routine. 'There were some lovely evenings and nights where we would just row and listen to our music,' added Frances. 'Helen had Alan Carr and Michael McIntyre on her iPod, so she would be giggling away. I think at that point all the iPods were still working, so we all had our own music. We didn't talk as much at night. We would just listen to music, and I think Niki would just be alone with her thoughts.'

SHIP'S LOG:

'There were some stressful situations on the boat that did sometimes bring out the worst in all of us. Each one of us had a moment, for sure – you can't possibly avoid having a moment on a 3,000-mile row across the Atlantic, no matter how great a person you are. We are all human. What was important was how we managed the situations. Our values kept us on track. It's so important to have values in life that you believe in and that you can remind yourself of in challenging times. Our principal and most important value was to try our best, and to put everyone else on the boat before yourself. Walk in the other person's shoes and you soon learn to be more gracious.

(JANETTE/SKIPPER)

CHAPTER 13

Hurricane

'And once the storm is over, you won't remember how you made it through, how you managed to survive. You won't even be sure whether the storm is really over. But one thing is certain. When you come out of the storm, you won't be the same person who walked in. That's what the storm is all about.'

HARUKI MURAKAMI

New Year's Eve came and went, with the only highlight being that Helen got to broadcast to Mike Bushell on *BBC Breakfast*, on whom she has a terrible crush. The giggling and hair flicking was only trumped by her delight at scoffing down a Peperami to celebrate, which even in this early stage of the race was enough to make everyone's mouth water.

'I was the only who had Peperamis. We all had snack packs with a big packet of biltong, which cost about £250. But I was the only one with Peperami, and I only had about five snack packs with it in. Every time I picked out a snack pack with a Peperami in it I was so excited. Then Niki would say, "Can I have one of your Peperamis?" And I'd go, "Yes, all right then." But I didn't really want to give it to her because I just loved it. Anyway, the day I spoke to Mike Bushell was a brilliant day because it was my turn to talk to *BBC Breakfast,* and it was Mike Bushell, who I really like, and I had a Peperami in my snack pack. That was the best day ever.'

It is extraordinary how very quickly food becomes an issue. Quite apart from the monotony of the wet and dry food that we had packed on board, our focus was very much influenced by the snack packs, and none of us had realised how much of a morale booster they would be.

'About five weeks before the row, we were all at Janette's,' said Helen, 'and we'd had a massive delivery from Holland & Barrett – they gave us loads of food for free, and at Janette's house we had boxes of all the snack-pack stuff. We were basically just putting everything in bags. Nuts, banana chips, Bounce Balls, flapjacks, small bags of sweet. My neighbour helped us do it because it took forever. As did Niki's dad. And we just grabbed stuff and shoved them into the 60 or so bags we had each.'

The individual snack packs were stashed away in the hatches with our names on, and every day someone would hand out one of your snack packs and that was it for the day. Janette would just throw hers over the side – she didn't like anything in them except the Mars bar. All the nuts and dried fruit would go, plus the bag of 'powder' (it was electrolyte powder). We would try to pour it away and the wind would blow it back all over us.

'If I did it again I would do my own snack packs,' said Helen. 'I would just fill it with stuff that I wanted to eat and that would make me happy. You have no idea how important it all becomes. I had one Mars bar a day and I saved that for the night shift. At night I would pause to eat it and that was my thing that I really looked forward to. At breakfast I would have the flapjack, but it was massive. For some reason I didn't like the chocolate flapjack, I liked the plain, and every time I got a snack pack mine would have chocolate bits in it when I just wanted plain things!

'Niki must have been very disappointed,' continued Helen. 'She did so much research and so much work on them. We just didn't like a lot of it. But that was our fault; we should've taken more interest. And they were so heavy as well. When we looked at other people's snack packs they took hardly anything compared to us, which was why Janette wanted to chuck everything over the side and get rid of a load of stuff. Niki had huge snack packs because she loves food. She had loads of sweets in hers. But sadly not a single Peperami.'

'You can only ask so many times what people want to eat. I tried and tried, but no one listened. I know now that all we really should have packed was chocolate, not healthy sports bars, but my heart was in the right place!' said Niki.

But frankly, we did have other things to worry about.

It was Ben who told us that a storm was on its way. A storm that would develop into a hurricane. Hurricane Alex. The first hurricane to form in the Atlantic since 1955, the first hurricane to form in January since 1938 and the first hurricane that any of us had ever been in, let alone experienced in the middle of the Atlantic in nothing but a small boat made of fibreglass that was low on power.

'You're just going to have to row,' Ben suggested – helpfully – on the telephone to Janette. The faster we rowed south, the less we would get caught up in the storm – sorry – hurricane.

Poor Ben. He kept telling us, but we didn't listen at first (for three whole days). We must have driven him mad. He could see the picture of the big swirly storm gathering on all his equipment back home. But we could not. So we were deaf to his entreaties. And then, finally, it was confirmed that a big one was heading right for us. Oddly, just as we turned to move south, we saw Greg. Far in the distance. On his own. Rowing.

Janette was straight on the radio. 'There's a storm! Go south! We all need to go south.' He couldn't believe it! We were so close and so helpful! He thanked us and off he went.

And so we rowed as fast as we could, as far south as we could, before it was scheduled to hit. We also had to pump as much water as we could, because we knew when the storm hit us we would be confined to our quarters for hours, if not days, and we'd need enough water in each of the cabins to keep us alive as the sea raged around us. We were growing increasingly anxious. Not one of us had ever experienced a hurricane before, let alone at sea. However, on the telephone we didn't want to worry our families, so it was agreed that the word 'hurricane' would not be mentioned. We could talk of 'high winds', things being 'a bit choppy' or just 'a bit of rubbish weather' being on its way. In fact, through our continuous downplaying of Alex we even managed to convince ourselves that it was just a small local event with nothing very much to see here.

And then it hit.

If you look up 'hurricane' on the Beaufort scale, the statistics are more than a little worrying, skimming past gales, strong gales, and 'major damage':

Hurricane Force 12

Observable Land Effects – very dangerous tropical whirling winds

Speed MPH – 76+

Effect at Sea – Phenomenal

Phenomenal? It's lucky none of us had read this as the skies began to darken on the morning of 12 January. As we put the para-anchor out again, soaking ourselves in the process, we could see the lightning and the driving rain coming towards us. All around us, the ocean was beginning to stir, and yet there was a moment when we, and indeed it, held our breaths, waiting for Alex to strike. Which he did, with a brute force 12.

We had battened down the hatches – Frances and Janette in the office, Niki and Helen in 'First Class' – and hoped that Charlie really knew how to make a self-righting boat. If she went over, would she really come bouncing right back up again? The most *Rose* had been tested was when we rocked her side to side on a bit of river in Burnham-on-Crouch.

The first waves were terrifying. *Rose* was lifted out of the water and then dropped from a great height over and over again, and we were thrown out of our small beds and spun around like socks in a washing machine. Sometimes the rise and fall was so great we'd hit our heads on the roof of the cabin before being dropped back down again onto our beds or the floor, onto some piece of equipment. Everything that was not pinned down, tied up or stored away flew about the cabin like an exorcist's Christmas party. We tried to keep in contact with Lee on the satellite phone and the rest of the support team – it was of little comfort to know that the whole race had been engulfed by the hurricane. We had managed to row a little further south than most of them, so while some of the other teams were right in the eye of the storm, we were only catching the outskirts – but they were violent enough.

The wind howled, lightning shot across the sky and the thunder sounded like some HGV lorry about to plough into the side of the boat. And all we could do was lie there, gripping the sides of our bunks, unable to get flat or straight.

And it went on and on. At least with some hideous fairground ride you can get off, have a rest, exhale, take a bit of air before going back to the enclosed coffin to be shaken and bashed and thrown about again. We could not.

We spent 70 hours locked in our cabins – two nights and three days. Of pure hell.

'You're locked in. No way out. Nowhere to go. You just have to sit it out and wait,' said Janette. 'You go through all sorts of emotions in the first couple of hours. I don't know how we got through it, I really don't. Frances and I started to get terrible headaches due to dehydration and lack of oxygen. We were desperate to get some air into the office, so we opened up the rudder compartment just to try to let something in. A little puff. There's no actual air in the compartment because it's sealed and it goes into the sea, but there is a small amount that comes in as the rudder bounces in and out of the water. And that's all we needed. But the waves were ramming the door of the cabin so hard, and water started coming in. Eventually the whole place was soaked through.'

Frances and Janette tried to while away the time playing cards, but the cards kept flying everywhere. They tried playing I Spy, but ran out of spies. They tried to watch a film on an iPhone but it soon ran out of battery. They tried to nap but every time they dozed off another wave would crash into the side of the boat and throw them about the cabin. The conditions were so cramped and confined that they both started taking analgesics to deal with the muscle cramps and back pain.

And then it began to get hot. Extremely hot. After about 10 hours of confinement they took off all their clothes.

'I got used to Frances's bottom and tits in my face,' said Janette. 'I remember moving one of her boobs, thinking it was a pillow, at one point. I was trying to shove it out of the way. But they are just bodies at the end of the day.'

Time began to blur. Day became night and night became day. And all the time we were locked up in the coffin cabs. Frances and Janette opened their snack packs and started to ration out their chocolate. At one point they found the Chocolate Orange! Niki's mum's Christmas Orange! A shiny orb of deliciousness! Could they? Should they? We had, after all, only had one 'slice' each on Christmas Day. It took them all of three and a half minutes to polish it off!

But the real problem was water. With supplies running very low and unable to make any, as it was impossible for anyone to get on deck and use the hand-pump, Janette made a decision to break into the ballast. Just as we had used bottles of water on the estuary at Burnham-on-Crouch to keep *Rose* heavy in the water, so we had bottles of fresh water below decks. The race rules specify that if you break into the water you have to immediately refill the bottle with seawater so that your boat is not lighter,

Niki enjoying mango gin on her birthday.

Niki getting stuck in cleaning *Rose's* solar panels, which we did every day of the crossing, unless the weather was really bad.

Mid-row – loving life.

Ollie Verschoyle, the Director of Photography on the *Four Mums in a Boat* documentary for National Geographic, filming us rowing into Antigua after more than 2 months at sea.

Just as we arrived into the harbour and set off our flares.

e made it! No words can describe how we felt at this moment.

Arriving into Antigua: the final push before we rowed into Nelson's Dockyard, English Harbour in Antigua on February 25th 2016.

Immediately after the race, being interviewed by the BBC.

Frances – and her excellent tan – with husband Mark and sons Jay and Jack in Antigua.

In Antigua with Jayne McCubbin and Brij Patel from the BBC. They were both so supportive from the start.

A backstage meeting with the cast from *Mamma Mia* at the Novello Theatre in London, reliving our best musical moments on the ocean.

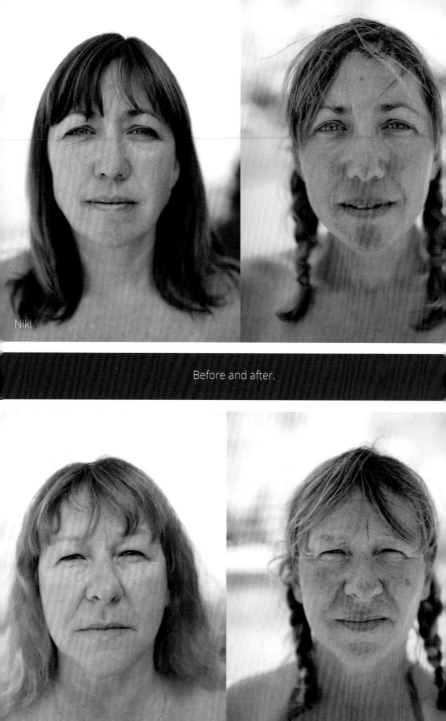

Niki

Before and after.

Janette

len

What a difference 2 months on the ocean makes!

ances

ber Estuary. As I watched her vanish over the horizon and out of my life, I was filled with sadness. But my sadness quickly turned to horror when I realised that amidst the previous evening's frantic throes of passion I had completely forgotten to switch the light on.

Fortunately, when I checked, no boats had run aground on the rocks overnight, so that was alright."

Preston's sex-filled first night on Loxley Head had certainly been an eventful one. But as he was to learn, it was hardly exceptional. The very next day, he had just heated up a box of microwave smokey fries when he heard a thundering clatter from the roof of his lighthouse.

manson

"I quickly bounded up the stairs and out onto the balcony just in time to see a bright orange helicopter settling down on the rooftop landing pad. I realised with relief that it was merely my monthly supplies being delivered. I waved to the pilots, and they clambered down from the cockpit and came inside. In the kitchen, as I made a brew and put another couple of boxes of chips in the microwave, they unzipped their bulky buoyancy suits and took off their helmets.

My jaw nearly hit the floor as I turned to talk to them. For standing there in the room were two of the most gorgeous, sexy women I'd ever seen. As they shook their heads to release their long golden tresses, allowing them to cascade across their shoulders in slow motion, they looked more like some of the voluptuous centrefolds in the magazines the previous keeper had left than helicopter pilots.

As we sat in the little round kitchen enjoying our tea and fries, we could hear the wind picking up outside. So much so that as night fell, as the girls got up to leave, there was a proper gale blowing outside. Up on the roof, their helicopter was rocking from side to side as the powerful gusts tore at its rotor blades. It was clear that it was now far too dangerous for them to take off back to the mainland.

temple

"There's only one thing for it, we'll just have to stay the night," said one of the sexy girls. "That's fine by me," I replied. "The only thing is, there's only one bed in the lighthouse."

"That's fine by us," the twins said in unison. I just remembered they were identical twins.

The next thing I knew, we were stripping off in my little round bedroom. Soon, their sexy lingerie lay strewn all over the floor along with my big jumper and boots, and we were all stark naked. Every five seconds, their nubile bodies were illuminated in blinding relief as the one million candle power beam of the Loxley Head light swept through the bedroom win-

dow, flashing out its warning of peril to nearby shipping. Suddenly, the twins stopped and sighed.

"We can only do it in the dark," they said. "Would it be okay to turn the light off?" I was thrown into a quandary. On the one hand, turning a lighthouse off at night is against every regulation in the Trinity House rulebook. It's the first thing they teach you on the lighthouse keeping course. But knowing that those two sexy helicopter pilots were lying naked in my bunk, just waiting for me to do them was too much of a temptation for a red-blooded man to resist. I reached out the side of the bed and flicked the switch. The light may have been turned off, but the twins were turned on alright. And it was electrifying.

TANKS A MILLION: Oil tanker crash could have cost Preston his job.

As darkness filled the room, the three of us began hungrily exploring each other's bodies in my little bed, frantically driving each other to ever greater heights of passion as the force ten gale raged outside.

bassey

Not being able to see seemed to intensify our other senses. The girls may have been unable to get their chopper up that night, but I had no such trouble, I can tell you. And as we reached a shattering simultaneous climax, I could have sworn the whole lighthouse shook on its foundations.

In the morning, I realised that the lighthouse had indeed shook on its foundations during the night. But it was nothing to do with my threesup. With the light switched off, a giant Panamanian oil tanker had run aground on the rocks, splitting its hull wide open. As I stood on the step and surveyed the damage, my heart sank. The sea was coated with thick, black slick of tarry crude dotted with dead and dying seals, gulls and puffins as far as the eye could see.

I got a proper roasting for that one, I can tell you."

williams

The oil tanker disaster had taught Preston a valuable lesson, and he vowed never again to let his sex life compromise his professional responsibilities. But that isn't to say that there weren't many more episodes when temptation was put in his way.

"I remember this one day, I had finished my dingbats book and I was just thinking about opening a couple of peperamis for tea when there was a knock at the door. Standing on the step were four women wearing rowing all-in-ones that left very little to the imagination. They were all attractive thirty-somethings - proper milfs who looked like they knew a trick or two. It was cold that day and I couldn't help noticing that their nipples were standing out through the sheer cloth. I asked them if they'd like to come in and have a cup of tea in the lighthouse.

They told me that they were four bored housewives from Yorkshire who had decided to row the Atlantic. However, they had got as far as Loxley Head before running out of supplies, and they had called in to see if I would sell them some food. I said that I could give them enough pot noodles, pop tarts and bags of Bombay mix to get them to Antigua. But I explained that money was of no use to me as there was nothing to spend it on on my solitary island home in the middle of the North Sea.

crabtree

The milfs had a quick confab. "Perhaps there's some other way we could pay you for our provisions," one of them said, winking at the others. Before I knew what was happening, they had taken their all-in-onesies off to reveal their sexy cougar bodies. There they stood, clad in their underwear, stockings and suspenders. Giggling, they began to drag me up the spiral stairs to my bedroom. I say drag me - to tell the truth I wasn't protesting too much.

Once inside, we got down to action. I'm too much of a gentleman to recount exactly what we got up to in there. Suffice to say, they may have arrived as a 'coxless four', but that all changed in my bedroom, I can tell you. Loxley Head lighthouse was designed to survive hundred foot waves crashing over it and we certainly tested its foundations to the limits that night.

thornley

The next morning, after a traditional hearty lighthouseman's breakfast of tea and cheesestrings, the milfs set off again, their boat filled with gunwhales with all the provisions they would need to get them to the other side of the pond - jars of hari-bos and bombay mix, a big box of monster munch and a catering-size bag of marshmallows. They had certainly earned it, I thought, as I patted my flat knackers.

I couldn't have been more pleased when I heard those ladies eventually reached Antigua, after rowing nearly five thousand miles. But I had to chuckle to myself when, at their press conference, they claimed to have made the trip in one continuous row. They somehow omitted to mention

their overnight stop-off at my house lovenest."

NEXT WEEK, Preston recalls the when a lifeboat full of Swedish stra arrived at the door after their er was sunk by a Russian sub caught in its nets. "Two minutes a container full of bacardi bre lost overboard from a Chinese ship washed ashore, and it was party time at Loxley Rock."

giving you an unfair advantage over the other competitors. Janette knew she could not refill them immediately due to the raging storm, but they were desperate for drinking water. So as the small fresh-water canisters ran out, they raided the bottles of fresh water below decks.

'We didn't have much choice,' said Janette. 'We were locked up in the cabins for so long, we didn't have a chance to get on the hand-pump.'

It was then that the madness set in. Janette and Frances developed 'cabin fever'. It's only after being locked in a cabin for three days that the expression can be truly understood. They started to laugh hysterically at anything and everything.

'Eating chocolate, burping, farting... everything was very, very funny,' said Frances. 'Janette farted terribly and every time she did I would say: "Was that really necessary?" At which point we would both dissolve into fits of weeping laughter.'

Up at the other end of the boat, in 'First Class', there was a separate kind of hell going on. Niki couldn't bear being locked up for so long inside the cabin. It was driving her crazy; she was claustrophobic and could not cope with being in such a confined space. Despite the thunder, the lightning, the lashing rain and the huge waves, she wanted to stay on deck.

'Even though our cabin was a little larger, we were bounced around even more, as we were at the bow of the boat. The heat and the lack of air in such a tiny space made me feel like I was suffocating – it was like being in an oven. I just wanted to get out; being lashed by the wind and the waves was preferable.'

And so she snapped. With Helen shouting at her to stay inside the cabin, Niki opened the door.

'Stay inside, Niki!' yelled Helen over the noise of the waves.

'I have got to get out!' Niki shouted back.

'You'll die out there!'

'I feel like I'm already dead!' Niki yelled back.

'Don't go!'

'I've got to.'

'Clip yourself on!' said Helen as Niki disappeared through the tiny cabin door.

'Of course!' grinned Niki, already giving Helen the thumbs up.

On deck, the waves and the swell were enormous. The wind was screaming and the rain was coming down at about 45 degrees, belting against the side of *Rose* like millions of sharp little needles. Dressed in her life jacket, with a double-clipped safety rope, sat Niki, gripping on for dear life as wave after wave smashed against or swept over the boat.

'It felt so much better to be out there. It was awful, awful, awful inside that airless, sealed unit – it was like a coffin. I was desperate to be on deck. I liked being on deck. I didn't mind the wild waves and the wind; I found them exhilarating. I enjoyed the freedom of it all. I just couldn't cope with being locked up.'

'Niki!' yelled Janette from the other end of the boat. 'Get back into your cabin!' Janette's voice was lost in the wind and the rain. 'Niki!' she tried again. 'Niki! NIKI!'

Eventually Niki turned around. She was soaking wet, lashed by the waves, her face was dripping with water, her cheeks were chapped pink in the wind and her eyes were round with a mixture of exhilaration and fear.

'I'm all right!' she shouted.

'No, you're not!'

'I'm fine!'

'Get back inside!'

'I can't!'

"Yes, you can and you will!'

Niki stood staring at Janette as the waves crashed over the boat.

'Get back inside, Niki! If you want me to order you, I will order you!'

'I had to be very firm with her,' said Janette. 'I had to yell through the wind and the rain to get her back inside the cabin, but she wouldn't go in the cabin. As skipper it was my job to keep everyone safe, and I was not happy that she had decided to be out on deck. I knew she was really struggling and I understood that – I don't like small spaces myself – but taking her chances up there on deck, rather than inside the cramped cabin, was not the right thing to do.'

Finally, after Janette's shouting and demanding, though not quite ordering, for her to get below deck, Niki complied.

We did all make occasional trips onto the deck in the end, braving the storm to get to the bucket, wearing our life jackets and with a double lanyard securely tied on. Usually naked but for the life jackets, a partner kept an eye out, making sure none of us was swept away.

'I think our experience was completely different from that of Janette and Frances,' said Helen. 'Niki was really hating it, struggling with it all, and my iPod was not working, so I had nothing but the stories in my own head. I tried to think about the nicest things – decorating my house, anything I could – and I also took the opportunity to sleep. To sleep as much as I could. And work my way through the snack packs that I had. The one good thing about Niki spending so much time on deck was that I could spread out in the cabin. But the noise was overwhelming – the waves, the thunder, the wind, the lightning – it was biblical. I can't believe Niki spent any time on deck. That was the last place I wanted to be. I didn't even drink any water, as I didn't want to leave the cabin to go to the loo. It was impossible to get out, hold on, take your clothes off and use the bucket and throw the whole of it over the side when you were desperately trying to hold on and not be blown off the boat or to ride the enormous waves.'

And then, very gradually, the storm moved on. There was not a moment when the sky suddenly cleared and the sun broke through and the sea turned pale blue and became flat and calm. There was just a moment when the sea looked rowable and the rain was less lashing, and frankly none of us could bear another night locked up in our cabins any more.

'We didn't emerge blinking into the sunlight,' said Janette. 'We just shouted across at each other to see if it was worth giving it a go – we had not been able to really speak to each other for three days. I gave Ben and the duty officer a call to see if anyone else had set off yet and were off para-anchor, and I thought let's give this thing a go.'

We picked up our oars and started to row. It was an amazing feeling as we dipped our blades in and out of the water, trying to make up the 20 miles we had lost. No one said very much, no one discussed it much – we were all quite shocked by what we'd been through and thankful to be alive – so we simply picked up where we'd left off. We had a job to do. We had survived a hurricane and now we needed to get to Antigua.

'We circled ourselves in a little bubble on that boat,' said Janette. 'It was our little bubble and not at any time did we really focus on if there was any danger or what sort of danger we were in. We put it out of our heads. "We'll be fine" was our motto. "It'll be fine." Never at any stage did we think, "We are on our own, in the middle of the ocean, with help more than 24 hours away." We just got through each day as it came. Each shift was our challenge. That's what kept us alive.'

SHIP'S LOG:

'Even though sometimes it is really tough, there are moments when you really have to try hard to picture the world around you differently so that you can get through. It was not nice in those cabins in the storm. Distraction can really work, but it takes some effort.'

(JANETTE/SKIPPER)

CHAPTER 14

Flow

'Sometimes you find yourself in the middle of nowhere, sometimes in the middle of nowhere you find yourself.'

ANON

Surviving the hurricane was a huge boost to our confidence. It was like the ocean had thrown all she could at *Rose* and us, she'd behaved as badly as she possibly could and had a full-blown tantrum, and we had managed. We had ridden the storm and we had come out the other side, still rowing. After our three days of confinement we had a new respect for the Atlantic. We had seen what she could really do, and we rather fell in love with her. It was like she was talking to us, teaching us something. All we had to do was listen.

'Actually, we became obsessed by the sea,' said Helen. 'We spent hours and days trying to work out the rhythm. In the mornings the waves would be choppy and confused, they'd come at you from all angles. At around midday the ocean would get sticky and then at night there'd be these waves that came at the boat and you'd hear them coming and you'd raise your blades so that they could travel under the boat and you'd feel like you were flying.'

'The ocean gave you so much,' said Janette. 'I really loved it. I got the peace and the quiet and the living-in-the-moment thing. There were no distractions. It's funny because there was the constant noise of the sea, but, on occasions, all of a sudden the sea would go really quiet and there'd be no noise and you'd be like… no noise? Most of the time you would hear the whooshing and crashing of the waves. But there were moments when it was like somebody had taken away all the noise. It's incredible out there. Simply incredible.'

'The mornings and the sunsets were the most beautiful,' said Helen. 'Particularly that morning shift when we'd start in the darkness and watch the sun come up, and you'd sit there on the boat, thinking, "Okay, what have you got for me today? Let's see what you can do."'

The more time we spent out there, the better we got at reading the waves and the more we found our own rhythm. We still had problems with our autohelm, our rudder didn't work properly and we still had to hand-pump our water, as our batteries never charged properly. But now that the weather was improving it was sunny, so the solar panels were coming into their own, we were approaching halfway and Frances suddenly appeared on deck in a bikini!

'Whatever is going to happen,' she announced, 'I am planning on getting an excellent tan.'

She looked fantastic in her polka-dot two-piece from M&S. Her stomach was toned, she'd lost more than a few pounds and she had a broad grin across her face.

'Right! That's it!' declared Janette, ditching the oars. 'I am trying on the shorts!'

Out came the turquoise shorts with the green piping for a squeezing-on ceremony. We held our breath and crossed our fingers as Janette puffed and pulled and tugged. At last, they stretched to the top of her thighs and a few inches over her buttocks.

'Ta-daaa!' she pronounced, attempting to parade up and down the boat. 'Nearly there!'

'Very nearly there,' encouraged Niki.

'Not bad,' confirmed Helen.

'Fortunately we have another 1,500 miles to go,' said Frances.

By now we were beginning to settle into a routine beyond eating, sleeping and rowing. At around 12.30 p.m. every day came one of the highlights: The Scores on the Doors! Everything would stop, even the rowing, and we'd pause to witness either Janette or Helen, although it was mainly Helen, emerge from the office with all the razzmatazz of a game-show hostess (albeit sporting little more than a fetid T-shirt) and we'd play The Scores on the Doors. Helen's Vic-and-Bob-inspired game wasn't hugely complicated, but we really looked forward to it on a daily basis. It mainly involved guessing how far we had rowed the day before, and how much further we had left to row. Actually, it involved *only* that. But it was dressed up with as many high kicks and jazz hands and pretend-trumpet hoots, whoops and handclaps as we could possibly execute in a 40-foot swell. We'd hurl those wild guesses around the boat – 25 miles? 40 miles? 65 miles? – with plenty of ooohs and aaaahs and nooooos thrown in. And the prize for the person who guessed the closest? A general feeling of smugness at being right – that's all. Often the mileage would be pitifully low, to which our communal response would be: 'At least we aren't going backwards!'

We developed hundreds of little games to keep us entertained and to keep our bored minds from wandering or flat-lining completely. There was the Fame Game, where we had to guess the names of celebrities. Helen was excellent at this, due to her fondness for edifying editions of *Heat*, *Hello!* and *OK!* magazines, and Janette was terrible. Her excuse was that she rarely watched the telly. Although, in reality, she was just not terribly good at playing the game. Instead of asking the correct type of yes-or-no questions – i.e., is it a woman? – Janette would immediately jump in at the deep end and ask, 'Is it Richard Gere?'

Although, oddly, she thrived at the Name Game – another word game where you had to come up with every name you could beginning with a certain letter of the alphabet. Jane, John, Jericho, Juliet, Janet, James, Jimmy… It did later transpire that she'd played it for hours with her children on the way to France, so she had something of a head start on the rest of us.

We also enjoyed the endless gift of Helen losing something. It happened every day. At least once a day, there'd be a pause and then she'd ask the question:

'Has anyone seen…?'

Quite how she managed to lose so many things in such a tiny space we never knew. She did eventually accuse us of stealing her things for comic effect. In fact, all we'd done was some tidying. There was also another fabulous timewaster we called Yacht? Tanker? Bird? This was a particular forte of Niki's, where we'd scan the horizon for hours looking for signs of anything other than white horses. And the first person to spot the first 'catch of the day' or 'spot of the day', as it were, got to write their 'spot' down on the cabin walls below.

The cabin walls were also little oases of joy, as we had encouraged friends, family and indeed other rowers at La Gomera to write us little messages of support inside the boat. So, in quiet moments, when we needed a boost, we'd lie down in the office and read motivational missives of support from loved ones and others in the race.

We even found ways of making our dreary food packs a little bit more entertaining. Janette used to pretend to be running a rather poor takeaway restaurant, where she'd bark our orders back at us, asking if we wanted pizza or egg-fried rice or a chicken korma. And then she'd simply hurl the same old boring beef stew at us as we pretended to thoroughly enjoy what we had 'ordered'.

These games entertained us for hours and made us laugh until the tears rolled down our cheeks. It is extraordinary how little you need when you are surrounded by people you love.

The further south and west we rowed, the more the weather improved, and despite our lack of batteries, when the sun was hot enough, we realised we could play our music on the stereo for a couple of hours in the afternoon and we'd still have enough power in the batteries for the night shift. We'd spend endless hours discussing what we should listen to, and invariably it would come back to the *Mamma Mia!* soundtrack, as each of us knew every single word. But what a difference those two hours made. The sun on our faces, riding the waves, belting out ABBA songs at the tops of our voices. We all had a favourite for different reasons, but just powering along, pulling on the oars in time to the music, wiggling about on our seats and feeling on top of the world, or at least on top of a wave, was enough to make all of us smile.

However, the sunshine did bring with it a different host of problems. The rules of the race dictate that you are not allowed to cover the deck of the boat with a tarpaulin or any other piece of material that might catch the wind and act as a sail, thereby assisting your ever-so-speedy passage across the Atlantic. The result was that the deck turned into a boiling sweatbox, with two even more boiling sweatbox cabins at either end. Rowing at midday was a deeply unpleasant experience. The sun would beat down relentlessly for the entire two-hour shift, burning our faces, lips, noses and shoulders, despite the huge amount of sun cream we slapped on each other. It was also painful to have so many cuts, nicks and scabs roasting in the sun. The front seat of the boat was the worst; it had a particular frying-pan quality to it, as you were first in line against the elements. There was a terrible moment as we crossed the halfway point when Janette nearly passed out with heat stroke and had to be taken back to her equally hot, sweaty cabin to get the sun off her head and drink a quick two litres of water.

But the hazy days, or those with a little cloud cover, were glorious. By now we had more or less dispensed with clothes. Helen had lost her chafe-free pants over the side on a gust of wind quite early on, and the rest of us slowly began to shed items. Aside from the constant rubbing and the sores we now all had over our backsides, hands and inner thighs, it was just so much easier to wear nothing, to be naked, than to be constantly trying to dry off wet clothes as yet another rogue wave doused us on the boat.

'You could never tell when they were coming,' said Niki. 'Sometimes they would go under the boat so you wouldn't get hit, but other times they'd go over the boat and they'd smack you out of nowhere.'

'And sometimes they would just come out of nowhere and cover you from head to foot like someone had thrown a bucket of water,' said Helen. 'And somehow the sea always seemed to know when I was coming off shift. I'd finish my two hours, ready to go to bed, and open the cabin door right when it landed. And then me and my bed would be soaking wet. It was far worse at night, because you couldn't see them coming.'

Rogue waves were also dangerous, as without warning they'd send us flying across the boat. Frances was ambushed one night just as she was coming off her shift and was preparing to go into the cabin.

'I was sent flying across the boat, garrotted by the safety rope, and hit my back on the boat as I bounced off it. When I landed I couldn't see anything. It was like a cartoon reaction, with stars circling my head. I went blind, it was dark and I could just see a silvery light. I couldn't see anything else at all.'

Janette and Niki were quick to react and hauled her into the cabin where she lay still, staring blindly at the ceiling. 'It was frightening. I saw it happen and my heart was in my mouth. It could have been the end of her as the safety rope caught her on her carotid artery, around the neck,' said Janette. 'She could very easily have died.'

But Frances was her usual sanguine self and made not an iota of fuss.

She simply had a couple of glucose tablets and a lie down. Her sight slowly returned, and she was back on the oars two hours later.

Helen wasn't quite so lucky. She'd spent the previous few days endlessly complaining about not being able to wash her hair and ostentatiously scratching it whenever possible. It had been over a month now and the longest she, and indeed the rest of us, had ever been without the use of shampoo. It was driving her mad. She had long since given up on brushing it as well. The black hairband she used to tie it up with was slowly becoming embedded in a giant bird's nest at the back of her head, and instead of sorting it all out in the salt and the sun and the wind, she'd simply wrapped the whole lot up in a headscarf like some crystal ball reader at the local fair.

The rogue wave hit just as Helen was getting off the oars. It could not have hit at a more inopportune moment. With nothing to hold onto, she was sent flying across the side of the boat and as the boat flipped down and then back up again a sharp screw sliced through her scalp, leaving her with a three-inch cut to the head and blood seeping into her hair. She didn't scream. She didn't really make much of a noise; she just sat in the bottom of the boat, holding the side of her head, her scarf slowly turning scarlet.

'Well,' she said, looking at each of us in turn, a bewildered expression on her face. 'At least now I get to wash my hair.'

'Be careful what you wish for,' said Janette, grabbing the medical bag as she went to inspect the gash in Helen's head.

'And no,' said Helen, taking off her blood-soaked scarf. 'You are not sewing me up like a pork chop.'

In the end, Janette decided it was impossible to suture at sea in such a tiny boat, bouncing all over the place – the last thing she wanted to do was stick Helen in the head with a needle – so she simply washed the cut and stuck it together with some plaster stitches.

We were physically beginning to fall apart. The hours, the days, the conditions, the sores, the cuts, the bruises from being constantly bashed by the boat and the sea, and the weather were really beginning to take their toll. Our hands were agony. They were calloused and split and covered in blisters that bled and wept all the time. Niki's fingernail bed was so swollen with yellow pus there was nothing to be done but for Janette to take a knife to it, lance it and for Niki to knock back a course of very strong antibiotics.

'I have a feeling she enjoyed doing it a little too much,' said Niki. 'But it was either that or lose the finger.'

Helen's feet went the way of our backsides, mainly because she persisted in rowing without shoes. She said the shoes gave her blisters, which were nothing in comparison to what had happened to her heels – all split with chunks of skin hanging off. But she carried on in her Christmas socks, wearing a pair of sheepskin, padded slippers that Niki had pulled out of the bottom of her Mary Poppins bag. They were apparently for the elderly, to prevent bedsores, but she'd given them to Helen right at the beginning of the trip. Helen liked them because they were cosy and they matched our individual sheepskin rugs that we used to put on our rowing seat to help with the chafing. Although, in reality, nothing could really help with the chafing. Painful backsides and swollen hands (to the point where we all had to take off our wedding rings) and puffed-up joints were things we had expected, but the little withered calf muscles were not. Who knew that not walking for six weeks would affect your legs? Our thighs were strong, but our calves had all but disappeared.

It was the beginning of February and the novelty of being on the ocean was wearing thin. As the currents slowed us down again, we began to feel that we might never get to Antigua. We had just under 1,000 miles to go and we were counting them down on a daily basis, which is never a good sign. We heard that Ocean Reunion (with Charlie's nephew Angus on board) had already won the race in record time. Row Like a Girl had arrived in Antigua and, against all the predictions, come in second. Atlantic Challenge, Atlantic Drifters, Oarsome Buoys, All Beans No Monkeys, Team Beyond and Row2Recovery had all finished already. We had visions of our families sitting waiting for us, staring fruitlessly at the horizon for our little boat to arrive.

Our confidence at getting through the hurricane, at forging forth across the ocean, was waning. We were finding it very hard going and harder still to keep on course, and no amount of *Mamma Mia!* could make it feel any better. Our autohelm was still not working and we were having to steer by hand in strong seas, which we had to do in shifts of 15 minutes each, as it turned out that steering was physically much harder than rowing.

A low was beginning to engulf the boat. We had a meeting to try and talk through how we were all feeling. We'd had a few of these since we left La Gomera, but they'd mostly been about food and what cabins we were in. This was a little more serious. We'd all had enough. More than enough. We could feel ourselves flat-lining. We would have to rally ourselves or slip into a deep depression. Janette's solution to our being marooned and isolated and frankly desolate was to suggest that we rowed harder, that we lengthened our time on the oars and rowed three up instead of two. It did not go down well.

'I want to get there now,' she said. 'I think we need to do more rowing. What does everyone else think?'

'I don't think we can row any more,' said Helen. Out of all of us, she was always the first person to speak up. 'The boat is being permanently rowed. It is never NOT being rowed. How can we row any more?'

'But if we rowed three up then we'd get there quicker,' Janette replied.

'Quicker?' queried Frances.

'The thing is, you are making it sound as if we're lazy,' said Helen.

'No, I'm not.'

'Yes, you are, and we're not being lazy. We physically can't do any more.'

'How about rowing more if you feel like it? If you've got a bit left in you? During the day, not at night. You can get up on the oars and row if you fancy it,' suggested Janette.

'My feeling is, we get there when we are meant to get there,' said Frances.

'I just want to get there,' said Niki.

We all looked at her. Over the last few weeks Niki had become a worry to us all. She was less and less talkative, particularly at night, when we would either row listening to music or we'd talk. But Niki didn't. She would disappear into her own head for hours at a time. She then started to complain about the noise we were making. It was almost as if she was in a situation where she felt out of control and she was trying to seize some of it back. It was clear that we were all finding it difficult, living on top of each other all the time.

'She'd complain about my music being too loud, that she could hear it through the earphones,' said Helen. 'She didn't like any noise at night.'

'Helen's earphones were SO loud!' replied Niki.

'She didn't like us talking on the night shift.'

'I was trying to sleep.'

'Janette and I decided to try to train ourselves to virtually talk,' continued Helen. 'She would say, "Think of a colour," and then I'd think of one and she'd ask what it was. And I'd say, "Green." And she'd scream, "Green! That's what I was thinking!" I don't think Niki was the only one going mad at this point!'

We were supposed to rotate accommodation, to share the luxury of 'First Class', where you could stretch out a little more and not need an analgesic to get through the extra hours of a night on para-anchor. But after a couple of weeks, Niki said she just couldn't go in there.

'I struggled with the cabins,' she said. 'I never realised I was claustrophobic before I went. It was something to do with the heat. I get really bad hay-fever-related asthma. When I was a teenager I used to be rushed into hospital and put in oxygen tents. I've always had a problem with my breathing, but only in the summer. When I was on the boat, when it was cold it was all right, but the hotter it got – and having to seal yourself into these little spaces, with no air… I've never experienced anything like it. By the end of the journey, I was having palpitations whenever I went into the cabin – almost panic attacks. It was awful, absolutely awful. I would try to be out on deck as much as I could, and during the day, rather than having a sleep, I would sometimes stay out on deck and just stand at the back to be outside. Eventually, we had an informal arrangement, which nobody ever talked about, where I would get into the cabin and shut the door, leaving a tiny gap, and actually just a little bit of air would come through, so I would lie with my face right next to the door and try to go to sleep as quickly as possible. Then the girls would come and shut it properly after I'd gone to sleep.'

Niki couldn't bear to sleep in the office, so Janette offered to stay in there for the majority of the trip. 'While it would have been nice to have had some extra legroom, I felt responsible as the skipper; I wanted to keep Niki in a cabin – any cabin. I didn't mind too much, as the navigation equipment was in there,' said Janette. 'The only person I didn't want to share with was Helen, as she was so messy! She used to wash herself with her wet wipes and leave them on the bed. She insisted she was going to recycle them as toilet paper later, as we had to ration ourselves to six wet wipes a day for everything. But actually, in the end, even Helen became quite tidy. She stopped walking around the boat asking everyone, "Where's my…?" and started keeping her storage nets near her bunk, quite nice and tidy.'

As things wore on, Niki became obsessed with the speed of the boat.

'She would ask every other minute from the back seat,' said Frances. 'It was everybody's favourite seat because you had a little bit of shelter and you were right by the loo; however, you were reliant on the people in front of you to look at the speedometer, so she would always be asking, "How fast are we going? How fast are we going?" In the end, we more or less just said, "D'you know? I can't see. The sun is shining on it. I can't see how fast we're going." She was very sad, missing her family. I don't think she realised the effect she was having on the rest of us. It was the hardest thing for me. I would always say, "We'll get there when we get there. Don't worry about it." But she couldn't understand how anyone would think that was a reasonable response.'

'I missed my family so much,' said Niki. 'I was desperate to talk to them, desperate to see them. My children are a little bit younger than everyone else's and perhaps I felt they really needed me. I was at a very low point and I think the more you get told you shouldn't do something, the more you want to do it. So the other three kept saying to me: "We're going to get there when we get there. You don't need to work out when we're going to get there." But that's what I spent hours doing. I quite enjoyed it, actually. I think the pain of my idiotic coccyx injury and the terrible claustrophobia I felt about the cabins meant I was desperately trying to take my mind off things, off the thought of being enclosed in an airless cabin, so I found myself doing the mathematics of miles done and miles to go. Working out, "Right, we've done so many miles today, so if we average that, then we'll get to Antigua around this date." It was something to do. It was something to keep my mind occupied. It was like counting sheep. I probably got a bit frustrated. On our boat everyone was quite happy to just take as long as it took, to go with the flow, whereas a lot of other boats, they were more like I was, working out estimated times of arrival and pushing more. I wasn't pushing to get there in a certain position in the race. I just wanted to get there to see my family.'

Helen suggested that Niki start calling home and talking to Gareth more often. Although Janette spoke to Ben every day, albeit briefly, the rest of us were sparing in our contact with our families – partly because it was so expensive and also partly because a lot of the conversations didn't go terribly well! Janette's children were almost never home when she called; Helen's were at boarding school and having their own brand-new experience, although she did once memorably spend 15 minutes asking her mother for shampoo. The conversation went something like this:

Helen: 'Hi, Mum. I need some leave-in conditioner.'

Mum: 'Levin conditioner? What's that?'

Helen: 'Leave in.'

Mum: 'Levin?'

Helen: 'No, leave in – as in *leave in*.'

Mum: 'Levin?'

Helen: 'No, leave it in.'

Mum: 'Leave what in, dear?'

Helen: 'Arghghgh!'

And then they were cut off.

No, phone calls were not that easy. Frances's children were busy with their friends and one of Niki's sons brilliantly passed the phone back to Gareth, complaining that he couldn't carry on talking to his mum, as his Shreddies were getting soggy. Which is as it should be, really. The last thing we wanted was for our children to be sitting at home, weeping into sodden handkerchiefs, staring at the phone. The truth was, we were more needy than they were. Our husbands, on the other hand, were always positive and upbeat, but when your only news is that the flapjacks are too big, or you've been hit in the face by a flying fish, it's quite difficult to have a conversation.

But the extra calls to Gareth only made a small bit of difference, and soon it wasn't just the constant need to know how fast we were going; Niki then moved on to food. 'She was so worried about her food running out,' said Frances. 'She started not eating, even though she needed to eat.'

'I started stockpiling all my nuts and fruit and shouting at anyone who was throwing their food away, saying, "No! Give it to me!" I was like a squirrel and I had little batches of it everywhere,' said Niki. 'They got very frustrated, but I was probably just trying to take back control.'

And by now, she wasn't the only one. Firstly, Frances had a low spell early one evening, before we moved into our night-time routine. 'It was about three weeks before we finished. 'I'd been finding some of the night shifts more worrying as it was harder to stay on course during the nights. For some reason, when we went off course it always took longer to bring the boat around at night compared with during the day. The night I felt sad wasn't even a particularly rough night.' 'Weirdly, we all had different things that we hated,' said Niki. 'I couldn't stand the cabins, and both Helen and Frances hated the boat being hit by massive side waves in the middle of the night. They really didn't like it at all.'

'There was no high drama that night,' Frances says. 'The thought simply crept into my head that there was a chance we could be hit by a big wave, capsize, and the safety lines might break, so we wouldn't be able to climb back on board. I felt that I'd been self-indulgent risking my life when my children needed me to at least do my best to stay alive until they'd grown up. I could just imagine the headlines about how irresponsible we'd all been. I finished my shift and shed a few tears behind my sunglasses. Janette gave me a hug and a kiss and told me it would be all right.

'I went into the cabin and tried to sleep but I couldn't, so I listened to some music until it was time to row again. When I got on the oars two hours later I was fine. It seems almost irrational, but after that night the longer we were out on the ocean the less worried I was, because I trusted Rose, and her ability to stay upright in all sorts of seas, more and more.

'Helen was always so certain that we were going to get to Antigua because her angel cards had said so. She was totally confident that there was nothing to worry about. But for those two hours, doubt had found its way into my mind. I'd spent my whole life being responsible and doing what was expected of me, and it had been quite a leap of faith to enter this race and do something so out of the ordinary.'

Janette's way of dealing with the stress of being on board was to laugh, hysterically. 'I did this a couple of times – I just laughed manically. Honest to God, I went mad. I can remember one night, I was in front and Niki was behind me, and I'd been laughing at Helen's legs because they looked so funny. Skinny legs with socks on the end. They just looked like sparrow legs. It kind of set me off and I started laughing and I could not stop. I couldn't row because I was laughing so hard. I was in hysterics and I knew that Niki was sat behind me, miserable and very fed up, and even that made me laugh. It wasn't helpful for Niki, because she was down in the dumps and I'm hysterically laughing for about an hour. Laughing was my release, whereas crying was Niki's. We all had something.'

'I cried and she laughed,' said Niki. 'I was sitting there in my own little world, dreaming away, and then all of a sudden Janette just started laughing, and she laughed for an hour, hysterically, to the point where she couldn't row, she couldn't sit on her seat. It wasn't laughter. It was hysteria. It happened to her a number of times.

'If you ask Frances and Janette what they struggled with mentally on the boat they would say they did not. But both Janette and Frances became students again, laughing and making jokes. And Helen and I would look on. They both dealt with stress through laughter.'

In fact, the only person to maintain a firm grip on her sanity was Helen. Although on dry land she is probably the quirkiest of all of us, on the water she was the most balanced! Her strategy, such as it was, was to keep calm and keep buggering on. She was determined, focused and did not deviate.

'A woman of steel,' said Janette. 'A bit like a robot!'

'One of the duty officers, Ian Couch, said to me that you see people's true personalities when you're on that boat. Their true personalities will come out, their strengths and weaknesses. You will see the real person,' said Helen. 'I always knew we would make it across. I never had any doubt in my mind. Maybe that's why I didn't have a wobble or a moment.'

'Helen is a lot more mentally strong than you realise,' said Frances. 'I think because we have both lost parents, we've seen somebody close to us go through that, and it makes you tougher. We know that's as bad as it gets, and you do survive. So there's been that big crisis for us and we've moved through it. You realise that you are not in control of life. We don't know how the story will end, but if we all think positively it will end well. We just needed to work through this.'

And so we did. We needed to pull together; we needed to help each other. Otherwise we would lose exactly what we had come to find out here in the middle of the Atlantic. And that is what we did. Together.

'The strength of our team is each individual member. The strength of each member is our team.'

'One afternoon,' said Janette, 'when Frances and I were rowing, we started discussing Niki and how she seemed so low and how we could help her through the difficulties she was having. We were trying to work out why Niki was so miserable, and what we could do and how we could help. I was really feeling sorry for her because I thought it must be awful for her to feel like that on this tiny boat in such a confined space.'

'Is there something wrong?' asked Niki, poking her head out of the cabin.

'What?' asked Frances.

'Only I couldn't help but overhear you talking about me,' said Niki.

'Well, actually, now you come to mention it,' said Frances, 'I would like to say something.'

'They were talking so loudly,' Niki said later. 'It was impossible not to hear them!'

'Fortunately, Frances was the one who was sat right near her at the back, because I think Frances is quite good at dealing with things like that,' said Janette.

What followed was a firm and frank discussion about how Niki's mood was affecting the group, and she admitted that she really needed our help to keep her mind off missing Gareth and her family. Helen popped her head up like a meerkat halfway through the conversation, only for Janette to indicate very quietly that she should bugger off.

'Niki was very brave,' said Frances. 'She didn't get upset at all. She just said she was finding it hard and asked if I could help her. She admitted that she was a person who liked to be in control and at that moment she felt as though she wasn't in control. She was especially struggling with the uncertainty of not knowing how much longer we were going to be out on the ocean. She found the feeling of being adrift unsettling. She said she'd started to feel particularly isolated.'

'The only problems we had on board,' said Helen, 'were when we stopped talking properly to each other, when we withdrew into those tiny cabins with our own thoughts. So we decided to hold more meetings where we discussed how we were feeling. And we would go over conversations, saying, "You hurt me when you said this. I need you to listen when I say that."'

So we upped our meetings and gave each other carte blanche to discuss whatever was bothering us. Whatever anyone had said, or however anyone had behaved – it was aired. We were extraordinarily honest with each other and we had a no-sulking policy. Otherwise things festered. We were living in a very small, confined space, with zero privacy and no escape. We all agreed that if some feedback was a little too punchy, we'd add 'just saying' (usually in a sing-song voice) at the end of the sentence to take the sting out of the tail!

We'd had a phrase that we often used in the build-up to the race. 'It'll be fine,' we found ourselves saying all the time. 'It'll be fine' even though we got on the wrong train. 'It'll be fine' if we don't quite have the sponsorship money at the moment. 'It'll be fine' even though we've only managed five hours of training this week. But as we found ourselves very alone on the ocean, stalked by our own demons, we decided 'It'll be fine' was perhaps not positive enough and we (at Niki's instigation) decided to borrow from the fine words of Pollyanna and started to play the Glad Game. So every negative situation had to be turned into something positive.

'If something shit happens, you have to find a reason to be glad about it,' explained Niki. 'In the film and the book, the storyline is all built around this game. The Glad Game. So we played the Glad Game. "I'm glad the water-pump is broken because I get to stay on deck a little bit longer and talk to my friends." That sort of thing. That was the challenge. The more difficult the problem, the more fun the challenge, and the more you did it, the easier it got to find the "glad" in things.'

Eventually we were 'glad' we only had Bounce Balls to eat in our snack packs, we were 'glad' we had to ration each wet wipe to be reused at least twice before ending up in the toilet bucket, we were 'glad' we had no autohelm, 'glad' we had no lighting at night, 'glad' that Niki was teaching Helen to steer, 'glad' none of us drove with her at night as we found out she couldn't see in the dark, 'glad' we only had 500 miles left to go, 'glad' we had not washed our hair in two and a half months, 'glad' our calf muscles had withered to nothing, 'glad' our chafe-free pants had flown overboard.

Except that Janette was not too happy about the last one. 'I have never seen so much fanny in my life!' she said. 'There was fanny in front of me, fanny to the back of me, fanny in my face, fanny on my head, just fanny, fanny, fanny, everywhere! And they're hideous! I have no idea what my husband is thinking!'

The level of nudity was fine; it was the proximity of the nudity that, perhaps quite literally, got up her nose.

'There was one point when Janette complained to me, "Helen, take your vulva out of my face!" I was, to be fair, bent right over trying to stick plasters on my feet. But she's right; there was a lot of fanny. Sometimes you'd open the cabin door to find an arse in your face, as someone had put surgical spirit on their backside and were cooling it off in the air. Or maybe they were just giving their buttocks an airing.'

'The worst bit was walking around the boat with your pants off, legs apart, scuttling like a crab,' said Janette. 'There'd be a wave and suddenly someone would tumble towards you, fanny in the face. For some reason, Helen was the worst. She'd walk through as you were sitting down, rowing, her legs akimbo – there was nothing you could do, nowhere to go. You'd get more information than her gynaecologist. Frankly, I saw enough fanny on the Atlantic to last me a lifetime.'

Fanny was not the only vision we saw. Much like we did during those two nights we spent on the North Sea, we all, at one point or another, began to hallucinate, although unlike on the North Sea it took much longer for these visions to come. But they were just, if not more, vivid and also oddly personal and profound. Maybe it's the intense loneliness of the sea that allows your brain to play and fill in the gaps, to compensate for the boredom. Or maybe in the quiet and calm, you have time for reflection, space to explore your feelings or your deepest thoughts.

'I'd be rowing along and I'd think, "What are these houses doing here?"' said Janette. 'And there'd be a whole row of houses and a red telephone box. I'd be thinking, "I'm rowing in the ocean. How can they be there?" I saw a lot of flyover bridges. I'd be rowing away from a bridge. And trees. I saw a lot of trees as I was rowing along at night. They were particularly vivid. And I saw a lot of houses. I could see the bricks, the windows, the grass in front of the houses, sloping down towards me.'

'I heard a choir,' said Helen. 'Janette saw an angel. She kept saying to me, "Look, Helen, there's an angel, there's an angel." And she saw this angel figure, just small, sitting by the navigation lights. I'm afraid I didn't, for once! All I could hear, for the first two weeks, was a choir, singing in my head.'

'There's something about death, dark skies and stars,' said Frances. 'My mother's name was on the boat, I was rowing for her, for Maggie's. I thought, "She is with me all the time." Especially during the night. Not during the day, really. I didn't think about her so much during the day, but at night I felt her presence – she was there with me, looking down. It was an odd feeling because I'm not sentimental like that at all. But I really did feel her and it was incredibly comforting.'

'I always felt my father was there. His name was also on the boat,' said Helen. 'I always felt there was somebody behind me. I was always turning around to look, trying to catch him out. I remember being in the cabin when I was feeling really ill and sort of asking for him to be there. I felt his presence. I felt his support, like he was looking after me. After I saw Janette's Great-Aunty Rose on the North Sea, if we were rowing together at night, we'd chat about it a lot. Janette would say she could smell eggs and bacon. She said there was somebody with us who likes eggs and bacon. She could feel somebody with us. I'd be saying, "Well, my dad liked a cooked breakfast but he wasn't that bothered." We were trying to think who it might be, and then, in the end, for some reason, we came up with Frances's Aunt Edith. Who unfortunately doesn't seem to exist. Then Janette would say, "Somebody's with us who likes a floral slipper. Anyone? Anyone partial to a floral slipper?" Then we'd rack our brains trying to think of someone. It was really funny.'

But then the more we felt the rhythm of the sea and surrendered ourselves to its power, its charm, the more we achieved what in meditative terms is called 'flow'.

'I had moments where I forgot completely about responsibility, because the sea does that to you,' said Janette. 'Looking at those stars, it does take your mind away. It takes your mind to a place where you've never been before. Well, where *I've* never been before. It is a bit like meditation, I guess. It takes you completely away from yourself. Night-time was amazing. I liked it better than the day. Whether it was rough or calm, I loved the night because I could see all the stars, and I loved it when the moon came out because I could see everything then. Sometimes at night you can hear and see the fish. When Niki and I were on duty one night there was an enormous pod of dolphins. She saw them first. She's so good at spotting wildlife. She always saw everything first. There was a massive pod of dolphins and we'd stopped rowing to watch. There were loads of them flying through the air, twisting and jumping, all lit by the moon.'

'As soon as we saw wildlife, we all downed tools,' said Frances. 'We'd all stand up, but we also didn't want to damage any of the animals with our blades on their heads. So we'd pull them on board and watch the turtle or the dolphin.'

'One night, it was round about sunset,' said Janette, 'Niki and I were rowing and all of a sudden we saw a whale come steaming past us, really close, on a mission, just going for it. Normally they'd stop and circle us for a while. They'd just circle around the edge of the boat and keep circling until they worked out who we were. The night-time was spectacular. It was a dome of stars; often I'd mistake them for boats because they're quite low. They look like they're on the horizon. The clear nights were particularly beautiful.'

We used to refer to the moon as our bedroom light and would wait for it to come up every night. It was extraordinary, the difference it made. We could read by the light of the moon. We could see each other, see the ocean – without it the world was very black. Its cycle was fascinating. And the full moons were breath-taking, with the whole ocean glittering and shimmering before us. We would also row towards it, keeping it to one side of the boat. We could always tell when whoever was steering had fallen asleep at the tiller (mainly Janette), as the moon would suddenly appear at the wrong side of the boat.

'We had one night where I just looked behind me. It was really calm and it looked like a path of fairy lights in the air,' said Helen. 'I said to Frances, "Am I seeing something? Can you see?" It just looked so magical. And she said, "Yes, I can see what you are seeing."'

'It was phosphorescence,' said Frances.

'A footpath of sparkling lights,' added Helen, 'like the yellow brick road from *The Wizard of Oz*. I remember thinking, "It looks so magical, am I hallucinating?" We felt really close to space, the stars – the moon was our friend. We couldn't wait for the moon to rise as that meant we had light. It's amazing how much you can see by the light of the moon. That was definitely one of the best moments. That, and seeing the whales close up.

'We didn't see many. There'd be days and days and days when we didn't see anything other than weird birds. We'd ask ourselves where these things had come from. We were thousands of miles away from land. And they looked like mini-dinosaurs. They would swoop down. I remember Niki shouting at me, "Helen, there's a sign, there's a sign! There's a whole bunch of feathers for you, right there!"'

But it was the whales we really loved. We'd been warned that they were dangerous; one flick of the tail and the whole boat would go under. Yet we never felt worried or at risk, which was probably foolish of us. We just felt immensely privileged to see something so beautiful in the wild. Particularly when we were visited by a mother and her calf.

'She was huge and grey,' said Helen. 'And then the baby just came over, right next to the boat, and lifted its head and blew. That was a really special moment because we were all mums in the boat, and we felt the whale trusted us with her baby, that she knew we were the same. That we would never harm it. It was a really important moment. Sometimes it was like the ocean read our thoughts. Earlier, when Niki had an infected finger, there was a possibility that she might have to leave the boat. We were phoning Caroline. We were phoning Thor. We were phoning everybody about her infected finger. It was all very much touch and go, as, if it went on much longer, she would be in serious trouble. Then we made the medical decision that we were going to have to lance it. She went into the cabin and Janette got the scalpel and sliced into the skin and was squeezing all this pus out of her finger, but that's when the big pod of dolphins arrived. We'd had quite big waves that day and we were all tired and Niki was in pain, but then we just saw all these dolphins flying through the waves. It's like the wildlife came to us just when we needed it most...'

And the longer we were out there, the more we appreciated the little tricks the weather used to play on the ocean. We could sit in the boat and watch a small squall develop. A little black cloud would appear out of almost nothing and we would see it heading towards us. We'd been rowing in bright sunshine, waiting for it to arrive. Then we'd close our eyes as it approached, in anticipation of the rainstorm about to be unleashed upon us. It would soak us out of nowhere and then disappear, leaving a stunning rainbow in its wake.

'They would span from one end of the horizon to the other,' said Niki.

'Arching across the whole sky. They were absolutely beautiful. They were like a reward for surviving the rain storm in the first place.'

And then, of course, there were the sunsets.

'Pink and grey clouds,' said Frances. 'When it was cloudy it was more beautiful than ever, because the pink and orange would bounce and reflect off the sky. The light was extraordinary.'

'It is absolutely magnificent out there,' said Niki.

'I felt like I was on another planet,' said Janette.

'It was like we were on a huge round table and we were the centre-piece. And the clouds were travelling around us,' said Frances. 'It was a privilege to witness such beauty. It was something none of us shall ever forget. It was as if we were guests in another world… for a while.'

SHIP'S LOG:

'Some of the best moments in our lives are the hardest – when our mind and body are stretched to the limit, when we take up the challenge and flow with it. There were many times on our journey when we were completely involved in an activity, which became our full focus, and we were in flow. We found our strengths collectively and we worked with them together to achieve things we did not know we were capable of.'

(JANETTE/SKIPPER)

CHAPTER 15

Antigua

'Our greatest weakness lies in giving up. The most
certain way to succeed is always to try just one more
time.'

THOMAS A. EDISON

It wasn't until the arrival of the second support yacht that we realised
quite how lonely we had been. We had not seen another face, another
person, for nine weeks. We had become so wrapped up in our own world
that it was almost a revelation that anyone else or anywhere else existed.
We were so used to our routines – rowing, sleeping, eating, making hot
water (Helen), cleaning the solar panels and toilet (Frances), checking
for water ingress, replacing seat wheels and doing bilge duties (Niki) and
monitoring rubbish (Janette), as well as the endless rowing – that when
Manfred Tennstedt (the skipper of the support yacht) announced over
the radio that they were coming to see us to check on how we were
and to get some footage of us for a documentary, we became giddy to
the point of hysteria.

Helen was on lookout, scanning the horizon, scampering up and
down the boat, looking for any signs of life other than flying fish and
dinosaur birds.

We were now, by this stage of the race, rowing three up during the day,
with one of us steering (we had long since given up hope of repairing

our autohelm). It was exhausting and we were shattered, but we had little choice. Our progress was being hampered by squalls and currents determined to send us off course, so after another of our many meetings, we all decided we would have one last crack at it, one final push to get there before the end of February.

'I had the number 22 in my head,' said Helen. 'So I was convinced we were going to get there on 22 February. Someone told me 22. I had this feeling. Niki was always saying, "We're never going to get there. We're just going 2 knots or 1½ knots the whole time." I said, "Niki, we don't know that." They say that when you get to a certain point the trade winds and the currents will help you, so I just knew that we would speed up at some point, but that time never seemed to come. Our families were waiting to book their flights. I kept saying we would be there by 22 February, that we'd speed up, but we were only going 29 or 30 miles each day and we had over 200 miles left to row. Gareth and Mark were asking when to book for Antigua, and Carsten was telling them it could be March. But I still had this 22 in my head. Anyway, as we crept up to that date I knew it wasn't going to happen, and so did the rest of our families. They all had to change their flights.'

So when Manfred arrived with the dawn on 23 February, he could not have appeared at a more opportune moment. We were down to our last. We were on our knees. We'd drained all the reserves of determination, energy and character that any of us had left. We knew our families we waiting for us to arrive, they were desperate to book their tickets, but we were still up to a week away from English Harbour, Antigua.

The sun was beating down and the waves were calm as we rowed, pausing occasionally to stare out at the sea.

'When did they say they were coming?' asked Frances.

'Today,' said Janette. 'They said today.'

'Shall we call them on the radio?' asked Helen.

'Let's give them a bit longer,' said Janette.

'But they said today,' confirmed Niki.

The anticipation was building by the hour. What were we going to ask him? What news did we want to know? It was so ridiculously exciting, the thought of having a visitor, out here, in the middle of the ocean!

'There they are!' declared Helen, pointing off towards the horizon.

'Where?' asked Janette, squinting.

'There. That speck.'

'Are you sure?'

'It'll be a turtle,' said Frances, still rowing.

'Or another flying fish about to hit me in the face,' said Niki.

Niki was always hit in the face by flying fish. None of us knew why. It was just always Niki and always in the face, especially at night. They'd come at her under cover of darkness, like kamikaze fighter pilots, and she'd get smacked in the chops when she least expected it. And then Helen would spend the next 10 minutes screaming as the fish flipped around in the dark and we tried to grab hold of it to chuck it out of the boat. Sometimes we'd fail. Sometimes they rotted for days before we could find the source of the terrible rank smell.

'NO! I promise you,' promised Helen. 'It's a boat.'

A boat that took an eternity to arrive. We watched for what seemed like hours, for *Skye*, the Talisker support boat skippered by Manfred and his girlfriend Jemma, to get close enough to make contact. First, it was waving distance, soon it was hollering, then shouting, then shouting and waving and hollering. Questions were batted back and forth. How were we? How were they? What was their gossip? Who had finished? Seemingly nearly everyone. Out of the 26 crews, 18 were already home. How was Antigua? Amazing. What was the atmosphere like? Electric. Was it packed? Rammed. We should enjoy it when we get there. Take our time. Come in slowly. Relish every second.

They took out their cameras and started to film us rowing along for a documentary on the race.

'He's not harnessed on,' said Frances, looking across at the boat.

'No,' agreed Helen, glancing over at Manfred as he swung over the side of his boat, wielding his camera. 'How terribly dangerous. One slip…' And she screamed.

Manfred had hurled himself off the side of his boat and was swimming towards us. Seemingly, he was unimpressed at the idea that it would take just one rogue wave to sweep him away from us; one rogue wave between him and Guadeloupe and the coast of Venezuela.

'Morning,' he said as he swam through the waves.

'It's like coming across a real-life merman,' declared Helen. 'Covered in tattoos.'

'How are you all feeling?' he asked as he came towards us.

We were so impressed by his swimming. We were so impressed by his calm in the water. That manly one-armed front crawl, holding onto his camera. We were just so impressed by his being there. We had so much to say, so many questions, we were all tripping over ourselves, trying to speak. We were so starved of company, so starved of information, that anything he said we laughed at, anything he told us we found fascinating. What was going on in the outside world?

It was odd. We had been in a bubble for the past nine weeks. And we loved our bubble. We'd deliberately created it. It was our protection. Our way of dealing with the enormity of what we were doing, rowing 3,000 miles across the most unpredictable ocean on earth. Our world had become us and the boat. The closest thing to us was, in fact, space (so the tweet we received from Tim Peake was something we really treasured). Also, after so many days at sea (63 at this point), we had felt, like the dolphins, the whales and the flying fish, that we, too, had become part of the ocean. We had become creatures of the sea. We understood it better. We respected it more. We had fallen in love with it. We bashed ourselves less as our ability to read the waves improved. We could predict the sideways rogue waves coming a mile off and were ready for them. We could see mini-storms coming and would put on our wet-weather gear and sing loudly to ourselves as the rain poured down. It was like we'd been battling an enemy, a bitter enemy, that didn't want us there, but after weeks of exhausting manoeuvres – of attack and counter-attack – we had grown tired of the war and used to each other's company. We'd come to some sort of harmonious agreement to put up with one another, at least until we reached Antigua.

But it was this bubble that saved us, the bubble that made us think of nothing else other than getting across the ocean. It was our focus and our security.

And Manfred penetrated that bubble as soon as he jumped into the water. Yet none of us seemed to mind. In fact, we were delighted. Whatever we had been looking for out on the waves, we had surely found by now. Our time was up. We needed to come in.

'So,' said Manfred, swimming around *Rose*, 'the idea is to film you cleaning the underside of the boat.'

'Cleaning the boat?' asked Janette.

'Yes,' he nodded, taking a quick glance at *Rose*. 'How many times have you done it?'

We hadn't. We hadn't cleaned *Rose* once. It had been suggested to us that we clean the barnacles off the bottom, but frankly the waves had been so big and the current so strong that none of us had dared set foot off the boat. We hadn't swum or been in the water at all during the nine-week crossing. We had been in the zone – the eat, sleep, row, repeat zone. We had admired the ocean, we had fallen deeply in love with it, but we had not immersed ourselves in it at all. Perhaps we'd been too busy trying to cross it.

'You haven't?' Manfred looked surprised. 'Row Like a Girl cleaned the bottom of their boat three times. It will increase your speed like you won't believe. You'll get to Antigua at least a day sooner.'

So Frances and Niki attached themselves to long safety wires and hurled themselves over the side, with scrubbing brushes to scrape off the barnacles, limpets and seaweed that had attached to the underside of *Rose*. She was, frankly, filthy – an extraordinary amount of wildlife had hitched itself to our undercarriage for a free ride across the Atlantic.

'This is fantastic!' yelled Niki, splashing and diving in the water. 'I can feel every single muscle in my body relaxing!'

'Heaven!' agreed Frances as she swam under the boat.

'Why haven't we done this before?' asked Niki.

'The sharks!' shouted Janette from on board *Rose*.

'We haven't seen one of those for at least an hour!' laughed Niki. 'This is brilliant.'

It was one of the highlights of the trip for Niki and Frances, like being a guest in a magical world – swimming in an aquarium, surrounded by curious little fish and larger dorados who were gratefully feeding off the loose barnacles they'd scratched and scraped off the bottom of the boat. It was a moment of relaxation and joy, feeling at one with nature and the environment, and they were also enjoying the company of Manfred. Not only did it feel fantastic to be in the water, there was something very special about sharing the experience with someone else, swimming alongside them.

Niki climbed back onto the boat with all the elegance of those French gazelles, whereas Frances needed some assistance. Quite a lot of assistance. Fortunately, Janette was on hand to haul her in. Helen, meanwhile, cleverly filmed the whole magical, once-in-a-lifetime, never-to-be-repeated experience, only to cover the entire screen with her fat finger! Go Helen!

We had been told on numerous occasions by Ben and Carsten to clean under the boat.

'It'll make a difference,' they'd said. 'You should do it.'

And what a difference!

'We simply didn't realise the impact it would have,' said Helen. 'Who knew a few barnacles could slow you down that much? But right then and there we doubled our knottage. Janette argues that at that time the wind had also changed and the currents moved, but as soon as Niki and Frances cleaned under the boat, got back on and Janette and I started rowing, it was an oh-my-God moment! We went from 2 to 4 knots at a stroke. Everybody could see that we were now going faster. Ian Couch, the safety officer, phoned up and asked, "Have you cleaned under your boat?" I said we had, and he said they could tell, as we were going so much faster. If we'd cleaned under our boat sooner, we would have quite simply got there a week earlier. It does make that much of a difference.'

So as the sun set and we waved goodbye to Manfred and his crew, we turned up the ABBA, put *Mamma Mia!* on at full blast for the seventy-fifth time that trip and danced and sang as we rowed. Suddenly *Rose* was like a knife through butter. We could almost smell the land; we kept imagining the lights, the noise, the warm welcome in the harbour, the hugs from our families and friends. We did 58 miles in one day! Followed by 69. It was hard to believe the end was in sight.

We started to talk about it, imagining it; we were counting down the miles now. Every mile we ticked off with a loud 'Ker-ching!'

'Fifty-five miles left!' shouted Niki.

'Do you think you'll be emotional when you get there?' Janette asked Frances.

'Emotional?' asked Frances. 'I should say so. I am on the edge of crying all the time. I could conjure up a tear just thinking about it now.'

'And you do realise that when we get there, we'll hold a world record?' asked Janette.

'A world record,' nodded Frances.

'The oldest women to have ever rowed the Atlantic!' declared Janette.

'Ker-ching!' came a shout from Niki on deck. 'Fifty-four miles left.'

'And we shall celebrate with rum and chocolate,' said Janette.

'Is there anything left of the mango gin?' asked Helen.

'I think we only have brandy,' said Janette.

'Brandy?' asked Frances.

'I was keeping it for emergencies.'

'And we didn't have any of those?' asked Frances.

'In the meantime,' said Janette with a flourish, pulling something out from behind her back. 'I give you… OLIVES!'

The announcement of olives sent a frisson of excitement around the boat. We had eaten nothing that exotic or exciting for two and a half months. The closest any of us had got to a culinary experience was when Helen found a spare shepherd's pie behind Niki's snack-pack collection and had guzzled down the whole 1,000-calorie event in one sitting.

'It actually said on the packet "to share". I thought, "Sod that. A thousand calories? I could do with those." It was delicious. I don't think I have ever felt so full, so replete, in my life!' said Helen.

So we gathered on deck to ceremoniously open the tin of olives that Janette had thoughtfully bought in France and carried on board *Rose* for the enjoyment of her crew.

'Ta-daaa!' she announced as she pulled open the tin.

It turns out that Janette's French is as proficient as her pre-race workout.

'Bugger!' she said, looking inside the tin. 'What the hell is that? Bloody mackerel?' She sniffed. 'Bloody mackerel in bloody olive oil!

Bugger that!' She put down the tin in disgust. 'How are you supposed to know that from the sodding picture?'

The rest of us were delighted. Mackerel? It tasted like ambrosia. It was oily and greasy and packed full of salty deliciousness. There were three slivers each, which we handed round with great ceremony. We each devoured our share, making ecstatic moaning sounds, as if we had never tasted anything so fantastic. Nine weeks of packaged meals must have taken their toll, as our bodies were clearly craving something. Vitamins. Omega-3. Oils. The fish almost made us high while we were eating it.

Another thing our bodies were clearly craving was a shower or a wash of some description. We'd wet-wiped ourselves all the way across the Atlantic. We'd used wet wipes as toilet roll because toilet roll would never have lasted nine weeks on the sea without becoming a sodden, mushy mess, but now we were down to our last few wet wipes. So Janette made an executive skipper decision: we could crack open the grab bags. The grab bags are so-called as they are the bags that you 'grab' as the ship goes down. They are emergency pre-packed kits that are supposed to save your life as you float about in the Atlantic, waiting for help. They contain food, torches, rockets and, most importantly, fresh water.

'We each had two sponges that we cut in half,' said Helen. 'We had a bucket and we had a tiny bit of shower gel and we stripped completely naked and shaved our legs and under arms and covered ourselves in shower gel. I don't think I have ever felt so fantastic after a wash in my life. I remember thinking to myself, "Why haven't I done this before?" If I did this race again, I would do a body wash once a week – I would – because it made me feel so much better. Although, I suppose, sometimes you've got to reach the nadir of filth in order to realise quite how nice it is to be clean.'

Packed in small plastic bags labelled in German, the *wasser* hair wash was a game-changer.

'The excitement was mounting,' said Frances. 'We were so focused on arriving that we didn't even notice a massive cargo ship approaching us. It appeared out of nowhere. We, of course, immediately got onto the radio for a chat. Calling out to them, saying, "*Rose, Rose, Rose…*" attempting to make contact. But they ignored us, as if to say, "Go away, you needy old bags, talk among yourselves."'

Ker-ching!

We were about 30 miles out when we suddenly saw what looked like a large cloud over the ocean. It was a distant white glow on the sea. A halo.

'It was like the Resurrection; all it needed was a heavenly choir. None of us could understand what it was,' said Janette. 'And then Frances stared, narrowed her eyes and said, "That's the light pollution coming from Antigua."'

It was like a mushroom of light floating above the sea. It was beautiful because it meant we had almost made it. We were nearly within sight of land. We were safe. If anything happened now, we could be rescued. But at the same time, as we all stopped rowing and stared, we realised where we had been, where we had come from. We had passed through one of the last pristine wildernesses on earth. During our journey, we'd seen nothing man-made – no plastic, no pollution, nothing. We had become totally at home, in tune with nature. Our skin was clear, our lungs had inhaled nothing but fresh air for months. And now it was about to be over.

'It suddenly hit home,' said Frances. 'I felt very sad – I was overcome with sadness. After all this time and all this preparation, after all this great experience, these were our last few hours of rowing. These were our last few hours with *Rose*; I thought, "We'll never get back in her on an ocean again. We'll never row another ocean. This is the end of a really amazing time. The end of our dream." I felt bereft.'

'Even I felt really quite sad that it was ending,' said Niki, 'despite all my anxiety about getting there. It wasn't just the journey; it was the whole thing. We'd been planning for so long and we'd done so many things together – so many exciting things – and we'd learnt so much. It was the feeling that this was going to be it.'

We braced ourselves. And then Janette rang Ben for a weather report.

'He said, "The weather is fantastic. If you carry on at the knots that you're going at now, it's going to get you in when it's dark." For the whole journey we'd been hoping and praying for the wind to keep going in the right direction, the tide to go in the right direction, and that's all we wanted. And the moment we didn't want it to happen, it bloody did. The wind was going in the right direction; the tide was right. We'd cleaned our boat and everything was good with us, and we didn't want it to be. Ben said, "You really need to think about what you are doing. You really need to think about putting your anchor out and coming in when it's light. It's too dangerous." I got off the phone and I looked at them all and I shook my head.'

We all knew we shouldn't enter an unfamiliar port at night. We'd done it once before on the North Sea and nearly rammed ourselves into the harbour wall. It was extremely dangerous. We had all read the port notes as well, in the almanac for English Harbour, which said that if you're not familiar with the port, if you haven't been there before, then don't enter during the hours of darkness.

We had to make a decision. We were approaching 20 miles out, and at that point you can't change your mind; you have to tell the harbour master if you are on your way in, and inform ABSAR (Antigua and Barbuda Search and Rescue). We had a meeting, a conversation, where we all eventually agreed that we had to park up, put out the para-anchor for the very last night and sit it out. We were so near and yet still so far. It was an extremely counterintuitive move. Having rowed our hearts out for so long, having pushed ourselves to the limit, having emptied all our reserves, to suddenly have to moor up and spend another night, our last night, on the para-anchor was, for some of us, profoundly depressing.

'I was furious,' said Helen. 'I couldn't cope with much more. I just wanted to get there, really. I wanted to get off the boat. It was like waiting for Christmas Day. You know when you're a child and you really can't wait for Christmas morning? I was ready to burst. I had absolutely had enough.'

'It was probably one of the favourite nights of my life,' said Frances. 'The night of waiting was just so full of expectation and anticipation. We knew great things were going to happen the following day and I didn't want it to end. We were so used to our own company and it had just been enough. Now other things were about to encroach on our bubble. I was very happy to prolong that experience for one last night.'

So we cracked open the last of our alcohol, which was tantamount to three sips of brandy each (from a small bottle very kindly provided by Sam, one of the grandfathers at our children's school), and finished off the last of the emergency Mars bars and prepared to sit out the night. But the waves were huge and the current was very strong, and there was another race going on around us, which meant two of us had to be on deck on watch all the time. We had 60 feet of ropes hanging overboard and if any of the sailing boats came between us and the anchor, we would capsize. The irony of potentially coming so far only to lose *Rose* with 20 miles to go was not lost on us.

'We were so stressed,' said Helen. 'It was such an uncomfortable night. We were getting bounced around and there was this sailing race going on, so we were on the VHF radio all night, trying to contact the boats and warn them about the anchor and all the ropes.

'There was one point when I was on deck and there was a sailing boat that wouldn't answer the radio, so we were on deck with our torches, shouting and waving, saying, "We're here, we're here and we've got a ruddy great anchor out!" We were flashing the torches. They did eventually alter their course, but they never responded to us at all.'

Meanwhile, Janette was still in contact with Ben, who was following our progress. The sea that night was rough, with some strong currents and, despite our anchor being out, we were still being pulled towards Antigua. At about 3 a.m. we made the decision to retrieve the anchor and begin the final leg of the journey. Moments after Niki and Frances had pulled in the anchor, an enormous wave hit the boat and Janette, who was steering, watched in awe as our speed climbed for a brief but terrifying moment to over 14 knots. Thank goodness Janette was able to keep Rose's nose facing into the wave. If that one wave had hit us on the side, our race could have ended very differently!

All night long we could see the lights of Antigua as we kept to our two-hours-on, two-hours-off watch shift. We would still have to row tomorrow. It would not be a quick trip, as we still had another three to four hours of solid work at the oars to get us into English Harbour. Janette kept on insisting we rest and try to get some sleep. But none of us could; aside from the anticipation and the ever-circling yachts, we suddenly had a signal on our telephones. We had crossed the threshold; our toes were dipped into the pool of civilisation.

We had kept a blog during the voyage – but it was very hard to write the entries and then get them transmitted over the airwaves. Janette and Niki had spent time in La Gomera learning how to use the special live mail system with data compression, designed for boats. The data was transmitted from Janette's laptop, via the satellite phone, which had a dial-up connection like a really old modem, and transmissions could only be sent when the boat had enough power. It was a laborious process, according to Janette: 'It would only send if the sat phone stayed connected, and if it didn't stay connected you had to start all over again – very frustrating. It was a nightmare and took ages in the hot sweaty cabin.'

Janette wrote the first entries, but eventually everybody added contributions. Not all of the transmissions got through immediately, though. One blog written by Frances on Christmas Day was delayed by the power problems on the boat, and was only sent in early February – by which time she'd had to rewrite some of it as the Christmas references were out of date.

Now we were no longer off comms! Frances was the first to notice. 'Suddenly all these text messages came flying in,' she said. 'We'd only had the satellite phone all the way across the Atlantic, and now all of a sudden all these messages of support that had been floating around in the ether for months landed! And we started reading them out to each other.'

'They were so positive,' said Niki. 'It was very emotional. There were a few tears as we read what people had sent us. And then the Facebook messages came through and some of them were extraordinary. We simply could not stop crying as we read them out loud to each other.'

Ladies… you are an inspiration to all of us working mothers. Setting a goal, training hard and working together as a team with good humour, even when things get very tough. With best wishes to you all from a sunny but chilly Hampshire. X

Well done all of you. A tremendous effort. You are amazing and an inspiration to us ordinary folk. Well done and keep digging deep. Best wishes.

Reading your entry at 00.39 gives me the inspiration and kick I need that the pain I feel right now is nothing in comparison to the courage you all have to keep rowing. Thank you.

In what has been one of the most depressing and bleak periods of my life, the one thing that has put a smile on my face has been reading about you four amazing ladies. Thank you for being a constant source of hope and inspiration.

Absolutely amazing. Our friend has been inspired to do this for his fortieth, literally because he saw your story and was blown away! What an achievement. Stay strong, stay brave, stay a team.

I don't have a bad day while you're out there!!!! Take care, keep smiling and rowing. You are my heroes.

It's hard at the time, as is any great achievement, but one day you will all look back on this and walk 2 inches taller for the rest of your lives. Wishing you all a great journey. It's what life is all about. You are encouraging SO many people to live a better and more fulfilling life than you can possibly imagine. Hope the weather is kind. Keep smiling.

Fantastic blog and your adventure has motivated me to do something that little bit crazy :-) Maybe not as adventurous as what you guys are doing, but something special :-) Keep going, girls. Everyone is very proud of you and I've been telling all the Aussies about you! X

It is amazing to hear of what you are going through, you are fantastic. I was reluctant to go out for a run tonight (windy, wet, cold, just didn't want to go), but thinking of you and what you are achieving changed my attitude sharpish and I shifted my butt out that door! Take care. Here's to fair winds to Antigua!

Fantastic to read your blog. Am addicted to your progress! First thing, before letting out the dogs, I check your speed and position and then throughout the day! Well done, girls. You are doing brilliantly! So proud of you.

Keep going, ladies! You have no idea the effect you are having on us all. So inspiring and proud for women everywhere. We are thinking of you all. Hang in there. The Prosecco is chilling! Sending you love – Jeannie. Eat, sleep, row, repeat! xxx

Amazing, inspirational, strong team of women. You're excellent role models for my teenage daughter. Well done, from Leeds, Yorkshire. #thisgirlcan

Really inspiring, watching you all. I am nervous about travelling alone, yet seeing all of you conquer so much has given me a kick up the backside. Stop feeling sorry for myself and get up and on. Well done. Incredible. Best of luck with the next challenge, whatever that may be.

Girls, u r shamazing!!! U have inspired me… Have signed up for beginners rowing course. Watch out – that record of yours is looking shaky!

The level of support out there was humbling, and we'd had no idea!

'A friend of mine sent me a text, saying, "I can see you on Yellow Brick, you're only a few miles out. Bet you never get this message,"' said Frances, 'and so I replied instantly. She said, "Oh, I'm crying now!" It was really lovely.'

'I texted Lucy because Lucy and Henry weren't in Antigua,' said Helen. 'So I texted them to say we'd be there in the morning, just so they didn't hear it from anybody else. I wanted to let them know that we had done it and that we were safe. Lucy was in her French lesson when she got the message to say that we were nearly there. She replied saying how proud she was of me and how happy she was that we were all safe. She said she'd let Henry know. I then got a message from the mum of the boy sitting next to Lucy in French, who'd obviously passed on the news! She was apparently in tears at the joy of our arrival! It was a very special moment. I was incredibly impressed with the way my children had coped with such a huge change in their lives. They were my inspiration. Both their parents had gone away at the same time, which had not been part of the plan, but they had not moaned, complained or anything. They had just got on with it in a positive way. I was extremely proud of them. And could not wait to see them when I got back.' Helen later found out that one of Henry's teachers had been moved to tears reading what Helen had blogged about her children – coincidentally, just as the teacher was marking Henry's schoolwork.

At sunrise we saw land for the first time in two and a half months.

'It does not look real,' said Janette, staring. 'It looks like somebody has just dropped a piece of land there in the middle of the ocean. It looks completely out of place, cluttering up the horizon.'

We had 10 miles to go as we packed up our things and gave *Rose* a final tidy. She was about to meet her public, so we wanted her to look her best. We were also trying to occupy ourselves as we waited for the support boat to escort us in. Helen had been trying to raise ABSAR for the last few hours on the radio. We'd all been listening to her flirting with other boats on the emergency channel 16. It was good to hear that after nine weeks on the Atlantic she had not lost her touch.

And then we saw it. The rescue boat coming towards us over the horizon.

'There they are!' Janette's voiced cracked. 'Over there!'

'Oh my God!' Niki stood on the deck, her hands over her mouth. It was impossible to believe it was nearly over. We could see some people waving on the deck. Not long now. Our on-board radio crackled down below in the office. Frances leapt at it.

'Hello, ladies!' said Carsten over the radio. 'Congratulations! Welcome to Antigua! You are world record holders! You are the oldest women's crew to have ever rowed the Atlantic! How do you feel?'

He'd been the one who'd pushed us off all those weeks ago in La Gomera. And his was the first real voice of home that we heard.

We were ecstatic! We were leaping about in the boat, hugging and kissing each other. We had done it! Against all the odds, all the doubters, we were officially the oldest women to have rowed the Atlantic. It was an extraordinary feeling.

'And you've come twenty-second in the race!' exclaimed Carsten.

'Twenty-second?' asked Helen.

'Yes, well done!'

'I knew 22 had to come in somewhere,' said Helen. 'It wasn't the date, it was our position!'

We were giddy, we were shaking, we were crying, we were hugging each other. We'd done it! We'd made it all the way across. We'd finished. Well, almost…

There was the small matter of rowing into the harbour first!

So we settled down for one last push. With Janette, our skipper, at the helm we set sail for the port. None of us had any idea what to expect.

'We were really worried while we were on the Atlantic that there would be nobody there to see us in,' said Helen. 'And I had a dream that we rowed into this industrial marina with nobody there. We were saying we were so late coming in that no one's going to be there.'

Three miles left... Then two miles... We were rowing three up, as we couldn't wait to get there. Carsten was on the radio alongside us, shouting words of encouragement. Then, as we neared the harbour, the sea teamed with little RIB boats buzzing about us. On board were groups of people filming, taking photos, shouting and waving at us.

The official finish line for the race was a staging post just before we entered the harbour, which was marked with buoys. The foghorn sounded as we crossed it, there was cheering from the surrounding boats and we stood up and hugged each other again. We had actually done it! We were handed champagne, the Yorkshire flag and huge signs saying, 'We've just rowed the Atlantic!' and then we lit flares while we posed for photographs!

'It was so emotional,' said Janette.

'It hit you all at once,' said Frances. 'And then suddenly we realised... SHIT! Our hands were on fire!'

Seriously, on fire. Not just a little bit burnt. Really quite badly burnt by the flares we were all holding – completely incorrectly, of course: upside down (the instructions were in Spanish).

'We were so emotional and happy we didn't feel it at first,' said Janette. 'And then suddenly the pain hit us! We were burning our own hands!'

They dropped the flares as Niki brilliantly leapt at the medical kit and pulled out the burn cream, hurling it at Janette. She and Frances slathered their hands with the stuff before we got back on the oars. We still had to enter the harbour. With half the crew's hands dripping with Flamazine, we powered around the corner as best as four middle-aged mums who've just rowed an ocean possibly could. The noise was incredible. All these horns started blasting, and we could hear the crowds cheering. Then one of the many super-yachts moored up started to play 'Here Come the Girls', 'Don't Stop Me Now' and 'Ladies' Night' at full blast over their sound system. We heard people shouting our names and we saw all these faces. It was magnificent and disorientating at the same time.

'All these little RIBs were coming towards us with people in them. There were faces, faces everywhere. All smiling, all cheering,' said Janette.

There were so many little boats crowding around us, so many people yelling and waving and crying. It was completely overwhelming. The blasting horns, the cheering crews lined up on deck on the huge yachts. We didn't know where to look, what to take in, who to wave to.

'In one of the tiny boats were my sister, Jane, and her husband, Ricardo. I didn't notice them at all!' said Janette. 'In the same boat as them was a couple we'd met in La Gomera, Ruth and John, who'd sailed down to Antigua to meet us. I didn't know my sister and her husband were going to be there, so I'm waving at Ruth and John, and Ricardo and Jane are sat in the same boat as them, but I didn't see them. The whole thing was very surreal.'

Slowly we came in, weaving our way through all the little boats, listening to the wall of sound. Janette was still at the helm, grinning broadly. On the quay we could see our families waving and crying. They had Yorkshire Rows banners and T-shirts. We were desperate to get there. Finally, as we pulled in alongside the quay, Janette threw the ropes. No one can remember who caught them. We were all so overwhelmed; we were moored up, about to step onto dry land, at last.

'We were all dying to leap off the boat,' said Frances, 'but we had to sit there while people took more and more photos. And then we were released.'

Niki and Frances leapt off the boat first. 'I could just see Mark and the children on the quayside and made eye contact with them as I came in,' said Frances. 'Then I got off and gave Mark a huge hug. And then I hugged the children. Apparently they'd been arguing before I arrived. They'd said, "Who do you think she's going to hug and kiss first? You don't want to be third, do you?" So it was fortunate that I did a double hug and hugged them both at the same time!'

'I was so disorientated,' said Niki. 'I was like a rabbit in the headlights. I was so excited to see Gareth and the children, but I found it very hard to speak. I just wanted to keep hugging them all. I had spent the entire journey dreaming of this moment when we were all together again. With the attention and the crowds, I think I was completely bewildered. We were all looking around like we could not believe it. It was a sensory overload.'

Janette was the next off the boat. 'It was hard to walk. Ben came towards me and put his arms around me, and I held on to him so tightly, as if I'd never let him go. I was sobbing and sobbing, shaking all over, and he just kept saying, "It's OK – you're here, I'm here, it's OK".

'When I did eventually let go of him a bit, he said, "Look who else is here!" and there was my sister Jane and her husband Ricardo. I'd had no idea. I let go of Ben and threw my arms around Jane, saying, "I can't believe you're here – oh my God, thank you, thank you for coming". I couldn't really stand; Jane and Ben were holding me up.'

'It was very powerful to watch,' said Helen. 'I was still on the boat and I couldn't believe what I was seeing. Janette crying. I have never seen anyone cry like that before.'

'I was so, so relieved,' said Janette. 'I was utterly relieved. I had done it. I had brought them all home safely. It felt like a mammoth weight had been lifted off my shoulders. I had been responsible for other people's mums and wives, and I had really felt it. If we had not made it, it would have been my fault. We were safe. Those girls were safe. That was my sole purpose. If it didn't work out, if something went wrong, I was the skipper and I was the one going down with the ship. I was the one who had to keep everything together.'

So Janette wept and wept. 'I think my sister was a little surprised!'

Helen came off the boat. 'Neither my husband nor my children were there,' she said. 'Richard was in the Isle of Man with his new job and my children had exams – Lucy had her GCSE mock – so my mum very sweetly came on her own. It was lovely to see her. She's 81 years old!' So apart from her mum, there was no great reunion for Helen. 'It was odd. I came off the boat and just started chatting to people. I said hi to Bella and Olivia, from Row Like a Girl. I have to admit I was a little jealous of those who did have their children there, but Lucy's education was more important. I'd see them all soon and it was lovely to spend some time with my mum, and in the end, perhaps it made the next few days a lot easier.'

In fact, the next few days were very odd indeed. Straight off the boat, we were taken to be photographed and interviewed. None of us could walk – our calves were so withered and our balance so confused, after all those days at sea, that we lurched around like four drunks on a hen night. Carsten and all the race officials had to support us, hold us up, as we walked. In our first interview all you can see are our confused faces and rictus smiles as we hug each other and sway from side to side in perpetual motion. At some point in the chaos and the hugs and the questions, Janette and Frances were handed some ice cubes to help with their very badly burnt hands.

The confusion and the melee continued; there were hundreds of people asking for photos, slapping us on the back. There appeared to be people from Yorkshire everywhere. 'Hey, we're from York!' we heard. 'We're from Bradford! We've been waiting for days for you lot to come in!'

And after we'd spoken to a litany of cameras, answering the same questions over and over – were we proud? Amazed? Stunned that we'd made it? And would we do it again? – Janette and Frances were taken to a medi-centre to have their hands bandaged. And Janette promptly collapsed.

'I had a giant wobble,' she said. 'My legs gave way under me and I very nearly passed out. It was the shock of finishing, the release of responsibility and perhaps my severely burnt hands.'

While Frances and Janette were being bandaged, Helen and Niki ended up eating a slap-up brunch on their own at the restaurant on the harbour where everything was laid out with proper napkins, knives and forks, and little pillows on the seats.

All we really wanted to drink was Coca-Cola – there was something about the mixture of bubbles and sugar that was exactly what we craved. So we did! Some very thoughtful friends of Frances arrived at the quay with a giant cooler of joy, packed with champagne (plus flutes), beer and gallons of chilled coke. Lovely. And just what every transatlantic rower ordered!

We were also desperate for a bath and some quiet time to reflect. Our sudden re-emergence into the real world was proving to be a lot more difficult than we'd anticipated. The noise and the speed with which everything was moving were completely disorientating. We had not thought there would be so much interest; we hadn't realised how many people would want a piece of us and how many questions there would be. We were constantly being asked to comment on something we ourselves had yet to digest.

'I didn't want to speak to anyone initially about the row,' said Niki. 'I had so many thoughts going through my head, so many emotions I was trying to deal with. I found it very difficult to communicate. I just wanted to hear all about what Gareth and the kids had been doing – it seemed so long since we'd had that chance to talk.'

It was that age-old thing we were all too familiar with, of trying to be all things to all people, and just ending up being ripped in half.

While Janette and Ben had sensibly booked into a small place in English Harbour, where all the action was taking place and where we had to be for all our media commitments, the rest of us were in an all-inclusive resort on the other side of the island.

'When we got to the hotel, everyone knew who we were,' said Niki. 'Our families had been there a week already, and so everywhere we went everyone wanted a chat and a photo. I wanted to see my parents, my children and my lovely husband, but at the same time it was all so very overwhelming.'

'We were all a bit down and a bit odd,' said Helen. 'And frankly a little bit off-kilter. Personally, I was just desperate for a bath and to wash my hair.'

We all went into our own separate (luxury) bathrooms. Frances dyed her hair, Janette gave hers a deep conditioning treatment, Niki had a blow-dry and Helen stood under the shower, pouring coconut oil all over her stiff block of hair, hoping and praying she could get it to move in any way at all.

Helen's hair was a disaster. 'I could cope on that boat with 40-foot waves, the hurricane, two hours' sleep and everything. I just could not cope with what happened to my hair.'

Back on day two of our journey, Helen had made a fatal error. Unlike the rest of us, who'd opted for plaits and who, despite the increasing filthiness of our hair, had continued to brush it and plait and re-plait it, Helen, as she simply could not bear to touch her own dirty mop, had tied it up in a bunch and left it.

'Apparently, it was the worst thing I could have done. If you talk to proper sailing people, they'll tell you never to wear bobbles other than at the end of a plait. It was a schoolgirl mistake! But I had ruined my hair. The others had all gone and had showers and they all looked amazing, and I still had this bandana on my head and this matted mess, thinking, "What on earth am I going do?" Everybody told me I needed to go to a hairdresser. One of the *BBC Breakfast* crew told me I'd look lovely with an Audrey Hepburn pixie cut, as it was obvious that I was going to lose the lot! So my first night was just miserable. I looked crap and I went to bed at 9 p.m. I think my mum was a bit annoyed, as she wanted to go out partying! At 81!'

All of us seemed to adapt to sleeping back in a normal bed relatively easily. Stories that we'd read about other rowers rowing in their sleep, sobbing all night or waking up feverishly to start their shift did not apply to us. Frances dreamt about rowing. Niki was just relieved she could breathe properly, and Helen and Janette were out cold after one glass of wine. The only real problem was our painful buttocks, our hugely swollen hands (we were still unable to wear our wedding rings) and our inability to walk. We each had to hang onto the lavatory every time we went to the loo. But frankly we were used to that.

The next day we woke up at 3 a.m. to do a live interview with *BBC Breakfast*. 'I remember thinking, "I can't believe that I've been on a boat for 67 days, only having an hour and a half sleep, and I've got to get up at three o'clock, my first night in my bed,"' said Helen. 'I think Mark was a bit annoyed... He wasn't happy that we were being asked to do that, but I could understand that *BBC Breakfast*'s Jayne McCubbin had flown over to Antigua, and the show had been so supportive of us, every step of the way, so we had to – we wanted to. They had been so very kind to us in the past.'

In fact, the next few days were quite fraught as we struggled to fulfil all of our commitments and be mums.

'My children were very bored with me being so busy,' said Frances. 'It was the most expensive holiday we've ever had,' said Frances. 'And it's my children's least favourite.'

'I wasn't torn, because my children didn't come,' said Janette. 'But I could see that everyone else was. All the rowers, the race organisers, the TV producers, all those people we had got to know over the years, were all in Antigua and they wanted to go for a few drinks with us.'

The second night was the most difficult. There was a party for everyone who had been involved in the challenge and there was one question: were the husbands going to come? Or were they going to stay at the hotel and look after the children?

In the end, Gareth came out, leaving the kids with Niki's parents, Bunny and Pete, and Mark stayed in.

'Mark said to me, "This is your gig, it's your party, so go and have a fabulous time,"' said Frances. 'He didn't know many of the people who would be there that night, and he said he didn't want me to feel I had to spend time with him when I should be celebrating with the other crews and race people. And, of course, there was no one else to look after the boys.'

'I really wanted Gareth with me,' said Niki. 'So he came.'

'Ben was in a slightly different situation,' said Janette. 'He had been there every day, every step of the race, so he also knew a lot of the people involved. But it was very difficult for the other husbands. We were all kindred spirits; we'd been through the same experience, which was very bonding. We were all being salty sea dogs together, and letting our hair down. Well, most of us were.'

Back to Helen's hair…

'Bella, from Row Like a Girl, said there was a really good hairdresser in English Harbour, so I went to her. I remember there was a boy sitting next to me in the chair and he said: "Oh, I've got a dreadlock, I've got a dreadlock!" And I said: "Look at this, mate." And he went "Urgh!" The hairdresser was lovely and she poured loads of coconut oil on my head, and then I sat in a chair and basically she was pulling out the lump, hair by hair, using a needle. But you could tell she was thinking, "This is not going to work." I was in there for about eight hours.

'Sitting next to me was this lovely woman, an American called Jessica, but her nickname was Gassy, and she said: "Oh, are you one of the Yorkshire women?" I said yes and explained the story of the hair. She said: "Do you know what? I'm going to help you get your hair straight." Because the other three, my dear friends who I had just rowed the Atlantic with, clearly had no interest in trying to sort my hair out whatsoever. My mother couldn't do it, and I couldn't do it on my own. So Gassy got out of her seat and, while she was having her hair highlighted and covered in foils, she started on mine. Then she was on the phone to her friend Jackie, saying, "I've got one of the Yorkshire ladies here. I need your help. She's got a massive dreadlock and we need to get it out." She was amazing. I was then pulled out of the hairdresser's to be interviewed by National Geographic and, as I left, Jessica said: "Come back tomorrow and we'll sort your hair out."

'She was like an angel. It was like I'd put it out there. So the next day, I took a taxi with my mum to find Jessica and it turned out she was a chef on a super-yacht. Unfortunately, my mum couldn't manage it up the gangplank of the yacht, so we sat on a bench in the harbour as Jessica picked at my hair with a meat probe, which was the finest, sharpest bit of metal she could find in the kitchen. And we just chatted and got to know each other while she was trying to unpick my hair. That was day two.

'On day three, my mum and I went back to see Jessica again. I sat down again and this time there was Jackie and someone called Jane, who's actually from Antigua, all having a go. I took loads of paracetamol, as it was now beginning to hurt. Before it had been so rock hard that I couldn't feel a thing, but the closer it got to the scalp, the more it hurt. Janette came past at one point and started to laugh, saying only *I* could have so many people working on my hair. It was the princess delegating... again!'

Eventually the dreadlock disappeared and Helen returned to the disbelieving hairdresser, whose mouth slowly opened in shock.

'I booked in for a colour, a cut and a wash, and it was just the most amazing thing. I had my hair back. It was in a terrible condition, but at least I didn't have to have it shaved off. Now Jessica emails me and we talk all the time. I don't know what I would have done if I hadn't met her. I'm so *glad* now that that actually happened to my hair, because I've met this lovely woman who I'll probably know forever.'

We wound up our interviews and started saying our goodbyes, getting ready to go home.

'We didn't want to let it go,' said Frances. 'And yet, in a way, we needed to. It was time for us to get on and do other things.'

The night before we left, we were all sitting in Janette's bedroom overlooking English Harbour. There was talk of watching one of the last two boats come in – Rowing for Rascals. But frankly we weren't sure we were up to it. We'd watched Coventry Five-O and Thrift Atlantic Energy arrive a few days before and both Janette and Frances had broken down.

'I didn't cry when we finished, but I did when I saw Coventry Five-O arrive,' said Frances.

'His daughters were there for Thrift Atlantic,' said Janette. 'His little daughters. They ran and yelled. It was so emotional.'

So we sat up in Janette's room, having a final farewell glass of wine as we looked at our extraordinary photographs, taken before and after the race.

'The befores were taken in La Gomera,' said Niki. 'They were very close up and all you can see are these very chubby, stressed, tired faces. The afters were taken as soon as we arrived on the other side in Antigua. We all looked five years younger. We looked completely different. There were no bags, no jowls – we were shining. We looked better. We all looked so, so happy.

All in all, we each lost between 1½ and 2 stone. We all dropped at least one dress size.

'Guess what?' said Janette, appearing in the doorway of the bathroom.

'What?' said Frances, turning around to see the vision before her.

'I can fit into the sodding shorts!'

It was true. The green-and-turquoise piped shorts were over the hips and fitting nicely around the waist. They were still a little tight over the thighs, but who was really looking? They were on! And that's what mattered!

'Well,' said Frances, raising a glass. 'To the real reason we crossed the Atlantic in the first place!'

SHIP'S LOG:

'When you accomplish something you have been wanting so much, the feeling is absolutely out of this world, and when you accomplish it with three other strong and amazing women there is nothing quite like that girl-power feeling. No one can ever take your accomplishment away from you. It will stay with you for the rest of your life.'

(JANETTE/SKIPPER)

CHAPTER 16

Re-entry

'The only time you should ever look back is to see
how far you have come.'

ANON

Of all the books we had read, all the people we had spoken to and
all the advice we'd sought, we never questioned or considered what it
would be like to return home. We had been so focused on the race, on
getting to La Gomera, and then we had been so determined to finish,
to cross the ocean, that we had not really thought about what would
happen afterwards.

'We planned to get to Antigua. That was that,' said Helen. 'But we
didn't plan for what happened later. We all felt weird when we got home,
and we had some serious communication problems. It is a massive jolt to
the system. I would say to any other teams, just plan for when you get off
the boat and be really careful, because there were a couple of teams I met
who said they'd fallen out with their rowing partners afterwards. I think
it is quite easy to do. We worked really hard at being friends across the
Atlantic and it worked, but what we didn't plan for was how we would
feel when we got off the boat.'

The speed, the noise, the voices and the bustle were unexpected, but
so was the media interest in our story. Suddenly we were asked to give

interviews, guest on radio shows and go on various TV shows, which some of us were much less enthusiastic about than others.

But we had commitments and we also wanted to raise money for our charities, and what better way to do that than exposure? Although the kind of exposure that Helen achieved on *BBC Breakfast* was perhaps not completely what she, or indeed we, were after. Poor Helen. No one is quite sure how it happened but during an interview, as we sat on the sofa with Dan Walker and Louise Minchin, chatting about our trip, they showed some footage of us rowing – only for the camera to pull back and reveal that Helen was devoid of chafe-free pants. Naturally, viewer outrage ensued and pictures of Helen's pixelated bits were plastered all over the newspapers.

'Of course it was me! It had to be me. I wasn't that bothered, to be honest, only it was difficult for my children, as it started trending on Twitter and my son was shown the footage on the way into homework club. But truthfully, I just felt very sorry for the editor. People can make mistakes, poor chap. He was so apologetic. I went up afterwards and said I was fine about it.'

We went from Ant and Dec to *BBC Breakfast* to *This Morning* to *Welcome to Yorkshire*. For the first couple of weeks after we got back our feet did not really touch the ground. It was an extraordinary whirlwind, which we did enjoy, but at the same it taught us to watch what we said and look out for each other, because it's very easy for one person's flip-pant joke to become someone else's grave offence. And there were a few moments over those first few days when one of us, particularly Helen, became very upset. Hugely upset.

It wasn't really anyone's fault. We had yet to get home, we'd been on the go ever since we'd touched down in London, Helen's fanny was trending on Twitter, which is enough to make anyone feel more than a little vulnerable, and then Frances cracked a joke – a silly joke at a press conference about Helen's night-time steering.

'It was a stupid joke, but what a salutary lesson in what not to say to journalists!' said Frances.

The next day her glib comments appeared in a newspaper, out of context and without any of the gentle humour attached.

'I felt Frances had embarrassed me. She'd said something about me nearly killing them at sea due to my bad steering. This was a joke, but in print it didn't come across like that. We were in a hotel room, going on *This Morning* the following day, when I read it in the bath. Frances and I were sharing a room and I just felt like I'd had enough.'

'I was mortified,' said Frances. 'I would never pretend to be perfect, but the last thing I would ever do is intentionally hurt the feelings of one of my friends. Helen refused to speak to me until the next day. It was a very long night.'

The following morning we all had breakfast together before going to the TV studios, and over the croissants and coffee, we talked it out – not just the night-time steering comment, but everything that had been said at one point or another that had caused upset. Eventually we were all in tears, saying how much we loved each other.

'This was my low point of the entire experience,' said Frances. 'Ironic, in the end, that my low point didn't happen on the boat, but after we had completed the race and were back in the UK.'

'We were all in tears over the breakfast table. We had mainly all kept it together on the boat, and then we were really struggling on dry land. I don't think we realised how tough it had been. But we were much stronger for that argument,' said Helen. 'We're more like sisters now. I think we probably were when we had that huge row. I don't think I would have had that row with them all if I hadn't felt so close to them. We've been through all the emotions we could possibly go through. I do think we are very close together, and we'll always have that special bond. Always.'

'They are like family now,' said Niki. 'And part of it is because it's not superficial. With a lot of friends you've never had a falling out, and you've not built a relationship. It's always been nice and easy. Whereas we've been through such a lot together these three years – we've had good times and bad times, we have all bickered and got through it. I think that's when you get to a really deep relationship: when you can get through all that and still want to be with each other. It's quite nice when it's not perfect. It's just sharing that level of experience and being able to get through it. But it wasn't just about the Atlantic, because the Atlantic was just a little part of it. The harder bit was leading up to that start line. That was the true test, I think. The Atlantic's going to challenge anybody. Everyone's going to go through similar stuff on the Atlantic, but before that, to get to where we did and to do what we did together, that was the difficult bit.'

Having lived and breathed as a foursome for so long, we had become so used to each other's company that we all felt it very profoundly when we came home.

'I was taken away from them straight away, because Ben and I had a nice hotel to stay in in Antigua, just the two of us,' said Janette. 'But I was a bit jealous because I thought, "They're all together still, and I'm not." And for the first couple of days I thought, "We should have all booked into the same resort, we should all have been together." But then I was so glad to see Ben that it quickly disappeared. It was lovely that it was just the two of us, but I also needed to be able to spend some time together with the girls so that it wasn't too traumatic, the separation. And it was a separation. It was definitely a separation. I do feel very close to them now and I really do miss the intimacy that we had on the boat.'

'I'd had enough of everybody initially when we got back,' said Niki. 'But after about three or four weeks, slowly but surely I wanted to see them again, and now, if something happens, I always want to pick up the phone and share it with them straight away. It's nice now that we've started to put more things in the diary. When we first came back we were doing a lot of Yorkshire Rows stuff, which was fine. We were seeing each other, but all we were doing was turning up at an event, having to be very sociable, and then leaving. It didn't feel like the old days – having a laugh, sitting around and sharing our gossip. We've started to do that again now. We've started doing yoga together and other bits and pieces, and that's quite nice because I feel like it's gone back to how it was.'

For the first few days, we also found the pace at which everything was moving very disconcerting. Having been in our watery paradise for so long, we found even the most normal and banal things extremely strange. 'I got into the car from the airport in London and I could not believe how fast the cars were going,' said Janette. 'I was really distracted and I kept on telling Ben to slow down. I kept saying, "This is far too fast," and he said, "This is how fast you drive!" I suppose I had been travelling at two to three miles an hour for months, so anything over 25mph was going to get my pulse racing!'

Fortunately, our husbands, friends and family were incredibly supportive and understanding at our re-entry back into the world, just as they had been through those entire three years.

'They have all been amazing. We could not have done anything without every single one of them,' said Janette. 'The fact that there were so many people supporting us made us determined not to give up. When you've got people backing you and supporting you, you don't want to disappoint them. I think the support that we had from very early on, until we got close to the race, certainly got us to the finish line – the fact that people believed in us and were saying, "Go on, girls!" You didn't want to let them down.'

'It's only when you get back that you learn what everyone else has been doing,' said Niki. 'Gareth had spent a lot of time keeping all our friends, supporters and sponsors updated on our progress through emails and Facebook. What a huge task! And on top of everything else he was dealing with, he did all that just for us. Good friends and complete strangers had also raised money through cake and cookie sales, sending all the money to our charities. And our lovely parents, Pete, Bunny and Karen, had helped to make things easier for Gareth and the kids while I was away. I will never be able to repay everyone's kindness and generosity – it does make you realise how much love and generosity there is out there.'

The good people of Burn village did finally turn off their Christmas lights in honour of our safe arrival. We also learned that a regular at the Wheatsheaf Inn in Burn had put a £1 coin in a tin every night we were out at sea, as had many others, and together they'd raised over £1,000, which was fantastically generous.

'It's a real village community, and they'd followed us and supported us every step of the way,' said Janette. 'And when we got back we found out that the BBC had gone into the pub while we were at sea and filmed them. They were all doing this "Eat, sleep, row, repeat" rhyme, which is brilliant.'

And our husbands? Our children? Did they cope? Did they miss us? Were we as invaluable as we had thought? Did the world that clearly revolved around us collapse as soon as we had gone?

'As far as I can work out, they had real fun,' said Frances. 'Rather annoyingly, they almost didn't notice that I was gone! They just got on with things. They have such busy lives that even when I rang they were hardly ever there because they were off at their friend's house or at a party. They did also rather brilliantly accuse me of being quite irritating when I got back. I kept on saying, "That is not important! That is froth!" Now I'm in a much better place. With the passing of time, I can see that some things are completely trivial, and others are not, and others are worth making a fuss about! I am much more patient. But it is amazing how

quickly things return to normal. My boys did love the whole experience
and they loved that first day in Antigua when we arrived at the harbour.
They loved being in La Gomera as well, at the start, and seeing all those
fantastically fit sportsmen and women, and us, competing on a sort of
level playing field with everybody else. They got all that. If I overhear
them talking to their friends about it they say they're "so proud" of their
mum. And it's not often you hear that. I see that sometimes Jack will
put #yorkshirerows or something on his Instagram. Quietly, they're very
proud. In fact, my older one, Jay, talks about it a lot. And Jack, I think he
just wants to know I'm completely back, and I'm not going off again. For
all of us, to a degree, we're hanging onto the adventure because we've
had such a good time.'

In Niki's family the reaction was similar. 'They were very proud. I
think my father, Pete, enjoyed the whole thing almost as much as I did.
He was there every step of the way. And Gareth? He is so utterly proud
of me! Every so often he just stops, looks at me, gives me the biggest
hug and tells me how amazing I am and asks if I can believe what we
have achieved. It makes every hardship experienced worth it. Both my
boys had a lot of fun while I was away, as they had so much going on
and so many invitations and people visiting, but you can see that they
like us being together again. There were so many parents at school who
were very kind. It does make you realise that you have a lot of special
people in your lives.'

And for Helen it has always been about the positivity.

'I wanted my children to be part of the whole journey, which they
have been. They went to the North Sea. They went to Southwold. They
met Greg from South Africa and they met Ocean Reunion when we
rowed the North Sea. They met those amazing characters who are "can
do", who climbed Everest. Extraordinary people you don't get to meet
very often. I've got a great picture of Henry with Perfecto Sanchez, an

ex-army entrepreneur from New York who became the first American to
row the North Sea. He's a fantastic bloke and Henry's helping him fold
the American flag. So they would never have experienced any of that,
and they have absorbed all that positivity. They're talking about wanting
to do similar things and I just think that's why I wanted to do it, because
I wanted them to get that "I can do anything" mentality.'

'I really miss the ocean,' said Janette. 'It's addictive. I would love to be
back out there again – it is like being on another planet. Ben has sailed
a lot and understands what it's like to be out at sea for a long period of
time, so I am very fortunate that he knows how long it takes to cross an
ocean, and how difficult it can be to adjust to normal life afterwards. The
whole adventure was incredible.'

And what of us? What did we learn from rowing 3,000 miles, battling a hurricane, living in a space about twice the size of a family car
with nothing but Bounce Balls, whales, the stars and *Mamma Mia!* for
sustenance, company and entertainment?

Frances:

'What did I learn? That if you want to change your life, you can. If I can
do it, anyone can. Just because you are a parent and a wife and you work,
you can still have an adventure. Life is risky, but it's worth taking risks.
You never know what is going to happen or what is round the corner:
"*A brand new start or the bitter end.*"

'I think I am a textbook introvert – my favourite night out really is
staying at home and reading a book! I was worried before I set off that I
would struggle to be in the constant company of other people, but being
able to retreat into the cabin several times a day on my own proved to
be plenty of time for me to recharge. I don't think I would have enjoyed
rowing solo. I wanted to be able to share this wonderful adventure, and

the memories the four of us have of those weeks on the ocean will stay with us for the rest of our lives. No matter how hard we try, I don't think it's possible to accurately describe what it feels like to cross an ocean in a rowing boat, but the four of us do know, and we have a very deep bond as a result. This trip has made me believe that I can do absolutely anything. I have a place in the Marathon des Sables in 2018, and there is no doubt in my mind that I will do it. But I'll just do it on my own, and I'll go out there, give it my best, make some new friends and have a really great time. One of my favourite quotations is from Theodore Roosevelt:

> It is not the critic who counts; not the man who points out how the strong man stumbles, or where the doer of deeds could have done them better. The credit belongs to the man who is actually in the arena, whose face is marred by dust and sweat and blood; who strives valiantly; who errs, who comes short again and again, because there is no effort without error and shortcoming; but who does actually strive to do the deeds; who knows great enthusiasms, the great devotions; who spends himself in a worthy cause; who at the best knows in the end the triumph of high achievement, and who at the worst, if he fails, at least fails while daring greatly, so that his place shall never be with those cold and timid souls who neither know victory nor defeat.

'That really resonates with me. What matters is what we think of ourselves and not what others think of us. I was at this dinner on Friday night, talking to another lawyer whom I've only met a few times, but she seems very similar to me in lots of ways, and she said: "Some people just moan about it, and some people do something about it. And you *have* done something about it."

'My life–work balance is out of control again, but this time I can handle it better. I am now focusing on the Marathon des Sables. I can't wait. I am so excited. Fulfilling a dream doesn't fill a hole; what it does do is open up a world of possibilities that I want a bit more of. So I will keep doing events like the Marathon des Sables, and I am doing a London-to-Paris cycle ride. I still feel that restlessness. But I now have no regrets. If I were to die tomorrow, I think I have used my time well. I have met amazing people and have had extraordinary experiences and I have loved and been loved. A few years ago, because of my work, I felt downtrodden. I don't feel downtrodden any more.'

Niki:

'For me, I realised what it was to be patient. I was Mrs Structured. And not knowing when I was even going to get there was my greatest challenge. Everything was a chore – eating, sleeping, going to the toilet, changing and repairing the wheel bearings in my two hours. But I soon realised I could only do one thing at a time. It is like the art of Zen.

'Watching the waves on deck, flowing past the boat, you were always rowing and watching the waves flow away from you, the up and down motions, the cresting waves and the rocking motion of the boat – it was sometimes like being hypnotised. It could be incredibly calming and almost spiritual. I can remember at night, my favourite moments were on deck, the boat skimming across the waves, the stars lighting up the skies and listening to the sounds of the sea and feeling at peace with the world.

'It was my time, and it gave me a chance to think things through, stuff that maybe before I went I hadn't been happy with, to really try to understand it in an environment that's so removed from everything. It was almost like a therapy boat for me. Sometimes I was upset when my two-hour rowing stint was over. There is nothing like repetitive exercise to set your brain free.

'Since coming back, I've started to put in place some of the things I decided I would change while I was out there. And that's what I've found really exciting. Some of them are small, stupid things, like the frustration of constantly having to tidy up the house. Out there, I decided that actually I needed to simplify my life, simplify my house and everything in it. And I've started. I've been through every single item of clothing I have, and every book on my shelves. I've been through all sorts of stuff. I'm slowly working my way through the house and I am simplifying everything. And that's helped counterbalance that unsettled feeling – because I can see something I've got out of that journey. 'Normally, New Year's resolutions just go out of the window immediately – I'm not very good at keeping things up – but this time it's been easier. There've been so many things that I've done or I've changed since I've come back, and I would never have instigated that sort of change without the challenge. And I also decided to try and get more involved in my children's interests. I have been involved in helping out at my son's junior rugby for a number of years and I decided I wanted to do this properly so I've got myself qualified as a Level 1 Rugby Coach. It's not something I would have committed to previously but is important to me to show my boys that you can continue to try new things and do things a little differently. And this has led to me working with York RUFC to set up a brand new girls section for 11–17 year olds to offer them the same opportunities as the boys in our local area. You take the first step and all of a sudden all these other opportunities come out of it, quite amazing!

'One of my resolutions is to be less focused, because I am very detail-conscious. If you'd seen me as a child you'd have thought I should be living in some commune somewhere, painting pictures or making something. You wouldn't have me down as a conscientious, detail oriented businessperson in any way, shape or form. But I am trying to change. Normally I would be over everything. But now I'm not. 'I was really cautious before, and that caution seems to have gone. I feel liberated. I don't seem to overthink things in the same way. I am much less anxious and worried. I've slept better since I've come back than ever before.' The overriding lesson I seem to have gained from the journey we took is an real appreciation for those people who surround us. You do realise the happiness you have in life comes from being with your amazing family and friends, and not the 'stuff' you gather on the way.'

Helen:

'Everyone should have what they consider to be an adventure, no matter how small. There is opportunity everywhere. There are so many things you can do, achieve and contribute to, which before I would have thought I would not be able to do. Now I think, "Why not?" You don't have to be brilliant at it. You can have a go and be part of something.

'It's true what Carsten says. I didn't agree or believe him at the time, until I'd done it myself, because I thought, "I'm a 45-year-old woman, it's not going to happen to me." But Carsten says that the people he says goodbye to (because he shakes your hand when you set off) and the people he welcomes back to Antigua are very different people. When you step off that boat, you'll be a different person. And it is completely true. You have nine weeks of pure thinking time on that boat, and water's very emotional. When I stepped off that boat I was very different indeed.'

For Helen, even though she was perhaps the toughest of all of us on the ocean, her return to Yorkshire has been a little more problematic.

Her children, Henry and Lucy, have been amazing. 'I will never forget seeing them in Arrivals at Heathrow, with their shiny smiles! Their lives were by far the most disrupted – they had to board at school and stayed with their granny at weekends, but they had been so consistently positive about the whole thing. Henry plotted our journey on a chart, making a huge collage. He researched every team and told us all the time where we were on Yellow Brick.'

Every time Helen called home Henry would offer up some piece of advice or helpful hint. He was genuinely involved, right down to suggesting ocean-friendly shampoo. Lucy has now vowed to row her own ocean. 'She is like me – she won't stop! She did a 25-mile sponsored walk the other day and was one of the few to finish.'

However, Helen and Richard's relationship has moved to a different place. While he is living and working in the Isle of Man, she has – for the moment – opted to stay put in York while their children are at school.

'He's got his own adventure at the moment. He's very busy with that and he loves his new job, and his new life on the Isle of Man, so he's in a very different place. We've come back as different people and I definitely want to do more things and have more adventures. It was a difficult decision to make, but the right one. I think our children were not that keen to move either – their lives are here and they need to be listened to. Richard comes back and forth, and we go over there all the time. I know I can live independently quite happily.

'I have recently developed a real craving for mountains! Weirdly, I was sent a climbing rope in the post the other day – no one knows where it came from! I have looked and tried to work it out, but no one ordered it in our house. So, of course, it's a sign! I called up the local climbing centre and someone has just dropped out, so I am now booked in. I have climbed before, but now I'm taking it up again!

'This challenge has given me a real yen and a confidence to do things. I have gone back to work two days a week, and I want to do something with vulnerable young people. I don't think I could have been happy with a job on the Isle of Man, never leaving it. My focus is now the children, and getting them through their various exams. It sounds like a dual mid-life crisis, I know! But Richard was so miserable in his old job and I think he got to a point where he couldn't see what he could do to get out of it. And now he's fallen on his feet with an amazing job, plus he'd always wanted to live by the sea. Always. It's so weird how it all happened. I meditated and asked for a change in the household, and then this all happened. So it is all my fault!

'But that journey taught me how to be brave. It showed me that I can push my limits. When I was younger I didn't do lots of things because I was frightened of failing. I turned down my place at the London College of Fashion because I thought I wouldn't be able to do it. I would never do that now. Never. Richard gave me loads of confidence. And I gave it back to him. I told him, "You can go and change yourself," which he did. For me, the Atlantic made me realise that I could do a whole lot more with my life, and that I, in fact, need a whole lot less. I don't need half the stuff I have; it all seems very immaterial now. Our lives are very cluttered with a lot that is not very important.

'I think, for me, the success of our trip is that we're still wanting to do other things together. We haven't come off the boat and thought, "Well, I never want to do anything with them again." They are my best friends and they will be forever. And the other thing I have learnt? If you are suffering mentally, just sing! Preferably ABBA!'

Janette:

And Janette? Janette is the one who's convinced she's changed the least.

'What have I learned? I learned that I should have sat around and read the manuals before we left. We should have known how all our stuff worked before we set off. A lot of our problems could have been avoided if we'd only known how the equipment worked.

'What else? I never want to see Helen's fanny again! I still have visions of her walking towards me, naked except for her little socks and her life jacket, holding onto the ropes on either side of the boat!

'And what else would I change? Absolutely nothing. Readjusting has been difficult. Even now, I look at a lot of things and say, "Well, does it really matter?" When I came back I had to go straight to a meeting in the US, a leadership meeting that I go to every quarter, and I was sitting in the meeting and they were deliberating, like people do in meetings, with everybody inputting and discussing, and I just thought, "Why don't you just do it? Stop talking about it and just do it!" I must have been a little forthright because I remember one of my colleagues came up to me afterwards and she said, "This all must seem immaterial to you, having done that ocean row." She was right. It did. I asked, "Ooh, is it obvious?" And she said yes, because I was saying, "What are you waiting for? Let's just do it. Put those biscuits away and just get on with it!" But I have always been a bit like that!

'The ocean does settle you, if you let it. Even though it's rough, it's not scary. I wasn't scared in the storm. I knew we would do it. When you really believe in something, it happens. I knew it would be hard at times, but I always knew we'd get there. And I think that's why we did – we believed. That is the power of positive thought, and with that you can do anything.

'I also learnt how much I love the ocean. I am going back there in four years, this time with my husband, not rowing. We are selling up – well, not everything. We still have children to put through university and a business to run. But we are downsizing and getting a catamaran and going off to sail around the world. It's our dream, and you know what happens when you dream – it comes true!

'They are like sisters to me now, these girls, and it is great to have more sisters. I love all three of them, because they are all such different people.

'One of the biggest things I have realised is that less is more. You spend half your life acquiring stuff, material things, and then the rest of your life disposing of them, whereas what is really important is your friends and family and the memories you make, the adventures you have. These are what life is about. The kindness we offer to others, and the way we can help people in our lives, is what's important. Sometimes it takes an ocean to show us that. I have learnt so much and I am very grateful for the experience I have had. There are many paths we can choose to walk in life. We don't always walk them, even though they are there, and we should at least try them out. What have we got to lose?'

And what of *Rose*? To whom we entrusted our lives? Who looked after us for nine long weeks? Who kept us safe during those incredible three days while we were battered by a hurricane? *Rose,* who gave us so much joy?

Rose is up for sale.

'I love that boat,' said Helen. 'She's the fifth member of our team, without a doubt. So when she goes (which I hope she will do soon, because we need the money for the charities and it's all tied up in the boat) I might cry. Which is more than I did on the Atlantic.'

'I would love to keep her,' said Frances. 'I really would. But she has to go. We need to pay Janette what we still owe her, and the rest goes to charity.'

'She's not been in the water since we've been back,' said Janette. 'We took her to my niece's school. And we took her to Burn because of the lovely chap in the village who put in a pound to the pub collection every day that we were out at sea – apparently he got quite aggrieved when we were out there longer than we should have been! But that is it. It's weird, because I see her every day. She's in my drive. I see her bum sticking out of the shed that Ben made for her. I feel like I want to go and sit on her and just remember the feeling of being out there. I loved the night-time best. I'd be looking up, almost breaking my neck sometimes, just looking at the stars and rowing and thinking, "God, am I really here? Am I really doing this?" It was just… I can't put into words how it felt. It was amazing out there. I can understand how the sea can be a drug to people. I want to go back out there and have that experience again as soon as possible. Because everything in the world was taken away from me, and that meant I could truly be me, and in the moment. I've never had that feeling like I had out there on the sea. Maybe if I did some meditation or something I'd get there eventually. I see the boat and I think, "To get on her and go back out there would be incredible."'

'I think everyone should experience what we have experienced,' added Helen. 'Everyone should experience being out of their comfort zone. You learn such a lot. Having said that, an adventure is different for everyone. But everyone should try something new. That's how we ended up where we ended up. We had two hours to kill on a Saturday morning, so we decided to learn a new skill. None of us dreamed that learning to row on a river on a Saturday morning would lead to rowing the Atlantic ocean.'

'It is about saying yes,' said Janette. 'If someone asks you to do something, say yes before anything else. It's because I said yes to Frances that I went on this wonderful adventure that I never dreamed I would go on, something I never thought I would do in my entire life. When I was 25 years old, I never thought I would row an ocean. Never. Is it one of the things I am most proud of? Probably, yes – the feeling of accomplishment is huge. When we rowed into that harbour the feeling was overwhelming. I think we all underestimate middle-aged women. I do, we all do. We underestimate ourselves all the time. But I won't do that again. Never. If someone asks you to play a game of badminton, just say yes, even if you've never played before. If someone offers you a business opportunity, just say yes. If someone asks you to help them out, say yes. You can always change your mind, but start with a yes, as you never know where it is going to take you. The moment I stepped off that boat in Antigua was fulfilling, satisfying, gratifying, everything. The only other time I'd felt like that was on my wedding day! Women can be obsessed with proving their worth, but you are as good as you want to be. We must accept ourselves, warts and all, because we all have warts. And it doesn't matter.

'I will never allow myself to think I am not good enough for anyone or anything. I now know I have nothing to prove to anyone. I am who I am. I am proud to be me. I love my vices and I love my virtues, because that's what makes me me. Thank you, adventure, you have shown me something, but more than that you have given me the permission to be me.

'We helped each other on that boat. We became really good friends, and those girls are now part of my family, and we wanted each other to do well, because we're women. And we all came out of it stronger. I learnt from Niki to be more sympathetic. I learnt from Frances to be a lot more relaxed. And from Helen? I learnt to live in the now, to embrace feathers, and she made me laugh like I have never laughed before.

'I have to admit that after a couple of glasses of wine I have gone into that shed and climbed aboard *Rose*. I've been into the cabin and lain down and thought, "Wow, this was our home for all those weeks." When I see her there, in the yard, I ask myself if we really did take her all those miles across that ocean. I still can't quite believe it. I still can't quite get to grips with the fact that we did it. It's weird. I know we did it, but it does, in many respects, feel like a dream. Because it was a dream. It was a dream to do it. And it still feels like a dream... Our dream.'

SHIP'S LOG:

'Our last lesson, and one we still have to learn: how do you fit back into life when you have been on an adventure? We need to allow the feelings of the adventure to exist without suppressing them or pretending they don't exist. You can be very sad when you come back from an adventure. We should try to understand that it's normal to feel like that, so we can become more engaged with life again. If our lives were always operating at a high-intensity level, we would burn out. Learning how to accept the peaks and troughs will help us prepare for our next adventure, whatever that may be!'

(JANETTE/SKIPPER)

Epilogue

It's now two years since we rowed an ocean, fulfilling a shared dream, raising money for charity and taking ourselves into the record books to boot. We have spent quite a lot of the time since we arrived in Antigua talking about the experience – the interest our row sparked has been a constant, and rather humbling, surprise – but we have also been busy getting on with our lives, and so the publication of the paperback version of the book seemed like a good opportunity for an update.

When we first got home we all talked about how the Challenge had changed us (or not in Janette's case!) and what we had learned from the experience. Now that we've had another 12 months back on dry land, do we still feel the same? Has Helen used that mysteriously delivered rope to climb any mountains? Does Frances still believe she can do anything? Is Niki living a simple, stuff-free life? What new paths has Janette chosen to follow? And can she still fit into those shorts?

Janette

'I fully intended to keep working for several more years when I got back from rowing the ocean. The company I was working for is a really great organisation and the best company I've worked with. I understand that many people, when they sell their business, struggle to get on with the new owners, but that wasn't the case for me; the family who bought it are wonderful people and they gave me a lot of support before I set off on the row. However, once I was home, I realised that what I had missed most were my family and friends. I didn't miss the house or the car or the possessions, but I did miss Ben and the children, so I decided to try out 'retirement' (actually, I prefer to call it 'living the dream' otherwise it makes me sound old), and see if it was for me or not. And it is! I'm shocked that I am enjoying not working so much, but it's really, really lovely. I haven't stopped working entirely, but I'm just doing the work I love because, while my decision to leave the company wasn't entirely down to the ocean journey, a big lesson the adventure did teach me was that it's important to do the things that make you happy. And right now having more time for my family and friends is making me happy.

'It also means I have time to help other businesses as a mentor, which is very fulfilling, and I'm loving the inspirational speaking we are doing as Yorkshire Rows. We get to meet some truly amazing people and it's good to know that we are making a difference to peoples' lives.

'I'm not an 'adventurer' and athletic challenges aren't really my thing, but I have also agreed to help a friend run the London Marathon in April 2018. I am not a runner so, physically, this is a big challenge for me, but that's not why I'm doing it. (I don't need the challenge; I have spent my whole life working hard building a successful business!) I'm doing it because my close friend Kate has a friend, Anthony Rebori, who went blind in his twenties and who is running it for the charity RP Fighting Blindness. Kate and I will be sharing the guide running, being Anthony's eyes for him, and he wants to finish in a good time, so I will do my best to help him achieve it. He is just such a wonderful, inspirational person. I did a half marathon with him and Kate recently and thinking about him and his daily life was what got me round. I was in the cloakroom at his house just before we left for the race and his white stick was in the hat stand; it was kind of significant because it made me think about what being blind means. When it got hard on the way round, I pictured his white stick and it reminded me that he has to live with that all his life and that made me keep running.

'And yes, I can still get the shorts on; just.'

Niki

'I am still trying to simplify things; we carry so much in our heads and our houses and I sometimes find that stressful. I haven't quite got the balance right yet, but 'things' definitely don't have the appeal they once did and I am trying not to sweat the small stuff. I used to worry a lot about everything and now the little things that used to make me anxious or irritate me just don't. I find I listen to my kids more too; it's important for me to be in the 'now' with them. Just spending time with my husband and children is my happy time.

'I have also found a love for sport and the outdoors. The problem with starting to believe in yourself is that you want to try so many things. I used to think, 'Wow, that looks amazing but I could never do it,' now I just think, 'Wow that looks amazing, I think I'll give it a go.' Talk about a change of mind-set. The challenge now is not to sign up for everything I see!

'I do have a lot planned. I started running for the first time in my adult life last June and, with the support of some fantastic friends and my family, have managed a few half marathons, along with my first three-day ultra-marathon. I didn't actually run too much of the ultra, but it was a huge achievement to finish. All this is a build-up to taking part in the Marathon des Sables with Frances in April 2018.

'I said no when Frances first pitched it – I'm new to running and it's a six-day, 142-mile run in the Sahara Desert – but then I remembered that we weren't that great at rowing when we started, so I talked to the family and signed up. I've got myself a great ultra-running coach who has a fabulous attitude around what people can achieve and it just shows that belief, combined with support and advice in the right areas, can help people to do so much more than they think. The biggest thing I learned from the row was that it is okay to ask for help. I think there's a lot of pressure on women to be the perfect mum, the perfect wife, the perfect career woman – to be seen as Wonder Woman – but I've learned that you achieve more and have a better life if you ask for help when you need it. And what is so wonderful is that I've realised that most people love to be asked for their advice and support; I've made some closer and stronger friends and met some of the most amazing people by asking for help.

'I have also discovered that it's important to me to help others realise their potential, especially girls in their formative years. As well as initiating a girls rugby section of York RUFC with the full backing of the club, I have also been working with a local school to support girls' development and confidence. I've got so much out of the experience and would love to do more in this area.'

Niki's husband, Gareth, added, 'The positive impact the row has had on Niki, myself and our two boys is immeasurable. The idea that you can pretty much do anything if you put your mind to it has been greatly reinforced by her adventure!'

Frances

'I was feeling my age before we decided to row an ocean and now I don't; now I feel exactly the same as I did when I was in my twenties (with more adventures ahead of me than behind me) so, yes, I do believe that I can do just about anything. It's easy for women to lose their confidence as they get older, but completing the Challenge has given me a strong sense of self-belief. I love the fact that what we did has helped to boost other women's confidence too.

'As part of some coaching recently, I was asked when in my life I had felt the most happy, fulfilled and supported. It was an interesting question and, as I thought about it, I realised that the times when I have felt this way have all been when I've been outdoors and away from mainstream society. Mark and I did a London-to-Paris cycle ride last May and we left Dieppe so early one morning that we had the roads entirely to ourselves. Cycling through the Normandy countryside that day, just the two of us, with the sun coming up and just the cows and birds for company was really lovely and a day I will always remember.

'I am taking part in the Marathon des Sables partly because I'm chasing the feeling of being out in the wilderness with a small group of optimistic people again. It will be physically and mentally difficult, but I've found that the ultra-running world is very similar to the ocean rowing world; you are just another competitor and everyone wants to help everyone else as much as they can. In the wider commercial world, it can sometimes feel as though people are not looking out for each other, but these ultra-challenge events seem to me to be inclusive bubbles of positivity.

'My biggest priority though since the row has been to spend time with my sons. I know that they are likely to have left home for college or university within just a few short years and I want to make the absolute most of the time I have with them now whilst they are still living at home.

'I have also signed up to do A-Level Spanish. The exam is in 2019 and I haven't really got started with the studying yet (I do have a tendency to over-commit and under-prepare), so I may have to defer the exam, but I seem to need to have a constant challenge (or two!) on the go these days.'

Helen

'I've agreed to climb some big mountains (I'm even considering Everest!). I'm not sure when, but I've taken the first step and am starting an 18-month mountaineering programme in Scotland in January where I'll learn useful things like ice climbing and navigation.

'It all started because I really struggled when I got back from the row. I had this underlying sadness, which I think was a result of losing that adrenalin high, and I needed to find something else to fill the hole. When the climbing rope appeared, I took it as a sign (of course!) and decided to find a refresher climbing course. Someone had dropped out so there was a place immediately, which was another sign. When I was in New York to present the *Four Mums in a Boat* documentary, I met a professional climber called Angie Payne and she was the one to plant the seed in my head when she asked me whether I would consider doing a climbing challenge. The idea was further cemented when I met the amazing Sue Harper. Sue has sailed across the Atlantic and climbed Everest and she was interested in showing the documentary at a festival in Scotland. We met up in Harrogate and she asked whether I had ever thought of climbing Everest. Before I could say anything, she told me that she thought I could do it and offered to help. The conversation left me on a real high. It was the first time I'd felt like that since we'd arrived in Antigua, so I decided to give it a shot. I'll just start and see what happens. I might not get there, but I know I'll meet interesting people along the way and I will have learned a new skill.

'I've also decided to use the experience of that long adrenalin hangover to start a new career. We were told that our true selves would come out on the boat and they really did. On the negative side, that meant discovering that I am more rebellious and stubborn than I had thought, but I also found that I have natural coaching skills. These came out when Niki was missing her family so badly. She'd looked after me when I was seasick at the start and then, when she was struggling at the end, I helped her to develop coping strategies. I didn't know I could do that before the row and now I do, I am now training to become a post-adventure life coach.'

Of course, what we have done has also affected other people. Our children and husbands were very supportive at the time and they are all still proud of us. Helen's daughter Lucy, who was rowing before we decided to do the Challenge, has said that what we've done has given her the drive to succeed and she's determined to row an ocean herself one day, but none of the other children have any interest in following our footsteps; they all have their own dreams and lives to lead. They've lived with it for so long that their mum rowing an ocean is just part of normal life. And that's what's so wonderful. How great is it that they all think it's normal for mums to do these things? Frances' husband Mark summed it up like this. 'She has taught me and our sons the importance of saying "yes" to new challenges, that it is never too late to pursue a dream and that achieving that dream requires hard work and determination. And that in the process – the pursuit and ultimate realisation of a goal – your life and the lives of those you touch will be enriched in ways you could never imagine.

We seem to have inspired lots of other people too. We have all been surprised by the celebrity bit; we thought what we were doing was a private thing, but it turns out that four mums rowing an ocean is big news (especially if they do it without their chafe-free pants!) We've done some amazing things – we've presented Duke of Edinburgh Gold Awards at Buckingham Palace and been given honorary doctorates by the Archbishop of York on behalf of York St John University for example – it all feels slightly surreal but also incredibly humbling.

But the best thing about 'being a bit famous' is that it brings us into contact with so many people and we have been stunned by people's reactions. 'The loveliest thing about having done the Challenge is when someone says, "If you can do that, so can I," ' says Niki. 'It's like having Christmas and your birthday in one because I was that person once and now we're passing it on.'

A few stories really stand out. Janette remembers encouraging a lovely lady who worked at a bank in Bradford to give up her job. 'It was one of the first inspirational talks we did after we got back. We asked all the delegates to write down what they would do if time and money were no object and there was nothing stopping them from fulfilling their dreams. One of the ladies said she had always dreamed of running her own business but was too frightened to give up her job and take such a big risk. Two days later, the event organiser rang to thank us for coming in and told us that the woman had been so moved by our story that she'd handed in her notice and was off to do that very thing.'

Helen is most proud of encouraging Dianne Carrington, a woman in her sixties, to do her own Atlantic row. We were doing a talk at Maggie's and the fundraising manager passed on Dianne's details to us at the end. A few weeks later, this message from Dianne popped into our inbox, 'I've always wanted to do something big, challenging and exciting,' she wrote, 'but I've never had the confidence to try. Your photo of the arrival in Antigua brought tears to my eyes. You had built a bond and done it as a team so, whilst I lack courage, I would dream of doing it and find a team of like-minded ladies. Your enthusiasm and offer of support was the magic ingredient.' Dianne and her two team mates set off from La Gomera in December 2017.

And Frances loves the Facebook message that read, 'If four chunky birds from Yorkshire can do this, then we certainly can!'

We couldn't end the book without mentioning the fifth member of our team. Rose saw us develop from untried novices to seasoned ocean rowers.

Through the incredible highs and lows of our journey, we looked after her and she looked after us. She saw us all at our strongest and weakest, she put up with our terrible singing and she heard a lot of stories that we're glad she can never repeat to anyone.

Now Rose is helping other people achieve their dreams too. We finally sold her to a Dutch adventurer called Ralph Tuijn who is really active in the ocean rowing world. She has already helped him set the world record for Portugal to South America, (48 days, 10 hours and 53 minutes) and, as we write this, is out on the same route as Ralph tries to break his own record. She is also taking part in the Talisker Whisky Atlantic Challenge again at the end of the year and there's a chance that the team who take her will be four dads from Yorkshire.

We had to sell her because so much of our sponsorship money was tied up in her (we've raised around £110,000 for Maggie's and the Yorkshire Air Ambulance so far), but it was sad to see her go. It sounds silly because she is just a boat after all, but she was part of the team. However, her part in our lives is over and it's fantastic that she is still out there having more adventures, taking people across oceans and helping to make the seemingly impossible possible. And, because it's unlucky to change a boat's name, she will always be Rose.

The Letters

For Frances: When you want to get off the boat...

If you are reading this, you are probably fed up, thinking of home and wanting to get off that boat.

That's perfectly understandable – anyone undertaking the challenge you are engaged in would have dark moments when it all feels too much. Just remember: the darkest hour is always just before the dawn. Dawn may feel like a hell of a long way away right now, but you must take it little steps at a time, just like dawn breaking. The daylight creeps up on you in the morning: dawn doesn't just break and instantly it's light – it comes bit by bit, minute by minute, creeping so slowly that sometimes you can't even notice that it has got lighter, but it WILL get lighter, and lighter and lighter, until you are standing in the sunlight. With every mile you row, you are closer to the finish, and closer to your goal, and closer to us. Take a deep breath and move forwards through the darkness, and you will arrive at your destiny.

Love you,

Mark, Jay, Jack (and Daisy) xxxxxxxxxxxxxxx

For Helen: from Lucy, Henry and Richard

Dear Mum,

You will be reading this when you are probably feeling tired and sad. Keep going, keep rowing and never give up – we are all watching you and willing you on. We are all proud of what you are doing and can't wait to see you when you get home. In the words of Nick Grimshaw, 'Jussssssst dooooooo it!'

Love always,

    Lucy, Henry and Richard

    X

For Janette: from Ben, James and Safiya

Happy Christmas, Janette! We will be thinking of you today and all the way across to Antigua. If anyone can do this, you can.

Lots of love,

Ben, James, Safiya, the Callaus, the Wilkinsons and the Nixes xxx

For Niki: from Gareth

My darling Niki,

As you set off for this great adventure I just want you to know how very, very proud I am of you, not just for this, but for everything you do. I know sometimes I find it hard to express my emotions and feelings, but know this: I am totally behind you in the endeavour, which shows a great example not only to our children, but to me as well. I am so very lucky to be married to such a fantastic woman – yes, as I'm writing this letter I am wondering why I don't tell you that enough. You have shown us that if you put your mind to it, you can pretty much achieve anything, which has opened our eyes, for which we are very grateful.

I will be thinking of you every moment of every day as I have done for the last 25 years. This will be the longest we've ever been apart and I'm looking forward very much to seeing you again in Antigua and hearing all about this fantastic adventure.

We will of course miss you, but you will be absolutely fine. You have us very well drilled and trained in the art of time management! You have left us very well placed to make sure that we continue to stay well organised. I think I've even got the hang of the washing machine and the dryer.

I think, for us, the time will fly, as we will be busy with Christmas and the holidays and then back to school, and before we know it, it will be half-term, which can't come soon enough. I suspect the time may sometimes drag a little bit for you, however...

We are very much looking forward to plotting your progress.

I am sure that I have said it before, but make sure you make the most of this trip. Embrace it, enjoy it, work through any lows – think of us and all the support that is urging you on. Ride the highs for as long as you can and make the most of it. You are going to be a member of a very exclusive club – as you know, there are not many women who have rowed across an ocean, nevermind the Atlantic. There are also not many men who are fortunate enough to be married to women who have rowed the Atlantic, so it seems I am lucky enough to get a big upside without the effort!!

But most importantly, stay safe, take care.

All my love, always,

Gareth

XXX

For Frances: When the going gets tough ...

'Invictus' by W. E. Henley

Out of the night that covers me,
Black as the pit from pole to pole,
I thank whatever gods may be
For my unconquerable soul.

In the fell clutch of circumstance
I have not winced or cried aloud.
Under the bludgeoning of chance
My head is bloody but unbowed.

Beyond this place of wrath and tears
Looms but the horror of the shade,
And yet the menace of the years
Finds and shall find me unafraid.

It matters not how strait the gate,
How charged with punishment the scroll,
I am the master of my fate,
I am the captain of my soul.

Invictus (Latin): meaning 'unconquerable'.

Dig deep – you can do this, I know you can. **Invictus es.**

Mx